Passionate Communities

St

Ruthann Robson
Writer
Law School, Queens College
City University of New York

Leila J. Rupp
History
Ohio State University

Paula Rust
Sociology
Hamilton College

Ann Allen Shockley
Librarian
Fisk University

Elizabeth Wood
Musicologist and Writer
Committee on Theory and Culture
New York University

Bonnie Zimmerman
Women's Studies
San Diego State University

THE CUTTING EDGE

Lesbian Life and Literature

Series Editor: Karla Jay

The Cook and the Carpenter: A Novel by the Carpenter
by June Arnold
with an introduction by Bonnie Zimmerman

Ladies Almanack
by Djuna Barnes
with an introduction by Susan Sniader Lanser

Virginia Woolf: Lesbian Readings
edited by Eileen Barrett and Patricia Cramer

Adventures of the Mind:
The Memoirs of Natalie Clifford Barney
translated by John Spalding Gatton
with an introduction by Karla Jay

Sophia Parnok:
The Life and Work of Russia's Sappho
by Diana Burgin

The Angel and the Perverts
by Lucie Delarue-Mardrus
translated and with an introduction by Anna Livia

Paint It Today
by H.D. (Hilda Doolittle)
edited and with an introduction by Cassandra Laity

Heterosexual Plots and Lesbian Narratives
by Marilyn R. Farwell

*Spinsters and Lesbians: Independent Womanhood
in the United States, 1890–1930 and 1950–1980*
by Trisha Franzen

Diana: A Strange Autobiography
by Diana Frederics
with an introduction by Julie L. Abraham

Your John: The Love Letters of Radclyffe Hall
edited and with an introduction by Joanne Glasgow

Lover
by Bertha Harris

Elizabeth Bowen: A Reputation in Writing
by renée c. hoogland

Lesbian Erotics
edited by Karla Jay

Changing Our Minds: Lesbian Feminism and Psychology
by Celia Kitzinger and Rachel Perkins

(Sem)Erotics: Theorizing Lesbian : Writing
by Elizabeth A. Meese

*Bisexuality and the Challenge to Lesbian Politics:
Sex, Loyalty, and Revolution*
by Paula C. Rust

*Passionate Communities:
Reading Lesbian Resistance in Jane Rule's Fiction*
by Marilyn R. Schuster

The Search for a Woman-Centered Spirituality
by Annette J. Van Dyke

Lesbian Friendships: For Ourselves and Each Other
edited by Jacqueline S. Weinstock
and Esther D. Rothblum

I Know My Own Heart:
The Diaries of Anne Lister, 1791–1840
edited by Helena Whitbread

No Priest but Love:
The Journals of Anne Lister, 1824–26
edited by Helena Whitbread

Marilyn R. Schuster

PASSIONATE COMMUNITIES

READING LESBIAN RESISTANCE IN JANE RULE'S FICTION

New York University Press

New York and London

NEW YORK UNIVERSITY PRESS
New York and London

© 1999 by New York University

Library of Congress Cataloging-in-Publication Data
Schuster, Marilyn R.
Passionate communities : reading lesbian resistance in Jane
Rule's fiction / Marilyn R. Schuster.
p. cm. — (The cutting edge)
Includes bibliographical references (p.   ) and index.
ISBN 0-8147-8130-6 (alk. paper)
ISBN 0-8147-8133-0 (pbk. : alk. paper)
1. Rule, Jane—Criticism and interpretation. 2. Women and
literature—Canada—History—20th century. 3. Lesbians' writings,
Canadian—History and criticism. 4. Lesbians in literature.
I. Title. II. Series: Cutting edge (New York, N.Y.)
PR9199.3.R78 Z87 1999
813'.54—ddc21   99-6339
                                      CIP

New York University Press books are printed on acid-free paper,
and their binding materials are chosen for strength and durability.

Manufactured in the United States of America

10 9 8 7 6 5 4 3 2 1

For Meg and Judi

CONTENTS

ACKNOWLEDGMENTS

Jane Rule's work has taken me to many communities. Some—Galiano Island, Toronto, Vancouver, the San Francisco Bay Area—are on the map; others are created by her friends, her coworkers, and her readers, some named, many anonymous.

In her work and in her life, Jane Rule—after long years before publication, when she felt she was writing in isolation, without an audience—has been a community builder. I'd like to thank her and Helen Sonthoff for welcoming me into their community on Galiano Island, and for the good food, plentiful drink, and intense conversations that marked our visits together. Whatever reservations Jane might have about becoming "the raw material for someone else's work," she has generously opened her files and answered my questions about her creative process. Neither Jane nor Helen has seen this book before publication (nor did they ask to), and any errors it may contain are clearly mine alone. My deepest hope for this book is that it will encourage another generation of readers to find community and read resistance in Jane's work.

Thanks go to another "Jane Rule," Mrs. Arthur Rule, Jane's mother, who shared her thoughts about her daughter's work and her life during conversations at her home in Palo Alto, California. She is a model octogenarian, fighting homophobia in the communities she belongs to.

I am especially grateful that Jane put me in touch with Lynne Fernie, Aerlyn Weissman, and Rina Fraticelli when they were making *Fiction and Other Truths: A Film about Jane Rule*. They welcomed me to Toronto and to the world of independent filmmaking, and I was honored to be part of that prize-winning project. Lynne has continued to help me in my work and to stimulate my thinking. Thanks to all of them, I've been able to know Rick Bébout, a longtime friend of Jane and member of the editorial collective at *The Body Politic*, where Jane's column, "So's Your Grandmother," appeared for many years. He invited me to read his rich correspondence with Jane, a unique resource that gave me a glimpse into the daily workings of gay and lesbian politics over the last two decades and, just as important, into the growth of their remarkable friendship. I'm grateful, too, to the Canadian Lesbian and Gay Archives in Toronto, home to *The Body Politic* papers and the personal papers of many of Jane Rule's friends and colleagues.

This project enabled me to get to know Vancouver, Canada, surely one of the most beautiful cities in North America. My friends Jo and Henry Rappaport introduced me to the culinary and cultural treasures of their city; their hospitality and especially their wit made my trips to the archives at the University of British Columbia even more enjoyable. The staff members at the University of British Columbia Library Special Collections and University Archives Division—Christopher Hives, in particular—were always helpful as I read through the Jane Rule Papers in the summers of 1994, 1995, and 1997.

During the 1996–97 academic year, our dear friends Meg Quigley and Judi Hiltner offered us their beautiful home at Stinson Beach in Marin County, California, for a sabbatical year unlike any other. It was in that magical setting that I was able to write this book and to enjoy that other beautiful North American city, San Francisco. Our San Francisco friends, especially Estelle Freedman and Susan Krieger, Caren Kaplan and Eric Smoodin, Cappy Coates and Veronica Selver, and so many more, created an intellectual landscape that matched the physical landscape we learned to love and to which we eagerly return whenever we can. An unanticipated pleasure that year was the chance to meet Peg Cruikshank, a central figure in the passionate community of Jane Rule's readers and a shaper of lesbian communities herself. She generously shared with me letters that Jane had written to her.

My institutional home during that sabbatical year was the Stanford Institute for Research on Women and Gender. I'm indebted to that community of scholars for valuable comments on a paper that grew into a chapter of this book. In particular I want to thank Marilyn Yalom for her encouragement and for giving me a letter from Jane Rule to Mrs. Robert Anderson, "Gracella," in which Jane talks about writing *The Young in One Another's Arms.*

From beginning to end I have counted on the personal and intellectual support of colleagues and students in my home community, the Women's Studies program at Smith College. Donna Divine and Martha

Ackelsberg, part of the extensive, passionate community of Jane Rule's readers, have always encouraged me in this work. Leyla Ezdinli repeatedly helped me to develop the theoretical foundation of my readings. My gratitude, as always, to Gayle Pemberton, honorary member of the Smith Women's Studies Program. The Women's Studies program also provided material support for my trips to Vancouver and Toronto through the Conway Fund and the Quigley Fund. The Smith College Committee on Faculty Compensation and Development and the Office of the Dean of the Faculty also provided much-needed funding to travel to Vancouver. Rachel Noto earned special thanks for her sharp-eyed proofreading.

Karla Jay and Niko Pfund have been patient and encouraging as this project extended far beyond the initial, overly optimistic timetable I had envisaged. Despina Papazoglou Gimbel is the ideal managing editor: patient and insistent, and her team, Elyse Strongin, Andrew Katz, and Andy Fotopoulos, is exceptional. I also want to thank Sonya L. Jones, who edited a special issue of *The Journal of Homosexuality* (35: 3–4, 1998), which included "Inscribing a Lesbian Reader, Projecting a Lesbian Subject: A Jane Rule Diptych" (87–112). The issue was published simultaneously as *Gay and Lesbian Literature since World War II: History and Memory.* Parts of that article appear in somewhat different form in chapters 1 and 4.

The "we" in these paragraphs is neither editorial nor affectation. My partner in life and work, Susan Van Dyne, has been with me at every stage of this project. Our first visit to Jane and Helen's home on Galiano in the summer of 1992 crystallized my desire to write a book-length study of Jane's work. During our sabbatical year in 1996–97—and since—Susan has read every scrap of every attempt to shape the manuscript, sometimes reminding me that a walk to watch the seal pups might help renew my spirit. As Director of Women's Studies at Smith College, she has nurtured an intellectual community that would rival any university and that enables all of us to grow in our research and teaching. For nearly two decades, Susan has encouraged and challenged me to do the work I most want to do.

Sailing to Galiano

Jane Rule at Home

Poetry and fiction can sometimes do what theory has not yet learned: to speak a language of desire where there had been only silence or denial. Adrienne Rich has taught this to us, as have Audre Lorde and Monique Wittig and many other lesbian writers who refused to be silenced long before the current wave of queer writing. Jane Rule's fiction—and the ways it has been received and ignored—provides a rich ground for exploring the creation of a language of desire in a context of denial.

Born in New Jersey in 1931, Jane Rule matured as a woman and a writer in the decade following World War II. The postwar effort to restore order on the home front included a campaign to define healthy femininity as heterosexual, monogamous, reproductive, and domestic. At the same time, as Jennifer Terry and other queer theorists have amply demonstrated, homosexuality was intensely pathologized. Medical and psychological discourses categorized "homosexual" as sick and were joined by the politics of McCarthyism that marked "homosexual" as traitor. Kinsey was denounced in the early fifties for proposing a continuum of sexual practices and desire rather than an opposition between the healthy, reproductive heterosexual and the sick, sterile, degenerate homosexual.

Literary texts were bound up in the same models of deviance. The lesbian fiction available to Rule as a young writer, such as Radclyffe Hall's *The Well of Loneliness,* seemed to marginalize lesbians as congenital inverts; or, like pulp fiction, it was formulaic, requiring "heterosexual recuperation" at the end (the lesbian loses "the girl" or is killed off, marriage and nature triumph over deviant desire); or it was highly coded, like Gertrude Stein's work.

Jane Rule's work provides a way for understanding the cultural work of fiction. We can see in her early work (published and unpublished) a writer at odds with a culture she nonetheless values and wants to engage. To borrow Marilyn Farwell's phrase, Rule is caught up in heterosexual plots as she tries to create lesbian narratives. Her early struggles, often unsuccessful as finished texts, nonetheless enable her to devise strategies of resistance and subversion.

The reception of Rule's work—especially as articulated in letters from readers—illustrates the cultural work of fiction in another way. Rule's texts often create a special bond of reading between reader and writer. Who are these readers? How is that bond understood? Why have Rule's fictions been so vital to some women (and some men as well)? Why do these narratives continue to be important to many readers? Read in the context of 1990s queer provocations in theory, literature, and film, Rule's stories may seem understated. But along with increased queer visibility in recent years, there has been a return of pathologizing discourses that echo the medical and political languages of the fifties. Discourse about AIDS and religious and political campaigns to explain, contain, or excise queer sexualities in the body politic bear an uncanny resemblance to the languages about deviance in the 1950s. Rule's strategies of resistance and subversion continue to be useful to a population at risk.

The Journey: Crossing Over

The journey to Jane Rule's home cannot be rushed. To get to the ferry at Tsawwassen—a spit of land that separates Boundary Bay from the Strait of Georgia—requires three city buses from my temporary home on the University of British Columbia campus in Vancouver. I tuck *Inland Passage* back into my bag as the bus pulls up to the ferry dock. On this sunny June day, foot passengers with backpacks and cars with camping equipment wait for the boat that will take them to the Gulf Islands for a holiday weekend. First stop, Galiano Island, where Jane Rule and Helen Sonthoff will meet me at the Sturdies Bay dock.

I've been traveling for much longer than the two hours on buses. Along with many other readers, I first met Jane in *Lesbian Images,* herself a reader of lesbian writers, holding her own story up to the stories available. In that book, as in her own fiction, Rule was charting new territory: reading as a writer, but also as a lesbian looking for stories that would help her map what it means for a woman to love women and to articulate that desire in language. Her readings of other lesbians in that book led me to her own writing, which had been unknown to me before. I turned to *Desert of the Heart* and then was given a worn photocopy of *This Is Not for You*, out of print but passed around from woman to woman—a silent community of readers finding, at last, stories to give shape and meaning to our lives. For nearly twenty years I've been meeting Jane in her books, then in letters, and once, two years ago, in person. This, my second sailing to Galiano, is a return to territory now more familiar. I've been living with her letters, college papers, unpublished stories, manuscripts, photographs, rejection notices, and, finally, reviews in dozens of boxes at the University of British Columbia archives.[1] She is the only company I've kept for two weeks. Moving back and forth in time, I try to piece together her childhood, her first loves, her persistence as publisher after publisher turn down *Desert of the Heart*.

As I returned to the late fifties in her papers, I asked myself the question I'd asked when I first read *Desert of the Heart*: How did this middle child of an American middle-class family become Canada's most public literary lesbian? How did she find a way to write stories of lesbian lives that weren't punishing or tortured—stories that echo Yeats (as in the title of her novel *The Young in One Another's Arms*, taken from "Sailing to Byzantium") and *Pilgrim's Progress* (in the quest allusions of *Desert of the Heart*) more than Radclyffe Hall's *The Well of Loneliness* or pulp fiction? And how could it be that a writer so vitally important to readers throughout North America has been

1. The *Jane Rule Papers* are located in Vancouver at the University of British Columbia Library, Special Collections and University Archives Division. The collection includes thirty-six boxes (6.1 m) acquired from 1988 to 1993. The collection contains notes, manuscripts, drafts, galleys, and correspondence relating to her published and unpublished novels and short stories; biographical and autobiographical material, nonfiction manuscripts, and personal and professional correspondence; and reviews of her work and audio recordings of interviews and readings. I will identify items cited from the collection by indicating the box number and folder number in parentheses within the text along with additional information such as chapter numbers and page numbers when available.

ignored by the professional arbiters of literary reputation—academics, literary critics, and now queer theorists?

Taking a seat by a window in the ferry, I wait for the horn to sound the beginning of the hour-long voyage through the Strait of Georgia. Strange waters, these: the border between Canada and the United States follows a quirky, jagged line between the Gulf Islands in British Columbia and the San Juan Islands in Washington state, with Canada as often to the south of the United States as to the north.

As the ferry pulls out of the dock I think about my first trip to Galiano two years ago, a vacation with Susan, partner in life and work, to celebrate the completion of book manuscripts about other women writers. The closer we got to the island, the more apprehensive we became. How much of Jane's life entered her fiction directly? Would Helen, our mothers' contemporary who graduated from Smith College years before either of us was born (and where we both now teach), turn out to be the model for Constance in *Memory Board,* lovable but without any short-term memory? I kept looking at a picture of Jane on the back of *Contract with the World,* taken when she was the age I was that summer; what would she look like now, twelve years my senior and suffering from arthritis of the lower spine that sometimes nearly cripples her? What a risk she and Helen had taken, we thought, to invite us in as houseguests for several days rather than take the ferry ride themselves to the city. Or, simply, they could have declined an invitation from strangers. Later, when we confessed these apprehensions over one of many glasses of Scotch, Helen said (in full command of her short-term memory), "It's difficult for Jane to travel because of her arthritis, and we've found through experience that you can put up with almost anyone for two days." A welcome and a warning that made us all laugh.

On that trip, we had driven off the ferry to follow the directions to their house. There is only one main road the length of Galiano. We drove through an Emily Carr landscape of fir trees and red-barked arbutus, with occasional glimpses of the water. Later we'd explore traces of Indian middens on the beaches of this tiny island where the past and present mingle, but no landfill, no Savings & Loan, no gas stations have brought the most visible signs of the late twentieth century. Without their careful directions we would have missed the house—a cedar cabin tucked into a hillside, modest and unassuming from the road, protecting the privacy of Helen's flower garden and Jane's pool.

They greeted us like old friends and, after settling into our room, we joined them for sherry before lunch. Gradually we discovered the signs of other presences—little drawings and paintings by Elizabeth "Hoppy" Hopkins, Gerard Manley Hopkins's niece, who had been their neighbor and whose grave they visit on walks to the sea. *The Poseurs,* a portrait of cats preening, hangs next to a painting of foot passengers in bright summer gear descending from the ferry at Sturdies Bay. Dozens of Indian baskets hang in the living room, traded for trout caught by Jane's namesake great-grandmother, Jane Vance, in the Eel River in the Northern California redwoods early in this century.

We wondered when we made that journey—Susan a reader of American women poets—if Galiano were like Emily Dickinson's room. Did the island shut out the world but open up the freedom to create? When Jane and Helen moved there permanently in 1976, Jane had imagined long stretches of uninterrupted time to write. She was forty-five and had published dozens of stories, three novels, and written most of a fourth, but she dismissed these as "apprenticeship novels" and looked forward to writing the works of her creative maturity. But even so, she didn't ever close the door of that house to the outside world. Every afternoon in summer she invited all children, permanent residents and visitors alike, to swim in her pool while she kept watch. Every winter she and Helen would travel to family and warmer weather in California to ease her arthritis and keep the elaborate networks of their friendships and kinships alive. Island living, yes, but isolation, no. Once in Galiano, they took an active role in island life, acting as the "Bank of Galiano," making loans so that neighbors could start businesses or buy houses. It was after moving to Galiano that Jane assumed her most public political voice, writing a column, "So's Your Grandmother," for *The Body Politic,* the gay liberationist newspaper in Toronto.

The freedom to write that moving to the island promised didn't last, however. A short time after Jane and Helen moved to Galiano, Jane's arthritis was diagnosed and started to worsen. Although she would write three more novels and publish three collections of stories and essays, Jane had constantly to choose between pain and writing: the pain killers prescribed for her illness blocked the concentration needed for writing. On that earlier visit, I was only vaguely aware of these circumstances. Jane's hospitality and kindness require her to shield her guests from her own discomfort. As we sipped after-dinner Scotch one night, I asked what she was working on now. It had been three years since *After the Fire* and I was eager for her next book. "I've retired," was the unequivocal answer; further discussion was not invited. Her decision, while clear, had not been easy.

The foreclosure of future texts made me want all the more to return to Rule's early work. Crossing over to Galiano Island, I think about the twenty years that I've been reading Rule and about the ways I have learned to "read queerly." What did it mean then, what does it mean now, to be a lesbian writer—or reader?

Reading Then, Reading Now

What it means to me now to be a *lesbian* reader is informed above all by *feminist* ways of reading. Reading "queerly" is inseparable in my practice from reading "as a woman." Two maps for reading queerly have emerged for me in the last twenty years, each predicated on affinity and difference, identification and separation between the writer and the reader. The first is the model for feminist reading developed by Adrienne Rich in her foundational 1976 essay about Emily Dickinson, "Vesuvius at Home: The Power of Emily Dickinson." Traveling to Dickinson's home at a century's remove even as I am traveling to Rule's home at a generation's remove, Rich clearly stakes out the importance of recovering the cultural and geographic context of the woman writer and the equal importance of clarifying her own cultural location as reader. The affinities she senses with Dickinson as a poet writing against the expectations of her time and place are neither more nor less important than the differences that separate the two women, the two historical moments in which they think and write. Patricinio Schweickart returns to Rich's essay in 1986 to propose a paradigm for feminist readings of women writers that Rich illustrates in her reading of Dickinson. Schweickart pays as much attention to the rhetorical strategies of Rich's text as she does to its content, especially the use of a personal voice and Rich's choice of images to articulate her relation to her subject.

Schweickart focuses on Rich's organizing metaphors—of witness, travel, and "trying to connect"—arguing that the images delineate a process for feminist reading. "The first," explains Schweickart, "is a judicial metaphor: the feminist reader speaks as a witness in defense of the woman writer" ("Reading Ourselves" 46). The second, a travel metaphor, points to the importance of uncovering the writer's historical and cultural context. The third image—"an insect against the screens of an existence which inhabited Amherst, Massachusetts"—acknowledges that reader and writer are both separated and united by the text between them (47).

As I think about reading and rereading Rule, first as a stranger and then as someone I've gotten to know through texts and conversation, I think about our affinities and am reminded of our differences. As lesbians looking to literature to make sense of our lives, we came of age in different cultural contexts. Rule began her teaching career in the McCarthy years; pressure was exerted on schools to require faculty members to sign a loyalty oath that implicitly, if not explicitly, exacted allegiance to heterosexuality as well as to the American flag. In that climate, Rule left behind her United States citizenship and moved to Canada in 1956. Rule came of age as a writer at a time when Radclyffe Hall and Beebo Brinker were the most visible literary lesbians; in that literary context, Rule sought to map out new ways of writing lesbian desire.

Having come to adulthood and professional maturity in the post-Stonewall, queer-friendly decades of the seventies and eighties, I've been nourished not only by a political climate distinctly less hostile than the climate Jane left when she went to Vancouver, but I also have something she didn't have—her fiction. And yet the assertions of queer pride in the nineties have not replaced the verbal and physical bashing of the fifties; they barely cover over the continuing fear and loathing of sexuality not contained by heterosexual reproduction. The rantings of McCarthy have been taken over by talk radio, and the repercussions, less public but no less real, are felt in the daily lives of gays and lesbians who may or may not see themselves represented in the already defunct politics of Queer Nation. The space between the rhetoric of talk radio and the rhetoric of queer power may be, precisely, the space occupied by much of Rule's fiction and many of her readers. It is this space that I hope to explore in reading Rule: in part because she has been passed over by many other professional readers, but also because she has been important in an intensely private way to me and to many other readers.

As Schweickart says of Rich's essay, a feminist reading of a woman writer weaves—but does not blend—"the context of writing and the context of reading" (54). I understand that to mean that the feminist reader does not appropriate a woman's text or use it to authorize or validate her way of reading, but looks at the interaction of these different but mutually illuminating contexts, making clear her own stakes as she proposes an interpretation that accounts for the text she's reading and, ideally, can be extended (tactfully) to other readings.

The model for feminist reading provided by Rich and analyzed by Schweickart is complemented in my mind by the *bond of reading* between women writers and readers that Shoshana Felman proposes in *What Does a Woman Want? Reading and Sexual Difference.* Felman's book brings together readings she had done over many years, primarily of texts by Balzac and Freud, but newly framed in her book by readings of texts by women—Woolf, Rich, de Beauvoir. Felman discovers her own presence in her earlier reading, her personal stakes in interpretation visible only in hindsight and illuminated by later reading of women writers. She explains that in her experience as a critic, "[f]eminism . . . is indeed for women, among other things, reading literature and theory with their own life—a life, however, that is not entirely in their conscious possession" (13). Her goal is to unsettle apparent certainties about autobiography and personal writing that have become commonplace in recent years. She asserts that "*none of us, as women, has as yet, precisely, an auto-biography*" (14, emphasis hers). Positioned as "other" in language, women don't have a story, but must become a story, through the *bond of reading.*

Felman is primarily concerned with *sexual difference*, what it means to be(come) a woman and to read as a woman, which for Felman means to read as a feminist. Her insights, however, translate very usefully to thinking about *different sexualities*. Felman, like Rich, is interested in reading practices, specific engagements with texts. She focuses on the negotiation that constitutes the subjectivity of *both* the writer and the reader, an act of newly gendered reading that extends deconstructionist methods. She argues that the unconscious, unavailable at the time of writing, can be discovered later, through the act of reading. She looks at what it means to *assume* one's sexual difference in the act of reading: "assuming, that is, not the false security of an 'identity' . . . but the very insecurity of a differential movement, which no ideology can fix and of which no institutional affiliation can redeem the radical anxiety, in the performance of an act that constantly—deliberately or unwittingly *enacts* our difference yet finally escapes our own control" (10).

The potential implications of Felman's effort to read sexual difference for specifically *lesbian* writers and readers become clearer as she turns to Simone de Beauvoir's reading of herself as a feminist writer. Felman cites an interview conducted by de Beauvoir with Jean-Paul Sartre three decades after de Beauvoir wrote *The Second Sex*. Sartre misreads de Beauvoir by telling her: "You became a feminist in writing this book." De Beauvoir counters by saying, "But I became a feminist especially after the book was read, and started to exist for other women" (11). The book, Felman argues, is the site for a negotiation through which both the writer and the readers constitute themselves. Felman says that "feminism comes to be defined here almost inadvertently as a bond of reading" (12). "The bond of reading," argues Felman, "constitutes a renewed relation to one's gender" through a relay of "becomings." "*Becoming* a feminist is undertaking to investigate what it means to *be* a woman and discovering that one *is* not a woman but rather *becomes* (somewhat interminably) a woman; discovering, through others' reading and through the way in which other women are *addressed* by one's own writing, that one is not born a woman, one has become . . . a woman" (12, emphasis hers).

If one were to substitute "lesbian" for "woman" in the above passage, the allied projects of writing and reading queerly can be seen to participate in a similar bond of writer and reader, made possible, but not wholly contained by, the text. When resituated in the cultural context of North America from the late fifties through the eighties, the bond of reading enabled by a writer who *becomes* a lesbian in her fiction and, more importantly, through the ways her fictions are read, can be understood as doubly confirming—confirming the legibility of sexual difference *and* of different sexuality. Multiple bonds of reading in which difference is confirmed and conferred can be seen in readings of African American women writers and by other groups read as *other* or as *different* by the (falsely) unified white, masculine, heterosexual mainstream.

I know from letters I've seen in the archives, written to Rule over the last three decades, that other readers, like me, have read her fictions "with their own lives." Her fictions have enabled us to take our lives more into our "conscious possession."

Reading Queerly

On this return trip, as the ferry continues its slow but certain crossing, my mind filled with unsorted fragments of memory and manuscripts (published and unpublished) from the archives, I open *Inland Passage* to "Dulce," a story about subjectivities (and sexualities) redefined through bonds of reading. Jane had told me once that she particularly loved this story; she loved it because it didn't come easily, but when she'd written it she liked what she found there. I return to that story first, to meet Jane again in a literary landscape for which she had worked hard and which had worked for her.

Inland Passage, like most of Rule's collections of stories and essays, invites a consideration of what it means to read at different historical and political moments, specifically, what it means to read (and write) *sexuality.* Published by Naiad in 1985, *Inland Passage* contains twenty-one stories, some of which were written as early as 1963. Some belong to a series Jane dismisses as her "Anna and Harry stories," stories of straight domesticity intended for mainstream women's magazines. At least four in the collection were first published in the Canadian women's magazine *Chatelaine.*

"Dulce," previously unpublished, opens the collection. The story can be read as a parable for reading; its placement in the collection leads me to reconsider the other stories, to read against the grain of the middle-class domesticity of the women's magazine stories. Like many of Rule's stories, this one contains a number of autobiographical lures, bits of her own story reconfigured in a character who is, nonetheless, clearly *not* her: Dulce, like Jane, lives in Vancouver, was graduated from Mills College as an English major (shunning the courses in child development and dietary science designed to resocialize women after the war), studied Shakespeare as a young student at Stratford. Dulce becomes in the story a model reader of texts, though not a writer; a listener who asks the right questions, but not a speaker. The autobiographical details seem almost an effort to throw the reader off. The character is so clearly not Rule that she seems only to be teasing with the surface references. In another way, though, Rule demonstrates in this story Shoshana Felman's observations about women, memory, and autobiography: "Women's autobiography is what their memory cannot contain" (*What Does a Woman Want?* 15). The unconscious eludes memory but reveals itself in the gaps, contradictions and surprising turns of reading. The story is about secrets and silences and learning to read oneself by reading others. It is also about false keys to meaning, about not rushing to an interpretation that suggests that a single key will unlock the full range of possible meanings the story might generate.

Dulce presents herself at the beginning of the story as a twenty-one-year-old orphan whose desire is to give herself away, "having no use of my own for it." Claiming her orphan status is a way of drawing close to her older childhood friend Wilson, who was orphaned very young. A poet, Wilson plays the role of brother, teacher, and intellectual mentor to Dulce in the story. He dedicates books and poems to her; he's an absent friend who provides heterosexual protection by correspondence when she is at college and uninterested in the advances of the boys around her. Even Dulce believes in this screen romance, so when Wilson decides to move permanently to England, discovering he was "born on the wrong continent," she asks rather plaintively, "What about me?" Wilson can only say, "I'm sorry" ("Dulce" 13). Later, Oscar, a sculptor who is a mutual friend, reveals to Dulce in starkly homophobic terms, that Wilson is not a "real man": He's a faggot. . . . A queer, a homosexual" (14). Oscar then takes it upon himself to initiate Dulce into the pleasures of heterosexuality. She seems more an observer than a participant in their affair, and even as it progresses she rereads Wilson's poems and discovers meanings she hadn't been able to read before:

> I took down Wilson's first volume of poems and turned to the love poems which had always bewildered me. What I thought had been about unrequited love was instead forbidden, I could quite clearly see, but nothing prevented the reader from supposing the object to be female, married or otherwise lost to him. It was not, however, a better explanation. Had they been, in a perverse way, poems also for me, the only way Wilson knew how to tell me that he was incapable of loving me? (15)

Dulce is learning to "read queerly," to read encoded desire. She is learning to read beyond the apparent certainties of sexual identities; the gay subtext coexists with the heterosexual screen, props it up, speaks multiple desires rather than a single love story. She rethinks the names that Oscar has given to Wilson, names she'd heard before but never considered seriously. Wilson might be a "faggot," but he is also "entirely masculine." What Oscar takes as the definitive key to the meaning of Wilson's poetry, Wilson's homosexuality, is, rather, a key to understanding Oscar. He projects his own reductive understanding, occluding any other adjacent readings. Dulce understands that her new knowledge adds layers of meaning without erasing what had been there before. She can understand the coexistence of forbidden and un-requited love where before she had met only confusion. She can even read in the text some of her own story with Wilson, or at least his language doesn't exclude it.

Dulce also sees Oscar's sculpture differently now. "Compared to Wilson, Oscar was transparent, his work hugely, joyously sexual, his needs blatant, his morality patriarchal" (16). The gay text is multilayered, resists as well as invites interpretation, is darkly attractive. The (anxious) heterosexual male text is transparent, imposing; it reproduces the dominant morality which, in turn, reaffirms the artist. Ultimately, Dulce loses interest in the art and the man. When asked to choose between her dog and Oscar, she chooses her dog.

Just as Wilson's poems become less bewildering but more complex when Dulce reads beyond the heterosexual pretense, her own desire becomes more legible when she has an affair with Lee, another would-be writer, this time a young woman, who, with her daughter, moves in with Dulce. Dulce uses the same language to describe her sexual discovery with Lee that she used to describe her textual discovery in Wilson's poems: "My sexual bewilderment and constraint left me" (26). As with Oscar, however, the insight outlasts the relationship, and for essentially the same reason: just as Oscar projected his loathing of "queers" onto Wilson and confirmed his own heterosexual desirability with Dulce, Lee has internalized society's fear of "preying lesbians" and uses Dulce to exorcise her fear. While Oscar uses disgust of gays to prop up his own seemingly uncomplicated heterosexuality, Lee becomes suicidal with internalized homophobia. Only through writing a novel that misrepresents her affair with Dulce can she write homophobia out of her system and out of her future texts.

Lee's novel provides an opportunity for Rule to represent Dulce again as a reader of fiction, of sexuality, and of herself. Having apprenticed herself as a reader with Wilson's poetry and her own life, Dulce is a more suspicious, more canny reader of Lee's novel. Wilson's poetry had taught her to break through heterosexual codes to a gay subtext. Lee's novel teaches her that certain figures of lesbian desire are also part of heterosexual codes (like Oscar's insults), written to reassure heterosexual readers rather than to express lesbian desire. Dulce recognizes a misspelled, partial translation of herself in the villainous character named Swete. The writing of the novel allows Lee, more than her psychoanalysis or her brief marriage to her psychiatrist, to purge herself of the suicidal self-hate provoked by her lesbian affairs. After this first novel, Lee divorces her shrink and matures as a writer, eventually becoming "one of Canada's best known lesbians" (31). To unmask Swete as Dulce doesn't reveal who Dulce is, it reveals Lee's struggle as a lesbian writer in a society and language that only validates heterosexual romance.

The story concludes with Dulce, now Dulcinea to a whole generation of poets in western Canada who dedicate their work to her, as an old woman who prefers art to artists, the representation of passion to love itself. The last sentence of the story—that Rule worked so hard to create and that speaks to her still—is a metaphor for the lesbian reader, whose story can be told, but at a distance and not without traces of sorrow: "My real companions, in my imagination, are my counterparts throughout history and the world who, whatever names they are given, are women very like myself, who holds the shell of a poem to her ear and hears the mighty sea at a safe and sorrowing distance" (32). Dulce provides a model for reading queerly that demonstrates how reader and writer constitute each other through the bond of reading. As the consummate reader of texts, Dulce by the end of the story becomes a generatrix of the texts of others. Just as important, through Dulce's story a network of readers ("my counterparts throughout history and the world") rather than writers is given an embodiment, a presence in the text, and, consequently, in the making of meaning. The ending of "Dulce" is unconventional in many ways. While the final image creates esthetic closure, it maintains the possibility for multiple readings. Rule counters the conventions of artistic coming of age stories and of the lesbian coming out stories of the 1970s and 1980s. Dulce is a seemingly isolated, somewhat melancholy figure who is left without a work or a love of her own. A more conventional ending would have brought Dulce to a literary or erotic triumph, she would have come into full possession of herself. But such an ending would cover over the more ambiguous, multilayered readings Dulce herself has learned to make. She points the way to a different, more complicated set of connections than a seemingly more satisfying ending would have allowed. Rule shows that the negotiation between writer and reader, the bond of reading, is always in process, always inflected by the time and place of both writer and reader.

In addition to learning that reading queerly doesn't lead to closure but to an opening up of layered, sometimes contradictory meanings, Dulce gradually learns the curious interdependence of heterosexual and queer meanings. The series of displacements and discoveries (textual and sexual) Dulce experiences as reader of Wilson and Lee and lover of Oscar and Lee shifts the erotic and linguistic balance conventionally assigned to heterosexuality and homosexuality. Heterosexuality is defined against homosexuality, it depends on exclusivity, the radical separation of sexual meanings. If Wilson is homosexual, that is all his poems can mean, according to Oscar. Queer desire, on the other hand, can incorporate, coexist with, and illuminate heterosexual desire (and fear). The queer text (and queer sex) is not imitative and reductive, but a more complex, inclusive paradigm that does not depend on expulsion of an opposite, an other.

Rule shifts the erotic and linguistic balance in a series of relays, as Felman would say. The apparently uncomplicated confidence of Oscar's sexuality—and art—is supported by his defensive condemnation of "faggots." After revealing Wilson's guilty secret, Oscar confirms his own sexuality with Dulce. And yet it is after her heterosexual initiation with Oscar that Dulce is better able to know and name her own lesbian desire. Having written out her internalized loathing to an assumed heterosexual audience, Lee is able to become a leading lesbian writer, embarrassed by her earlier detour of denial. Dulce, meanwhile, reads beyond the pretense of the demonized lesbian to see a reflection of Lee's struggle rather than a distorting representation of herself. In each case, heterosexual imposition is the illusion, the incomplete, false, or falsifying reading, the source of pain. Rather than represent homosexual texts or desire as imitations or as pale reflections (not real men), Rule's story represents heterosexual readings as partial and heterosexual desire as anxiously supported by the phantom of the homosexual other.

This Not Quite Promised Land

As I finished "Dulce," I thought back to early, unpublished (Rule has said, "unpublishable") manuscripts I had read in the archives. *Desert of the Heart* was not Rule's first novel, though it was the first to find a publisher; she spent years working through other manuscripts for novels and short stories before she wrote the characters of Evelyn and Ann with such unapologetic clarity. In fact, *Desert of the Heart* was her third or fourth novel, depending on how you count multiple, radical revisions of novels she titled *Who Are Penitent, This Not Quite Promised Land* (in two entirely different versions), and *Not for Myself Exactly* (an alternate title for *This Not Quite Promised Land*), among other heavily reworked manuscripts. The negative titles would be echoed later in the 1970 novel that followed *Desert of the Heart, This Is Not for You*, in which Rule portrays from within a tortured lesbian subjectivity defined through internalized homophobia and denial. Thematically the traces of condemnation and repentance in these early manuscripts signal the struggle of the young Rule to break through literary and social restrictions to speak a different kind of desire.

Like Wilson's early poems in "Dulce," these fictions represent unrequited, forbidden, or dangerous heterosexual desire. The romance plots often stage uncertainty about gender performance, most frequently as lonely efforts by male characters to define manhood. In psychological isolation, feeling inadequate, these characters resist or conform to what they perceive as restrictions imposed by gender expectations. While male characters struggle with the exigencies of masculinity, female characters often recognize strength in one another. A few flashes that hint at the quality of Rule's later fiction capture this recognition between strong female characters. For example, one male character observes: "There can be, between two women, a sudden intimacy of direct recognition that, in comparison, makes even lovers seem remote from each other" (box 11, folder 2, 100). Reading forty years later, I can't help but wonder if crises of masculinity sometimes stand in for crises of femininity; the erotic charge of the "intimacy of direct recognition" seems barely disguised.

Gender transpositions and encoded desire in these manuscripts lead to insoluble technical problems concerning point of view and plotting. The various versions of *This Not Quite Promised Land* center on the thwarted love story of an Englishman (Derek Good) and an American woman. The woman character is suggestively named Page Benjamin, combining the youngest child and the beckoning page, the site of the writer's desire and struggle. In one version, their story is told (improbably) in a long retrospective narrative by Page's eventual British husband (Peter Sargent) from their Vancouver home decades later. One of the many problems with the narrative is that there is no plausible reason why Derek and Page's affair should be forbidden, much less why Peter should know such intimate details about it.

Rule's experimental manuscripts show a young writer trying to find ways to express sexual desire and discovering the imbrication of body and language, sexuality and social codes. In a sexual initiation scene, for example, Rule imagines erotic violence that merges pleasure and disgust, masculine aggression and female masochism: "Derek used Page's body with lust and brutality which she received, exalting in pain. He named her the foulness of his despair, and in those names she felt a wild joy. It was a shocking and magnificent night, out of which they came exhausted and free of any fear of separation" (box 11, folder 2, 27). In the margin, Rule has penciled "rewrite."

Using the map for rereading suggested by "Dulce," the struggle of lover and mistress, writer and blank page staged in this initiation yields multiple interpretive possibilities. The easiest way to read (and dismiss) these efforts would be to assume that heterosexuality is an imperfect, distorting disguise for a lesbian affair. We would assume that Rule is hiding the "real" lesbian subject behind a heterosexual screen in order to write for a mainstream audience. In fact, this reading *does* resolve one of the major flaws of the text: once Derek is read as the literary cross-dressing of a lesbian lover for Page, the forbidden aspect of their love becomes plausible. But this reading mimics Oscar's reading of Wilson: once you have the key, the text becomes transparent. If we imagine coexisting, layered sexual meanings (such as Dulce discovers in rereading Wilson after Oscar's revelation), we can understand the sexual initiation scene in a more complex way. If we imagine that Rule is simultaneously staging anxious heterosexual desire and forbidden lesbian desire, a relay of associations emerges. First, we can discern a model of a heterosexual erotic based on a coupling of male aggression (*lust and brutality*) and misogynist anxiety (*the foulness of his despair*) with female passivity (*she received*) and masochism (*in those names she felt a wild joy*). When read as a displacement, this masculine, pornographic model of heterosexual desire fades into a model of lesbian desire that is infected and inflected by heterosexual disgust. This reading acknowledges the heterosexual screen, the lesbian subtext and their imbrication. The lesbian aggressor, assuming Derek's role, uses Page sexually and speaks the sexual insults that name lesbian desire. She violates sexual taboo even while speaking the words that have always named it as taboo, foul, and forbidden. Sexual pleasure is derived from transgression. "Derek" uses the (blank) "Page" to claim the foul, despairing words that "name" lesbian desire in an erotic economy that only validates heterosexual desire. The misogyny of the heterosexual coupling transmutes into homophobia in the lesbian coupling. Reclaiming the demonizing language releases the shocking, wild joy that Page experiences; the union realized in this struggle is verbal as well as physical: (re)possessing language as well as possessing bodies. Whether the language has been reclaimed or merely repeated is moot in this early effort. Rule's injunction to herself to rewrite reveals how important she thought this passage was, but reminds her (and us) that it was not yet resolved.

If we reread *This Not Quite Promised Land* as about *both* heterosexual initiation *and* lesbian love in an anxious, homophobic culture, we can see the ways that heterosexual anxiety and lesbian denial inform each other. Further, we can imagine that lesbian desire is about more than transgression and the forbidden (*the foulness of despair*) even while marked through and through by the forbidden and by the violence of denial.

Rule arrived at the language of *Desert of the Heart* only after having navigated through the codes and detours of these first literary efforts. The first readers of *Desert of the Heart* in 1964, trapped in the unexamined contradictions of anxious homophobia Rule tries to unravel in the early manuscripts, responded to the first published novel with charged ambivalence. In chapter 4 I will discuss the ways this positive lesbian romance resignifies sexuality. At the time of its publication, readers reading in public—in the mainstream press, for example—were able to see only what they could already recognize: demonized lesbian characters and a reincarnation of Radclyffe Hall. David Benedictus in the *Sunday Telegraph* (February 9, 1964) provides an exemplary reading of this type: "The relationship between the two principals is a tortuous and tormented one. Nevertheless, this is a literate, compassionate and bitter book, a sort of well, well, well, of loneliness." Benedictus fails to engage the text and can only see a repetition of his own expectations. He forces Rule into a figure of the lesbian writer that doesn't, in fact, fit.

Readers reading in private, with their own lives, resembled Dulce rereading Wilson; they found a more complexly layered text and traces of their own story. One woman, writing from England, said: "Having only just discovered your novel *Desert of the Heart* I find that you have written my book for me. Oh not the same place, the same time or the same people. But it's the same sense, the same significance and the same expression. I have read and reread it about twenty times and you used all the words I would have used if I could have" (box 19, folder 9, 1971). For this reader, the language of *Desert of the Heart* matters more than particularities of plot and characterization. The novel is porous, multilayered and puts into play more than one narrative point of view. The lesbian reader discovers language to read and speak her own life without being constrained by preconceived meanings of lesbian desire. In this more intimate bond of reading, Rule is constituted as *a* lesbian writer not assimilated to a single model of *the* lesbian writer; in the same movement, her reader finds the words to speak her own life and therefore to possess it more fully.

The ferry horn sounds and cuts short my imaginary voyage through Rule's early work. "Dulce," then, will be my guide through the rich but unsorted, contradictory papers from Rule's experimental years. As I raise my eyes from the pages of *Inland Passage*, Sturdies Bay comes into view. Waiting for the ferry to release its travelers, I strain to see the islanders awaiting the boat. Towering over the heads of the crowd, two tall women greet their neighbors and scan the crowd of foot passengers. I wave to them, Jane and Helen, welcoming hostesses, good neighbors, gentle survivors in their adopted land.

Self-Reflections: Growing Up Midcentury, Middle Class, Middle Child

How did "Jinx" (or "Jincus," nicknames used by her family and friends to distinguish her from other friends and relatives named Jane), who grew up in a middle-class family in the United States at midcentury become Jane Rule, Canadian lesbian writer? There is, of course, no simple or ready answer to that question. A fully articulated biography is beyond the scope (and beside the point) of this book. My main concern is to investigate the fictional, specifically invented aspect of Rule's work, to examine the ways in which Rule as writer experiments with subjectivities, especially lesbian subjectivities, in language. In an essay called "I Am Alone Here," written in 1969 or 1970, Rule wrote: "My characters are not veiled portraits of me or the people I know. They are ideas embodied in metaphors of personality living in a world I invent for them" (box 18, folder 1). Like any writer who considers herself a realist, however, she anchors her characters and situations in her experience of the world. She has acknowledged in interviews that she constructs her characters with a composite of physical traits, gestures, attitudes that she has observed in her friends or herself. She understands this as a way of feeling responsible for them, connected to them, but does not see it as an invitation to read her work as *romans à clef* or barely disguised autobiography. In some cases a family experience suggests a way of dramatizing a situation. For example, the frequency of twins in her family—her father was a twin and there were both identical and fraternal twins in her extended family—makes its way into her fiction (in *Memory Board* and *Theme for Diverse Instruments,* among other texts) as a device through which to examine how the sole variable of gender redefines or resignifies the lives of two people who are identical in every other way.

I am not interested in uncovering autobiographical sources for her fictional situations and characters; I am interested in understanding the narrative contours Rule has given to her own story. How does Rule's work engage (whether she intended it or not) cultural problems and forms of social and psychic power? How does her work provide, in turn, a means for readers to resist naturalized forms of power? A body of diverse published and unpublished texts gives some idea about how Rule herself has considered the significant events and people of her life at different moments, seen from different perspectives. These self-reflections provide useful insights into the family and social conditions in which Rule was raised. I will look specifically at nonfictional writing to find fragments of autobiography, but not because it is "truer"; these, too, are invented texts and, as Margaret Atwood has said, only the very naive equate "nonfiction" with "true."[2]

With *Lesbian Images,* in 1975, Rule entered fully into the public conversation that was emerging about gay and lesbian history. Commissioned by an editor at Doubleday, Rule took on the assignment reluctantly because it is not the sort of writing she was particularly interested in doing. But she recognized personally and in the lives of her friends that a book that would complicate our understanding of the multiple meanings of "lesbian" through a recovery of the work of lesbian writers and the images they created (some positive, some negative, some deeply ambivalent) was needed. Significantly, she frames her introduction to the book with an autobiographical sketch in which she presents herself as both a reader and a writer. Shaped by texts herself, she has in turn been read (and misread) through the books she has written.

In the following pages I will consider Rule as a writer and reader of her life: what events and themes does she identify as significant in shaping a narrative of her childhood? What events does she dwell on, what kinds of things does she leave out? The overall narrative of the self that emerges from these texts tells the story of an idealized childhood in a loving, white, middle-class family. It moves on to an opaque and seemingly inaccessible adolescence during a war that took her father away for three years until she was nearly fifteen, followed by a literary apprenticeship to great books and the male themes they privilege. After a brief breakdown and a period of depression associated with abortive love affairs and rejected writing, the story turns to a settled if unconventional domesticity that provides the grounding for literary productivity.

The story of Jane Rule's childhood, her family, and the various places they lived can be pieced together from several narratives—published and unpublished—in which she looks back on her life. The introduction to *Lesbian Images* is one such document. The following year she did a

---

2. At a reading from *Alias Grace*, Palo Alto, California, January 15, 1997.

lengthy interview with Geoffrey Hancock for a Canadian journal that prompted her to talk about her life. A number of her essays, including many columns written for *The Body Politic*, presented occasions for self-reflection. At a time in her life when Rule was feeling her age and her arthritis and when she was feeling "stalled" in her creativity, her imagination unaroused by fictional possibilities, she started to write an autobiography she called *Taking My Life*. A manuscript version of at least part of the autobiography is available in the Jane Rule Papers at the University of British Columbia in box 13, but it is not dated. A typescript, dated 1983, is in the archives but unavailable to readers. A more finished, shorter autobiography was published as "Jane Rule" in an authors' autobiography series in 1994. Interspersed among the letters and manuscripts in the archives at the University of British Columbia are other fragments of self-reflection, some in a parodic mode, such as her mock entry into a "Mrs. Chatelaine" contest in 1968 in which she plays with the ways her life refuses to fit the categories given on a questionnaire designed to identify the model Canadian housewife (box 23, folder 1).

There are many details in the stories she tells that typify the white middle class in America at mid-century: an apparent stability defined by unstable institutions. In the wake of the Depression and again after World War II, middle-class privilege is threatened by economic uncertainty; her (provisionally) intact nuclear family is buffeted around the country because of national emergency or corporate whim. Jane Rule has often characterized her parents as "that myth rarely discovered outside of ladies' magazines, a genuinely happy and deeply devoted pair" (*Images* 7). She doesn't pretend that this marital harmony was achieved without effort, but she maintains that the effort was mutual and mutually rewarding.

Rule was born on March 28, 1931, in Plainfield, New Jersey, sixteen and a half months after her brother Arthur. Her parents were living in Westfield, New Jersey, in "the Gatehouse," an "impractical, storybook house" on property owned by her paternal grandparents (*Taking My Life* box 13, page 3). Her father, Arthur Rule, who had graduated from Annapolis, was working for his father in the construction business. The values of her father's family—in which the men routinely went to Annapolis or West Point—were military and Southern. A family farm still existed in Kentucky. Her mother, née Jane Hink, came from an affluent, old San

Francisco family. But the sturdy, complacent values that might be associated with the privileged backgrounds of each of her parents had been or were about to be tested in ways that are more typical of the white middle class in midcentury America than cultural myths would have us believe. Rule's maternal grandparents had divorced when their only child, Jane's mother, was four years old. Rule's maternal grandfather then married a succession of women but his existence was treated as a sort of family secret, facilitated by the grandmother's remarriage to "Colonel Packer," who took on the role of grandfather. Rule's paternal grandfather, whose business promised economic stability, went bankrupt by the time Rule was five years old. Rule's mother subsidized a move to Palo Alto, California, with a legacy from her grandmother, taking the young family closer to her own family of origin but creating a rift with her husband's family.

This was the first of many changes the family would experience over the next fifteen years. In California they lived first with "the Colonel and Mother Packer," and then in a small house of their own. Jinx attended multiracial public schools, and in the summer the family would take the ferry across the bay to Marin County (the Golden Gate Bridge wasn't completed until 1937) and drive another nine hours to what became for young Jane an enchanted landscape: South Fork, 240 acres of redwood trees on the Eel River in Humboldt County. In her draft of an autobiography, Rule says: "It was officially Paradise Ranch, named by a fruit rancher who owned it until he was killed by Indians and my great grandfather Vance bought it from his bank cheaply" (*Taking My Life* box 13, page 13). Without glossing over the hardship such an isolated vacation in rather crude conditions caused for her mother, who had to take care of her own family and assorted visitors, and aware that relations among various relatives were hardly ideal, Rule remembers those summers as moments of splendid isolation in nature where she learned to fish, to swim, and to love the old-growth forest. Looking back she wrote: "For me, the real landscape of summer could hardly have been more magical. Just sitting on the porch steps, I could watch lizards, toads, butterflies, dragonflies and chipmunks. In the early morning and at dusk, deer fed in the orchard. Wildcat and bear occasionally appeared at the edge of the deep forest. One summer skunks lived uncomfortably near under the house" (*Taking My Life* box 13, page 18).

Even at this remote outpost, she remembers being aware of the outside world: "I had a particular nest among the willows, altered in some way each year by the spring floods. There in hiding or sitting on a large boulder in view of the highway, I could spend hours, the sound of the summer traffic faint about the sound of the river, reminder rather than disturber of solitude" (*Taking My Life* box 13, page 17). In one of her first efforts to write a novel (*Who Are Penitent*, written during Rule's year in London, 1952–53, which I will discuss in chapter 2), Rule returned to this landscape of childhood, the integrity of the old-growth forest mirroring the innocence of childhood. At the end of the manuscript, she has her character return to that spot as an adult whose illusions have been shattered, whose loyalties and certainties have been sorely tested. Her last gesture is to return to the family property to settle a deal with loggers to sell the trees and the land. In the last scene, she witnesses the felling of the huge redwood that in childhood she had called "the cathedral." In spite of the importance Rule attaches to the South Fork landscape in her own reconstruction of childhood, it has rarely surfaced in her published writing. One exception is the character of Ruth Wheeler in *The Young in One Another's Arms* who remembers such a time and place and who links the destruction of the land in the name of progress with personal injury and death.

When Jane was seven, her sister Libby was born, and even as her place in the family structure was forever shifted from younger to middle child, the family itself was uprooted again. Her father's company required him to leave the Bay Area and move to Hinsdale, Illinois. Her mother was very unhappy there, and her father was away from home more often than not. The next year they were moved to St. Louis, where Jane witnessed racial segregation and the many indignities that children visit on each other in hostile surroundings. Rule says the frequent relocations she experienced as a child taught her a valuable lesson in cultural relativism. From issues as serious as segregation to relatively trivial questions of accent, taste, and fashion, Jinx learned that community mores vary significantly. "I think the moving around was very good in one sense. I learned very early that what a great many people thought of as 'values' were really 'manners', and that 'manners' shifted radically from community to community" (Hancock 60–61).

Rule begins an autobiographical sketch she published in 1994 with one of the rare good events that happened during their short stay in St. Louis:

> When I was ten years old, I put on my first pair of glasses and saw in-dividual leaves on trees, the small stones which made up the gravel drive, the letters on street signs. . . .
>
> "You mustn't mind having to wear glasses," my mother said.
>
> Mind? Since no one else in the family did wear glasses, I was the only one to understand what a miracle they were. I was the only one who could choose, if I felt like it, to retreat again into that soft, vague world of the nearsighted where other people's concerns and even identities blurred. Or I could look with new eyes and read a world I had only guessed at before.
>
> "Four eyes!" kids shouted on the playground.
>
> "Two better than you," I'd shout back, meaning it. ("Jane Rule" 309)

Not long after the Japanese attack on Pearl Harbor, Rule's father reenlisted in the navy and was assigned to preflight school in Orinda, California. The family followed him back to the Bay Area, where Jane was enrolled, for a time, at a private girls' school, Anna Head's, in Berke-ley. The family barely finished out the school year in Orinda. Mr. Rule had volunteered for overseas duty and would be shipped out from Seat-tle. In a 1998 essay called "I Want to Speak Ill of the Dead," Rule re-flects on her difficult, sometimes competitive, deeply important rela-tionship with her bigger-than-life father whose approval was never com-pletely forthcoming. She returns again to her grief at his absence from her life between the ages of twelve and fifteen when he went to war. More than five years after his death she writes: "If I never quite managed to forgive him for going away to war, how on earth am I going to learn to forgive him for dying?" (52). When Arthur Rule went to war, his wife and children moved back to Palo Alto. Back for a time in the public schools she had known earlier, Jane discovered that a Japanese-American classmate had been sent to an internment camp.

Thanks to her maternal grandmother's generosity, Jane was enrolled in another girls' school, the Castilleja School, in Palo Alto. A day stu-dent, Rule was both a part of the school and an outsider. Most of the stu-dents were boarders who came from very wealthy families. Her in-sider/outsider status and the vagaries of her immediate family's financial stability led her to understand that the world of upper middle class privilege of Mother Packer, which had been her own mother's world as well, was a thing of the past. The effects of the Depression and, later, the effects of mobilization in World War II gave her a perspective on seemingly solid social institutions that was distinctly different from her mother's generation.

Rule describes Castilleja (and the Anna Head School earlier) as a place where what had been liabilities in the coeducational classroom became assets.

> At twelve I was sent to a girls' school, grateful because I was already too tall, too active, and too bright to make anything but the most grotesque transition into heterosexual adolescence. Among girls I could still take pride in all those attributes my brother could carry into maturity without apology. I didn't want to be a boy, ever, but I was outraged that his height and intelligence were graces for him and gaucheries for me. Since I could not hide the one fault, I decided there was no point in hiding the other. In a girls' school to play basketball and argue the fine points of Latin grammar were not considered abnormal. (*Images* 4)

While she was at the Castilleja School, Rule developed a close relationship with a young married woman artist. The attraction she felt for her and a few unrelated episodes in which older women kissed her or flirted with her suggested—at least in retrospect—the possibility of sexual desire between women. She also read *The Well of Loneliness* during her high school years. During her senior year, Rule challenged the head mistress and was either expelled (the official version) or quit (Rule's version).

In the various fragmented narratives that Rule has composed about her adolescence, her parents, especially her mother, sided with her when she faced institutional injustices. When she left Castilleja she says: "The anger I felt at all authority was constant for me now. I wanted nothing more to do with any of them. Mother raged with me" (*Taking My Life* box 13, page 89). I will return to these stories in the next chapter because Rule has returned to them often in an effort to understand their meanings for her and for the world she inhabited.

While her family provided a sense of continuity and protection in a rapidly changing world, there were the inevitable physical and emotional difficulties. Her sister Libby was critically ill and nearly died before having a mastoid operation; her brother Arthur became increasingly restless; school was a place where Jinx could test her mind and where she developed a sense of her own powers—to amuse her classmates and to resist arbitrary exercises of authority by teachers and administrators. And yet she also had a sense of unreality and confusion about her interior life during adolescence. In *Taking My Life* she writes:

> I have been able to use quite a lot of the material of my childhood in fiction, but I have never been able to use the years of my adolescence. In the great range of characters in novels and short stories it is as if people between the ages of 13 and 15 didn't exist. Yet I not only lived through those years but taught students that age for two years with comprehension and delight.
>
> What has put me off, I think, is the odd blur . . . between emotional ignorance and dishonesty which characterized those years for me and misshaped my understanding for much longer.
>
> The troubled and troubling bond I had with my brother made me mistrustful of the few boys I knew, and I was physically so daunting, grateful . . . for the protection of a girls' school which could put off the question of how I could ever be a woman loved by a man. But I was frightened enough by that eventual failure to invent 'David', off fighting in the Pacific, my only fantasy life with him trying to decide how he would die, how I would mourn him. I loved all poems about the death of lovers. (65)

In an institutional environment that repressed discussion of sexuality, dealing with feelings for which she had no name, or that didn't fit the names she might have learned, she attaches heterosexual expectations to a fantasy figure she would like to kill off in the heroic mode available at the time. This, at least, would give a noble conclusion to a sexuality that she alternately feared and feared failing.

In contrast to the idealized, poetic death of her fantasy lover, Rule suggests that the war became visible in the broken bodies and minds of young men whom she saw at the Oak Knoll Navy Hospital where her sister was treated and where she later did volunteer work as a college student. She talks about the temporary absence from daily domestic life of a generation of men and the effect on boys, like her brother, who were trying to sort out their masculinity on the home front, too young for the military at a time when going to war is what "men" did. When her father came back home after the war was over, her brother's situation didn't improve.

Rule appears to have been very sensitive to the tensions between father and son, perhaps all the more so because in the awkwardness of adolescence she thought she was a disappointment to her father. Remembering her father's attitude toward her brother at sixteen and herself at fourteen she writes:

> At sixteen his son was a fair beauty, vain about his clothes, entirely bored with school, secretive about where he went, what he thought and felt, if he did either. If I had presented such an adolescence to my father, he would have been amused and indulgent. At fourteen, shaped like a telephone pole, I was stiff and awkward socially . . . I had no notion of what to do about my pimpled face or my long, limp hair. Since very few clothes fitted me, I was indifferent to them. The one mirror I couldn't avoid was my father's face. It was a cold surprise to recognize how much I disappointed him. (*Taking My Life* box 13, page 75)

Later her brother would get into more serious trouble, and the conflict between father and son escalated. When Rule was a student at Mills, her brother left the army for reasons she never understood. When she asked what he did with his time in San Francisco, where he was supposed to be taking college courses, he talked about people he was meeting in North Beach, the home of the growing "beat" culture which would produce works like Kerouac's *On the Road* and Ginsberg's *Howl*. In *Taking My Life* she says: "I remember the shock of recognition when I first read *On the Road*. . . . These were the cracked young men I knew, suicidal and violent, the human rubble of the War" (126). *On the Road*, published in 1957 after Rule had gone to Canada and as many as ten years after she observed the damaged young men returning from the war, provides a language and a framework after the fact through which to interpret masculinity in crisis. There was no equivalent available to her either during college or when she started writing for making sense of her own experience as a woman and a lesbian.

Shortly after Jinx entered Mills College in Oakland, California, the family had to move again (this time to Reno, before returning again to Palo Alto). She didn't move with them and would only return home for vacations or other temporary visits from then on. During her college years Rule started to write fiction herself; she observes in *Taking My Life*: "I . . . wrote obscure symbolic stories for my writing class. Most of my main characters were young men, violent and in violent pain. . . . The few realistic stories I wrote were about troubled relationships between fathers and sons. So much of my own experience didn't seem to me experience at all, a mixture of daydreams and nightmares, out of which I could make nothing. My brother's suffering was dramatic, full of grand gestures and observable defeats" (127).

In the unspoken confusion of her adolescent feelings about sexuality, in the family scenario where her father valued her brother more obviously and worried about his development, and in the stories available to her—the "great books" she was reading at Mills and the contemporary texts of angry young men—Rule encountered the marginalization or erasure of female experience. Her own experience is out of focus, unreal; the only narratives she knew gave form and meaning to the sorrows of young men. At college, as in high school, she encountered institutional repression of female sexuality. In 1992, the Mills alumnae quarterly, in the context of examining diversity on campus, asked Rule to write about what it was like to be a lesbian when she was an undergraduate. In the essay she wrote to respond to their query, she stresses institutional repression of sexuality in general during her college years and the denial of homosexuality in particular:

> When I was a student at Mills, from 1948 to 1952, it was an offense to be sexual, never mind of what orientation. Men were not allowed in our rooms. Even the doors of the smaller living rooms were to be left open if we were entertaining men. . . .
>
> Homosexuality was never mentioned, even by the visiting woman doctor enlisted specially to give us two lectures on sex, about which she confessed she was very embarrassed, but mainly she was there to inspire us to keep our virginity as our most precious gift to our husbands. (*Mills Quarterly*, July 1992, 11–12)

Students didn't necessarily conform to institutionalized repression— if they had, the instruction wouldn't have been necessary. In *Taking My Life* Rule describes elaborate courting rituals, the trade and barter of sexual favors and triumphant victories over virginity. Heterosexuality, if offensive, was at least acknowledged. Homosexuality was never given the reality of overt institutional censure, although through rumor and observation, students learned that faculty members were fired for "moral turpitude." In the essay for the alumnae quarterly, Rule suggests that institutional containment of sexuality was ideologically linked to the ideal of "objectivity" that was central to scholarly discipline at that time. English majors were encouraged to analyze and admire great works but not to consider too closely the lives of the writers who produced them, much less relate the substance of those works to their own deeply personal struggles. Sexual policing and literary objectivity, she suggests, were rooted in hypocrisy and had personal as well as social consequences:

> As the substance of literature seemed to be nobody's business, so our own substance was nobody's business either, as long as we kept silent about it. . . . Tolerance in those days was mainly a negative virtue, the learning not to say what might offend rather than attempting to understand and include the differences among ourselves. In a way, to be ignored is better than to be mocked and castigated. Fewer people rebel in such a climate. More people crack under the strain. (11)

More than forty years later, she looks back at that climate and remembers her own shame, fear, and confusion in the face of silence, ignorance, and bigotry.

After her sophomore year at Mills, Rule would make the first of many trips to England. That first summer she studied Shakespeare at Stratford and fell in love with an English woman fifteen years her senior, also studying at Stratford. When she graduated from Mills in 1952 she returned to England for a year as an "occasional student" at the University of London, where she lived in a cold-water flat with the woman she loved. During that year, Rule wrote her first novel, never published, called *Who Are Penitent,* which I will discuss in chapter 2. It is in many ways a tortured text, heavy with religious references and marred, like *This Not Quite Promised Land,* with problems of plot and characterization. It is not an overtly lesbian novel. The few references to homosexual characters and feelings are heavily coded. When, somewhat against her better judgment, Rule submitted the manuscript to a publisher, it was rejected. In the envelope with the rejected manuscript was a scribbled note she was not supposed to see: "Sick writing by an invert." In a 1994 interview Rule said about this experience: "I knew the novel wasn't well enough done to publish. But it really offended me. And that helped me to just put it away. I thought, I have to have a piece of work strong enough so that it can survive this kind of hostility."[3] A letter written to a college friend, Ellen Kay, in August 1953, at the end of her year in London, refers to the pain her first novel caused her: "The miracle has happened. We are having a sunny bank holiday! I am sitting in my bathing suit in the garden. I can feel my spirit uncurling into the sun, the heat baking peace into my tired and doubting bones. Somewhere in the dark shadows of my writer mind another novel is growing, and the hurt of this one is healing in the sun" (box 19, folder 2).

Rule had to return to California for financial reasons at the end of her year in London. Restless, eager to return to England, she was, briefly, a student in the creative writing program at Stanford. Unable to return to England, Rule went to Massachusetts, where she taught at the Concord Academy for two years. It was during this time that she met Helen Sonthoff, who was also on the faculty. The demands of teaching, uncomfortable living arrangements, and frustration in her efforts to write took a toll during Rule's first year at Concord. She went to England that summer looking for relief, but encountered even greater emotional difficulties. In another letter to Ellen Kay in November 1955 she reflects on her first teaching year that brought her eye strain, migraine, and "bruised bones"; then she writes:

> I was quite sick after I got back from California this spring, sick as I once was at college—the long greyness. I went to England, hoping for the recovery I had the first summer I went. But I walked into the most horrible nightmare of my life, right through the mirror. I can't really talk about it yet, but after a month I went to a mental home. I had lost 25 lbs., was unable to speak. I spent a month there flat on my back, with doctors and psychiatrists saying I must stay at least a year. I got up and walked out. Slowly, I have recovered. But my health is frail and precious. I don't think I'll be really well for another six months. (Box 19, folder 2)

The social and emotional world she had known had changed. Various lovers, men and women, had switched partners. Her English lover was

---

3. Unpublished interview with the author, at Rule's home in Galiano, June 1994.

now with a woman who was wracked with Catholic guilt and "infected everyone with a sense of sin that she felt." Rule had no commitment to monogamy or a code of sexual fidelity based on exclusivity, but everyone, she says, was enraged, confused, or exhausted. Her English lover, an Anglican, was considering a Catholic order of silence (a vow she never took). Although Rule suffered in the changed English environment, she didn't give up on her fundamental optimism. She ends the letter saying:

> But, Ellen the world is magnificent, and though what little strength I have goes to earning a living, I know a book grows, a book I will speak in full voice. I'm not afraid of anything. I am bewildered. I misunderstand. And now for the first time I am frail. But . . . soon I'll make a book that is what I've wanted to say.

Still unpublished during her second year at Concord, Rule decided she needed time to write and turned in her resignation in January 1956. Years later she summarized the situation by saying: "Badgered by ill health, discouraged by obstacles in a new relationship, I determined to leave Concord and use my savings, supplemented by help my parents offered, to give myself another year for writing" ("Jane Rule" 311–12). In the summer of 1956 a friend asked her to help him move to Vancouver. She anticipated staying a few months. Before leaving she wrote on June 20, 1956, to Ellen Kay: "Passion used to be very important. Now it doesn't seem so. I look to a world with a more promising future of dailiness. Well, quite simply, I want soon to have children. If I find no relationship vital enough to create and sustain new life, I think I may live alone, friendly in the world but not so involved. I've spent all the energy I want to at the beginnings of love. I would rather work on books and have friends" (box 19, folder 2). In October she sent a postcard from Vancouver saying: "This is a beautiful, beautiful world . . . to see, to live in, to work in" (box 19, folder 2). In 1994, she looked back on that time and wrote: "In November of that year Helen Sonthoff . . . joined me for a holiday which is not, even now, over" ("Jane Rule" 312). The decision to stay was, of course, more complicated, less definite. When she was able to write it gave her great pleasure, she wanted to "make books and children" (letter of December 5, 1956, box 19, folder 2). Even after Sonthoff and Rule started to live together, they considered moving to the

Bay Area, but finally decided to make their life in Canada and become citizens there.

During her early years in Vancouver, Rule supported herself through a variety of jobs: "free-lance radio broadcasting, TV script reading, paper marking and tutoring for the English department at the University of British Columbia" ("Jane Rule" 312). Early on, she and Sonthoff became involved in the Vancouver Arts Club. Eventually it was a theater club but initially it was a club for different kinds of artists and people interested in the arts (architects, painters, musicians, actors). They shared space with the New Design Gallery, the first selling gallery in Vancouver. In 1958 she took on the job of assistant director of the new International House opening on the University of British Columbia campus. Meanwhile, Helen Sonthoff joined the English department faculty at the university. In 1959 they bought their first house and subsidized the mortgage by creating a student apartment in the basement.

Rule left her position at the International House after a couple of years in order to have more time to write. In 1961 she finished the manuscript of *Desert of the Heart,* originally called *Permanent Resident;* she had also completed a number of short stories, but except for one magazine story she was still, at thirty, an unpublished writer. Rule decided to show the manuscript of her new novel to her parents. Reflecting recently on that time, her mother (who continues to champion Rule's work and to educate people about homophobia) said, "Before I read *Desert of the Heart* I didn't know Jane was a lesbian. I asked her why she was writing about people like that, and she told me. You know, people of my generation just didn't talk about those things, we never knew."[4] Her father wrote at the time:

> Mom and I don't like the subject matter, probably because we have found a satisfactory way of life that doesn't include that sort of thing. We don't know much about it and I guess it's human nature to fear the unknown. Then I imagine a lot of people don't like the kind of a story it is and yet will find it well done. The good brain you have skipped a generation as far as your pappy is concerned and I would be better able to understand a lot more of the book if I had a chance to discuss it with you. You should not

4. Conversation between the author and Mrs. Rule in Palo Alto, January 16, 1997.

have worried that either Mom or I should be shocked by it or distressed. We are not. To a degree it is to me something like modern painting or music. I don't know enough about it to understand and therefore am not going to like it until I'm better educated. That, you'll have to do. (Letter dated August 17, 1961, box 19, folder 8)

Rule sold the book to Macmillan in Canada in October of the following year, but they would hold publication until there was an English and an American publisher. The English publishing house Warburg accepted it by October 1963, but American publishers proved to be far more resistant. Rejection slips included comments such as this one from Norton: "I'm afraid the Jane Rule manuscript, PERMANENT RESIDENT, put me off on a couple of counts: chiefly the theme, of course, which is pretty familiar stuff in paper books of a certain sort. Miss Rule is not a bad writer, however. I wonder if she has something else we might look at" (box 19, folder 7). Her agent, Kurt Hellmer, wrote her a letter in October 1962 saying that Little, Brown had turned it down: "I don't agree with their reasoning. I also talked to the editor, and he said something even more foolish: that a novel about Lesbianism must be written better than WALL OF LONELINESS [sic] (sorry if this isn't the exact title, but it slipped my mind)" (box 19, folder 7). Finally, on November 1, 1963, Kurt Hellmer wrote: "I take great pleasure in informing you that the 22nd publisher to whom PERMANENT RESIDENT was offered, namely the World Publishing Company, today accepted your book for publication." World brought the book out in 1965 and remaindered it the next year.

Rule and Sonthoff were able to travel extensively in England, Greece, the United States, and Europe in their early years in Vancouver; their first extensive trip in Canada took place in the summer of 1962. Rule continued to write and in 1963 sold "No More Bargains" to *Redbook*, the first of many stories she would sell to women's magazines. "My Country Wrong" was the first story she sold to *The Ladder*, the publication of the lesbian homophile organization the Daughters of Bilitis, in 1968. Selling *This Is Not for You*, the second novel to be published, was every bit as difficult as selling *Desert of the Heart*. She completed the manuscript in 1965, but no one was interested in it. She became so discouraged that she stopped writing for a time. Finally, in 1968, McCall Publishing Company expressed an interest in the novel and asked to see her next effort, which would be *Against the Season,* as well. Grants from the Canada Council in 1968 and 1969 allowed her to finish *Against the Season* and to prepare her first collection of short stories, *Theme for Diverse Instruments,* for publication with Talonbooks, a small Canadian publisher which, unlike the big American companies, keeps titles in print.

Meanwhile, Rule and Sonthoff were creating a life together that quietly challenged accepted ideas of domesticity. Rule has always been protective of their privacy, creating a distinct line between their public and private lives. A parodic, and angry, response to a contest in a 1968 issue of *Chatelaine,* a Canadian women's magazine that bought several of Rule's short stories, reveals that Rule early understood the politics and commodification of domesticity. The contest asks, "Are you Mrs. Chatelaine?" (*Chatelaine,* September 1968, 128) and promises a first prize of $1000 plus a stereo with push button control panel, a fifty-six–piece set of china, a beautiful lady's watch, and, to nine runners-up, "an attractive Corning Ware Broil-Bake tray and chrome-plated serving cradle." To enter you needed to give certain facts about yourself (height, weight, age; your husband's name, occupation and income: "We're not being nosy—this helps to show us how well you manage"; children's names and ages) and information about your household (how often do you entertain, typical menu for a day's meals, type of home you have, special projects you enjoy, community activities), and finally, "Write a one-page description of your hopes for your children, and how you are laying the groundwork for their future. . . . Explain in a few paragraphs what you believe a wife should contribute to marriage and family life." The contest is presented on a full page of the magazine overlaying half of the smiling face of a young woman who peers out at the reader. In a cover letter to the magazine, Rule admitted that she didn't qualify: "I'm not single. I'm not married. And you've bought a short story of mine." She filled it out, though, because she wanted them to know what a bad idea it was in a magazine that has good intentions.

I don't know why [I filled it out] except maybe that a lot of my kids are in trouble at the moment and a lot of their parents are frightened for them, and I feel friendly and sad and teed off. Mrs. Chatelaine is a good straw woman for such a night. . . . Get her out. Mothers and Others don't want her. She's a smug little ad reader whose kid isn't yet in jail, and she doesn't exist. And most people who can afford the time to read *Chatelaine* don't need the temptation to create ourselves in her image. We're all smug ad readers with too many stereos and dinner plates already—or if not, we want to be. You want women in politics? Give prizes like scholarships and baby sitting money. (Box 23, folder 1)

In the answers to the contest questions, Rule identifies her mate as "Mrs. Helen Sonthoff," and she lists seven children, five not living at home, two living at home (in the student apartment). Among her "special projects" she says:

Late at night I sometimes answer form questions, to test my own sense of identity against the identity I'm supposed to have, to test my own life against the life I'm supposed to lead. It's more of a hobby than a research project, but it keeps me in touch with how hard I have to work in order to write clear, hopeful little love songs to Mrs. Chatelaine because she's the one who sends the checks for the kids. And I like to participate in the larger community. (Box 23, folder 1)

The early 1970s were a time of intense productivity for Rule. *This Is Not for You* came out in 1970, followed by *Against the Season* the next year. *Theme for Diverse Instruments* and *Lesbian Images* both came out in 1975, and by October 1976 she was correcting galleys for *The Young in One Another's Arms*. In 1979 she started writing a column, "So's Your Grandmother," for the Toronto-based gay liberationist newspaper, *The Body Politic*, which was fighting obscenity charges because of articles on man/boy love. In the early 1970s, Rule and Sonthoff were becoming increasingly involved in feminist activities with women students, faculty, and staff members at the University of British Columbia. Because Rule was a known lesbian she hesitated for a time to join feminist groups. In the introduction to *Lesbian Images* she wrote: "My reluctance to be identified with Women's Liberation at first was my concern that it be protected from the label of 'lesbian,' which my presence would encourage; but the issues mattered so much to me that I could not stay away" (10). Through her involvement in feminist discussions and studies of the status of women at the university, Rule was developing an analysis of gender and power in institutions and she was also developing an analysis of homophobia and how it affects men and women differently. In a lecture called "Voices and Silences" that she gave to a seminar on lesbian lifestyles in the fledgling women's studies program at UBC in October 1971, Rule said:

> Resisting social pressure is, or should be, a major concern for all women. We live in a culture determined to make us accept with delight inferior status not only as public persons but as individuals, self effacement and masochism the marks of maturity. All lesbians as women experience that pressure which is greater and more persistent than the pressure exerted against lesbians as morally depraved or emotionally disturbed persons who should be punished or cured. If we concern ourselves, for the moment, with resisting social pressure only as lesbians, we must not forget or delude ourselves that the larger and more difficult battle against cultural bigotry is the business of all women. (Box 23, folder 4)

The lecture includes a well articulated analysis of internalized oppression and how it erodes one's ability to act positively in the world.

Jane Rule and Helen Sonthoff have always been frequent and generous hosts. Their house was the center for an active social and cultural life. They had sold their first house and bought a larger one with a view of the sea, mountains, and the city in 1962. By the mid-1970s, however, they felt a need to escape from time to time from the intensity of their Vancouver social life. They bought a house on Galiano Island to spend the summer and occasional weekends. By 1976, Sonthoff was able to take early retirement; they sold their Vancouver house and moved full time to Galiano. Rule hoped to be able to write full time and get beyond what she characterized as her "apprenticeship novels" (*Desert of the Heart, This Is Not for You, Against the Season,* and *The Young in One Another's Arms*). Shortly after the move to Galiano, however, Rule had her first severe episode of rheumatoid arthritis which would eventually impede her ability to write full time. She and Sonthoff were able to spend a month each winter in the American Southwest (Borrego Springs, California, or Arizona) to relieve the arthritis, and in 1979 they put in a swimming pool at the Galiano house. The climate is mild enough to allow for swimming nearly six months of the year, another way of alleviating the pain of the arthritis. For many years they had open hours at the pool on summer afternoons for any child (resident or visitor) on Galiano who wanted to swim.

In spite of health problems, the late 1970s and the '80s were very productive years. In 1981, as a fiftieth birthday present to offer her friends, Jane published a collection of short stories and essays, *Outlander*, with Naiad Press, a small publishing company in Florida specializing in lesbian books. The head of the press, Barbara Grier, had been literary editor of *The Ladder* and knew Rule from those days. Naiad Press, like Talonbooks in Canada, commits itself to keeping the titles it offers in print. Nearly all of Rule's novels and anthologies continue to be available from Naiad to this day. The year after *Outlander* came out, *Contract with the World* was published and Rule started thinking about *Memory Board*. In 1985 she published two collections: *A Hot-Eyed Moderate*, which included essays, some of which had appeared first in *The Body Politic*; and *Inland Passage*, which collected previously published as well as unpublished short stories. In 1987, *Memory Board* was published, and Rule and Sonthoff, joined by Rule's parents, went to England to launch the book. In 1989 Rule published *After the Fire*, her last novel, and decided to retire. Hers has not been a quiet retirement. She has testified on behalf of The Little Sisters Bookstore to protest Canadian censorship practices, and she participates in the Canadian Writers' Union and other groups that assist young writers. From time to time she writes short, autobiographical essays such as the reflection on her father's passing; she continues to be a generous correspondent. She and Helen Sonthoff are active in the community on Galiano Island and, ironically perhaps, much of the social life they went to Galiano to get away from now comes to them on the ferry, especially in the summer.

Readers and Writers: "Language Is as Primal a Drive as Sex"

The reception of Rule's work has been vexed, from the resistance of mainstream publishers in the 1960s to recognize a lesbian text as anything but pulp fiction to the lack of attention by academic critics, even with the advent of queer theory. In 1985 Donna Deitch adapted *Desert of the Heart* for the movie, *Desert Hearts*, and brought Rule to the attention of a whole new generation of lesbians as well as to a broader audience. In 1994, the University of British Columbia bestowed an honorary degree on Rule; Rule used the occasion, characteristically, to thank and to challenge the institution. She accepted the degree "not only on my behalf but on behalf of my gay and lesbian colleagues who have worked so hard to make this university a more tolerant and welcoming place. I accept it, too, for those who failed under the heavy burden of prejudice." In 1995, the Canadian filmmakers Lynne Fernie, Aerlyn Weissman, and Rina Fraticelli, who had made *Forbidden Love* about Canadian lesbians and the bar culture of the 1950s and 1960s, made the documentary, *Fiction and Other Truths: A Film about Jane Rule*, which won the Canadian Genie award. Even with this visibility, Rule's work has not received the critical attention one would anticipate for a lesbian writer of this caliber whose works continue to be available in the mad rush of gay, lesbian, bisexual, and queer publishing of the 1990s. This can be accounted for in part by the fact that she has retired, and that her last novel was published in 1989. But a closer look at the ways lesbian identities have been formed since the mid-1960s in North America suggests that the strength of her writing, the deep bond with her readers, and the indifference toward her work by critics stem from the same source: her resistance to dominant narratives, whether they are sanctioned by the mainstream culture or by political and sexual subcultures.

When Rule started to think of herself as a writer and as a lesbian, homophile organizations such as the Daughters of Bilitis hadn't yet taken shape. There was, to be sure, a bar culture in the Bay Area, but Rule has never frequented bars. There was not as yet a feminist movement that could provide a community within which to rethink gender and, ultimately, sexuality. As I suggested in the reading of her unpublished novel *This Not Quite Promised Land*, the young writer in the early 1950s was slowly working out a language through which to articulate gender and sexuality in ways that exposed the unspoken assumptions of conventional literature and potentially suggested ways of writing against those expectations. Her letters also show her struggling with the mandates of middle-class femininity to marry and bear children and her own drive to write books and lead an independent life supported by friends.

Rule's first two published novels, *Desert of the Heart* (1964) and *This Is Not for You* (1970), which center on the struggle to claim a lesbian identity in a society hostile to lesbians and unsupportive of independent women, were both written before there was a homophile movement visible to most lesbians and homosexual men or a viable feminist movement. When the women's movement and gay and lesbian groups became active and visible in a way that even mainstream media had to recognize in the early 1970s, the primary means for women to rethink gender and sexuality were consciousness-raising groups and other community-based discussion groups and actions. Sexual identities became politicized in powerful and recognizable ways, but the groups within which they were fashioned also tended to regulate as well as facilitate lesbian identity formation. Recent efforts to define a tradition of lesbian literature have been shaped by the sexual politics of the 1970s as seen in retrospect. For example, Lillian Faderman's important anthology of lesbian literature from the seventeenth-century to the present, *Chloë Plus Olivia,* organizes texts from the twentieth century around the categories of 1970s lesbian feminism (the closet before the 1969 riot at the Stonewall Inn, amazons as the defining figure of lesbian feminism, and post-lesbian feminism after the 1980s). Like all first efforts at categorization, Faderman's taxonomy obscures as much as it illuminates. The anthology includes Rule with the amazons of 1970s lesbian feminism. This categorization doesn't account for the fact that Rule's formation as a writer predates lesbian feminism and that her more mature works complicate rather than illustrate the figure of the lesbian amazon.

Rule, first because of historical accident and then because of geography, was relatively removed from the lesbian feminist communities that were opening up new ways of thinking about sexuality. I don't mean to suggest that Rule was an isolated voice cut off from public discussion; on the contrary, beginning most visibly with her contributions to *The Body Politic* in 1976, she participated in public debates about sexuality, gender, censorship, children's sexuality, and pornography, for example, that have been central to feminist and gay and lesbian politics. In her political writing, Rule has often taken stands on pornography, censorship, and other issues that vary from the positions sanctioned by many lesbian feminist organizations. In her literary work as well, she is fully aware of the politics of representation and she has refused to adopt uncritically what she has considered to be a succession of political stances dominant in gay and lesbian, and now queer, discourse.

Because of her distance from lesbian feminist communities in the early 1970s and her entanglements with some of them because of her political essays in the late 1970s and 1980s, Rule was not adopted with the same enthusiasm as writers like Rita Mae Brown. Brown, unlike Rule, was formed in the lesbian feminist communities of the urban U.S. Northeast and celebrated daring, transgressive, lesbian rebellion in characters like Molly Bolt in *Rubyfruit Jungle*. While Rule was read and appreciated privately by many political lesbian feminists in the mid-1970s and later, as I've learned in countless conversations, her texts were not formed in and by those communities and tend to go against the grain of 1970s lesbian separatism and triumphalism. Rule was aware of the strain between some of the voices of lesbian feminism and her own sense of what she needed to write, and she sometimes responded to those critics in her column and in other essays. By the late 1970s Rule's work was too lesbian to be read without distortion by the mainstream press and too heterogeneous to pass the test of lesbian fiction among some lesbian critics. Further, as a Canadian, Rule has been overlooked by many U.S. critics, demonstrating once again that in cultural terms the border between the United States and Canada can be crossed easily by Americans but less easily by Canadians—with the notable exceptions of Margaret Atwood, k.d. lang and, more recently, writers like Carol Shields and Michael Ondaatje.

I will argue that the reasons that have made Rule problematic for mainstream and some lesbian feminist readers (her distance from the urban centers of the Northeastern United States and her tendency to resist sanctioned narratives of gender and sexuality whether they come from the dominant culture or from political and sexual subcultures) are the very reasons that she has been so important to a less visible, less public, more dispersed community of lesbian readers and to readers—lesbian or not—who are not satisfied with the narratives of gender and sexuality produced by more public and overtly political discourse both pre- and post-Stonewall. Rule's writing demonstrates and invites a textual reworking of sexuality and gender. As I will discuss in chapter 2, the narratives of gay and lesbian history that have been produced so far are based primarily on groups that are accessible through public documents or publicly visible institutions such as political organizations, bars, resort communities, and certain urban neighborhoods. The lesbian identities fashioned in these social and political communities are essential to any understanding of the history of gay and lesbian lives, but they tell only part of the story. A study of Rule's fiction and its reception gives access to a less public but no less important network of lesbian lives and ways in which readers have negotiated the terms of their lives. Text-linked communities formed by the fictions of writers like Rule overlap the social communities linked by geography and politics, but these communities are not coextensive.

In a little note on a notepad tucked in among her papers, Rule scribbled: "Language is as primal a drive as sex"(box 37, folder 3). Language is as primal a drive as sex in that we define ourselves and establish our place in the world through narratives. Defining narratives begin, perhaps, with family stories and scripts but are also produced at school, in the workplace, among friends (the stories that define the bar communities come to mind), among sports enthusiasts, television viewers, any activity that joins people through shared stories. Consciousness-raising groups allowed some women to resist gender norms sustained by dominant narratives in the 1970s and, through that collective resistance, to redefine themselves. Fictions (whether stories, novels, television programs, films or other genres) provide narratives that are publicly available and privately consumed. Rule's fictions incorporate multiple points of view, undermining the hegemony of a single explanatory model. And yet, her fictions are not apolitical exercises in relativism; in her mature work Rule orchestrates her narratives through a narrative subjectivity that establishes values but doesn't determine meanings. For example, lesbian sexuality is assumed as part of the range of human sexual experience at the same time that homophobic attitudes are assumed as part of the social landscape in which most of us live. Sexuality is neutralized as a moral category but becomes part of larger moral dilemmas having to do with responsibility, loyalty, and generosity, for example. Rule's fictions are characterized by resistance to the inevitability of accepted values, categories and conventions. Her narratives don't provide answers but create spaces in which the readers can imagine their own resistance.

The Politics of Fiction: Barbara Gittings,
Resisting Lesbian Reader

To illustrate the cultural work of fiction and the formation of a resisting lesbian reader, I'd like to turn to a 1974 interview with Barbara Gittings that Jonathan Katz included in his 1976 foundational book on gay and lesbian history, *Gay American History: Lesbians and Gay Men in the U.S.A.*[5] Born in 1932, Barbara Gittings is a nearly exact contemporary of Rule. Barbara Gittings's experience as a lesbian who struggled to understand her sexuality in the 1950s, particularly the way that fiction helped her to work through her sexuality, describes exactly the experience of many of Jane Rule's readers. Gittings was sought out by Katz because she was instrumental in establishing the first East Coast chapter of the Daughters of Bilitis in New York in 1958, and she edited *The Ladder* (the journal published by the DOB) between 1963 and 1966. Rule's first novel, *Desert of the Heart,* was reviewed in *The Ladder* in 1964, and she contributed seven stories and numerous letters and essays to *The Ladder* between 1968 and 1972, the year the magazine folded.

As a first-year student at Northwestern University, Gittings had a close (but nonsexual) relationship with another woman student that led to rumors about lesbianism. The rumors prompted Gittings to interrogate her sexual orientation and she turned to available authorities (medical and scientific texts) to try to understand what "lesbian" means. Gittings's first experience with lesbianism (and homophobia) parallels Jane Rule's in that the accusation preceded the experience, as I will explore in chapter 2.

What interests me particularly in the interview is that Gittings says that when she was labeled as a lesbian in the late 1940s, the label gave her something "to work with" (Katz 1985, 421). She had been living with "a hazy feeling" that she couldn't define; the label, however negatively defined, was at least a way to engage with discourses of sexuality. She stopped going to classes and went to the library. In her own words:

> I was very aggressive about finding . . . literature about homosexuality. I went through the stacks, I went through reference books, I went to medical dictionaries, I went to ordinary dictionaries, I went to encyclopedias, I went to textbooks, the chapters on "abnormal psychology," sections called "sexual deviations" and "sexual perversions." That kind of labeling affects your image before you get to the material. But it didn't bother me too much because I was so anxious to read about myself. . . . I remember a scientific study in which a group of male heterosexuals and a group of

5. I want to acknowledge my debt to Phillip Brian Harper, who called this interview to my attention.

male homosexuals were compared for microscopic measurements of their bodies—the diameter of the cranium, the circumference of the neck, the length of the nose, the length of the earlobe, the circumference of the hips—to see if there were significant differences between the two groups. The fact that it was about male homosexuals really didn't bother me that much. Most of the material was on male homosexuals. (421)

Gittings's experience is a textbook example of interpellation. Having been called a lesbian (though she had not "experienced" a lesbian relationship), she turns to authoritative discourse (medicine and science) to read her own body and desire—never mind that the bodies and desires being measured and mapped were male. Even though she doesn't see herself reflected in the discourses she was interrogating, she doesn't at first question their accuracy or relevance—she had no ground from which to do so. When she learned that the favorite color of homosexuals was green she thought she was wrong to favor blue. There was no opening in the authoritative texts for her to resist their authority.

Then she discovered another kind of text through which she could interrogate the meanings of sexuality:

What really changed my image and gave me a much more positive feeling about homosexuality—even though I still thought it was a misfortune that needed to be changed—were the novels. In some of the so-called scientific materials I read, there were references to fiction titles, and I began to seek these out. As I remember, *The Well of Loneliness* was the first book I latched on to. (422)

What she found in the fiction was a lesbian character with complex emotions with whom she could identify. Fiction provided an opening for the reader that authoritative texts did not. She goes on to say:

Then I began to find other books. . . . The fiction made a big difference, because here were human beings that were fleshed out in a dimension that simply wasn't available in the scientific materials. . . . I appreciated the novels because even though most of them had unhappy endings, they did picture us as diverse people who had our happiness. . . . The nonfiction literature gave me a bad picture of myself, a picture I had to work against. The fiction, despite stereotypes, despite unhappiness, despite bad characters, was much more positive. (422–23)

Gittings goes on to say that she longed for someone to talk to about the books she was reading and the thoughts they were provoking. She went looking for company in the bars. But she didn't find women in the bars who were reading the same books she was reading. When Katz asks her if she was looking for a sense of lesbian community in these books, Gittings answers: "Oh, very much so, although I wouldn't have put it in those words . . . at the time I would have said 'I'm looking for my people.' Then I was so glad to find that my people existed, that there was literature about them, and a literature that portrayed them as human beings. There was definitely a sense of community, and of history, conveyed by the novels" (423). The community Gittings was looking for (and found) in fiction finally materialized for her when she found her way to an early meeting of the original chapter of the Daughters of Bilitis in San Francisco in 1956. Gittings stresses that the DOB and *The Ladder* enabled women to take steps toward resistance to what we now call homophobic definitions of lesbians. Fundamental changes in consciousness were "fomented in the sixties, well before Stonewall. The one thing that Stonewall represents . . . is a sudden burgeoning of grass-roots activity" (427). She stresses the importance of finding a way for lesbians to negotiate a positive sense of themselves before they can move to political action and social change. Katz mentions that early issues of *The Ladder* carried letters from all over the U.S. from women in little towns who wrote to say how important it was "just to have the knowledge that the DOB exists, that the magazine exists." Katz cites Lorraine Hansberry, the African American playwright, who wrote two (anonymous) letters to *The Ladder* in 1957 in which she said: "Women, like other oppressed groups of one kind or another, have particularly had to pay the price for the intellectual impoverishment that the second class status imposed on us created and sustained" (425). In a letter written in 1957, Hansberry characterized *The Ladder* as a place for women to engage ethical debates, to develop an analysis of their own:

> I think it is about time that equipped women began to take on some of the ethical questions which a male-dominated culture has produced and analyze them quite to pieces in a serious fashion . . . the woman intellectual is likely to find herself trying to draw conclusions—moral conclusions—based on acceptance of a social moral superstructure which has never ad-

mitted to the equality of women and is therefore immoral itself. . . . In this kind of work there may be women to emerge who will be able to formulate a new and possible concept that homosexual persecution and condemnation had at its roots not only social ignorance, but a philosophically active anti-feminist dogma. (425)

The trajectory from being interpellated as a lesbian to searching authoritative texts for a way to define one's sexuality to finding a more inviting, complex narrative in fiction for renegotiating gender and sexuality to political action that Gittings describes in her interview parallels the experience of many of Rule's readers. Rule's fiction (as early as 1964) provided a place for lesbians to "find their people," to engage with a community that had a history and that was in process. Rule's fictions didn't reinscribe a pathological view of lesbians; rather, they start with the assumption that homophobia (and other oppressions) need to be resisted.

Readers Writing

Because Rule is an inveterate correspondent and cares about her readers, she has always answered personally every signed letter she has received about her work. She has told me that the occasional hate mail she has received is often sent anonymously, but readers who find her work useful—even very closeted readers who are frightened to write about their sexuality—sign their letters. Rule has kept the letters she has received about her work. Some are included with the *Jane Rule Papers* in the archives at the University of British Columbia, others are still in her private files. Many of the letters were sent by other writers and scholars (Adrienne Rich, Rita Mae Brown, Bertha Harris, Annette Kolodny, Peg Cruikshank, Lillian Faderman, to name a few), but I'd like to focus on readers who are neither professional writers nor professional readers. Having read through all of the letters available to the public (or made available to me by Rule), I noticed several patterns. Many are what might be called typical fan letters from readers who consume her books as entertainment or who criticize and offer advice about what she should do differently (there are too many good-looking characters, her characters smoke or drink too much, she seems to equate being fat with being lazy, she should turn to Jesus because only harm can come from lesbian relation-ships). But for many readers, her fictions are an incitement to write about their own lives, sometimes sending long letters that tell their own stories even as they tell Rule how her work has helped them understand their lives differently.

Many of Rule's readers are isolated by geography or social situation from feminist or gay and lesbian communities. A breakthrough text like *Desert of the Heart* (1964) continues to be revolutionary decades later for readers who have not had access to narratives of feminism and sexual resistance. For example, a forty-five-year-old woman in a small Ontario town wrote to Rule in 1993 after having chanced upon *Desert of the Heart*: "I found myself living a similar experience and your novel changed the way I view my world. . . . You succeed in pulling [your characters] into the mainstream of everyday living, where they have always been anyway, but now they are visible, credi-ble, they have dignity" (private files). Another reader from Toronto for whom fiction had always provided a way of organizing personal meaning wrote in 1971:

> It has certainly been an illuminating and emotionally shattering experience to discover an author who actually understands the convoluted female psyche. I must say that I understand myself better now that I am ap-proaching the end of the second novel, my second, your third. . . . Hav-ing read constantly since I discovered the Bobbsey Twins at six years of age, it strikes me as unusual, now, that I haven't encountered an author, until my fortieth year, who speaks my language, hence the emotional im-pact of your books. (Box 19, folder 8)

Another reader, a lesbian from South Australia, wrote in the 1980s: "Many people like me must have put pen to paper (or fingers to key-boards) and said 'Your fiction has changed my life, also.' Perhaps that is too grand and sweeping a statement. Your fiction has changed my per-ception of my life and my perception of myself in the lives of others" (pri-vate files).

Even readers who had access to feminist communities, such as a "womon" who wrote from Brooklyn in 1981, distinguished Rule's work from other lesbian texts available to her:

Like many lesbians I devour lesbian novels, short stories, etc. Seeking words, images that validate, acknowledge our lives, our reality, in place of mainstream culture which wills us with silence, or simply maims with distortions. . . . But the really good stuff is rare. Your writing is rare. . . . You acknowledge the contradictions that are our lives. . . . I feel validate by your writing, and empowered by it. As well as just happy by it. It makes for good company. Your characters are people who I recognize quite easily—complex, scarred, courageous, funny, inadequate, but trying. (Private files)

The story of another reader, recounted in the same letter from Brooklyn, exemplifies the way in which Rule provides an opening within seemingly all powerful institutions to imagine a way of resisting:

A friend of mine when she was a kid growing up in a claustrophobic New Jersey suburb discovered one of your early books in the local public library. It was the only book she had ever seen about lesbians. She was too afraid to take it out. But she did return many times to quickly read pieces of it, sitting on the floor in the aisle between the stacks of books. You were important to her.

A letter written a few years earlier (in 1977) by a sophomore at Mills College echoes this library experience in another way. She wrote that *Lesbian Images* was kept in the "locked cabinet of the Alumnae Publications section" of the college library. A thoughtful librarian colluded with the student and "released" the book for her to read. She was so excited by the first chapter that she wrote to Rule immediately to thank her.

Other letters from women who characterize themselves as "a big bunch of closet-dwellers" (box 19, folder 8, September 1975) show that professional women who didn't dare risk identifying openly with lesbian communities found Rule's work useful. In 1976 a woman wrote from West Virginia after having read *Lesbian Images*. She admitted that she found relationships among women confusing and complex, adding "having 'closeted' myself with another for years, I often feel the protection has denied me greater understanding of women. Public school teaching forces a guarded existence as well" (box 19, folder 8).

Just as significantly, Rule's fiction has been useful to readers who are not lesbians, to men and women who discovered in her work a way to rethink their relation to the social institutions that had defined them. For example, a woman wrote the following from London in 1964, having just read *Desert of the Heart*:

> I confess I came upon it quite by chance, and had no warning of its theme. For this I'm grateful for I might not have taken it from the library if I had had advance knowledge. . . . You made me think deeply about a human relationship which I should have found, before, completely unacceptable, particularly in my own life, and I confess that I've got an extraordinary comfort from reading it. (Box 19, folder 9)

Letters from straight readers sometimes show that Rule's work has helped them have a more tolerant or understanding attitude toward lesbians. A man from Georgia who identifies as straight wrote Rule that he saw the film *Desert Hearts* and was then moved to read the book and the script and to rent the video to watch the film again. He wrote: "I've never read a book like *Desert of the Heart* before, or anything else about lesbians. It kind of showed me a lifestyle I've never been exposed to before, I'm not gay or anything like that, but perhaps I'm a little more understanding now of people who are" (private files). Another letter from a man who identifies as straight reveals an ability to incorporate insights from a lesbian text into his own life. Lesbian resistance to heterosexual conventions of intimacy can be useful for rethinking heterosexual marriage as well. He wrote from Cincinnati in 1988 that he had found *Outlander* in a box of paperbacks: "You've never met me, but you've had a very powerful impact on my life, nonetheless. I am writing to thank you for opening my eyes about what a loving, mature relationship between two people ought to be. I truly believe that if I had never come across your book . . . it would not have been possible for me to have the happy marriage I have now" (private files).

Two letters in Rule's private files were written by a man from Belfast on behalf of his reading group which had discovered *Desert of the Heart* in 1965, not long after it was published. He wrote that in their world, controlled by Catholic institutions, they are limited in what they can read: "It was by chance, Miss Rule, that we came on your book here in Belfast, as we have, more or less local writers or Books from England, in our Public Libraries they very seldom get the Books changed. The Books are as old as the buildings themselves." He doubted his letter would reach Rule but wanted her to let them know how to get more of her books. She answered immediately and in his second letter he reiterated the difficulties of censorship and surveillance in his community and, therefore, their desire to read books like hers: "It is very difficult, Miss Rule, to try and explain to people outside Ireland the choice of books Catholic people are supposed to read, we have the Church, the Catholic Truth Societie, the Government and lots more societies who stop a lot of Books and Authors' work being sold in Ireland."

The most persistent pattern in Rule's letters from readers reflects Barbara Gittings's story: a voracious appetite for narratives that incorporate contradictions and that challenge readers even as they affirm them. The letters make visible a passionate community of women and men for whom fictions matter fundamentally and for whom Rule's fictions provide a means for rethinking their lives and their place in the world. That community of readers is epitomized in a letter from 1976 sent by a woman in New York state who had just discovered Rule's books:

> In the past week I've discovered your books and have read *Lesbian Images, Against the Season* and *Desert of the Heart* in great gulps, like eating peanuts. I just have to tell you how much pleasure your books have given me—and more than that. It's hard to explain, but as someone to whom books have always been tremendously important, I've been seeking books, whether fiction or non-, about lesbianism, that don't merely rehash all the tired, old political, psychological and sociological stuff that has become so tiresome. . . . I just wanted to tell you that it's such a joy to have discovered these books, which are, in my perhaps simplistic term, "real novels" which happen to deal with women who love each other, rather than "lesbian novels." . . . Your novels have transcended that; they are on a profounder level where people realize that there are no pat answers, that lesbians, like other human beings, must resign themselves ultimately to the existential choice of struggling on separately or struggling on together. (Box 19, folder 9)

Passionate communities of readers can tell us about narratives of lesbian subjectivity that are no less political though far less visible than the narratives of lesbian lives produced through more public documents and institutions. As Shoshana Felman's work suggests, and letters from Rule's readers confirm, readers can come into fuller possession of their lives through engagement with fictions. Lesbian subjectivities formed through fiction and the private practice of reading can simultaneously incorporate and contest narratives that dominate public discourse.

I would like to suggest one more reason why Rule's work has not been central to discussions of queer literature in the 1990s, which also speaks in a positive way to some of her readership. Because her lesbian characters have not, generally, followed the triumphal, transgressive, and often playful pattern represented by Molly Bolt in the 1970s, or by a character like Winterson's Jeanette in *Oranges Are Not the Only Fruit* in the 1980s, or the bisexual, transsexual, transgendered, or multiply gendered characters of the 1990s, she has been considered assimilationist or domesticated—two attributes disdained by queer culture. Many of her readers recognize, however, that so-called assimilationist politics (a desire to live a productive and open life as a lesbian in a heterogeneous, heterosexually dominant society) are often perceived as profoundly threatening by the dominant culture, less easy to dismiss than more confrontational, in-your-face demands and postures. Recent public resistance to the legalization of gay marriage, for example, shows that many middle and working-class heterosexuals consider the social acceptance (and legal protections) attached to family life and children to be a reward for good behavior. How, then, can the rewards of married life be extended to gays and lesbians, who, by definition, are sexual outlaws who refuse to behave according to society's rules?

Further, lesbian subjectivity is not a fixed, easily recuperated or contained identity in Rule's work. Lesbian subjectivity in her fiction is a continuing challenge to the very concept of a fixed identity and to the identity politics founded on such a concept. Lesbian subjectivity creates a position or a zone within the text from which to examine the ways that sexual, gender and racial identities are produced and policed. While countering the expectations of the most recognizable narratives of queer culture, Rule's fictions demonstrate the profoundly unsettling character of "queer" sexualities in a less obvious, more deeply textual way.

I will consider the narratives (historical, political, religious, fictional, medical) Rule has written against and the narratives she created to challenge or confirm her readers. Rather than look for autobiographical sources or an inscription of her self in her writing, I will look for a history of subjectivities. I want to emphasize by this distinction that subjectivities are both product and producer of language, text-based, inviting experimentation with various subject positions. A history of subjectivities invites multiple narratives and multilayered texts. While autobiography can be as multilayered as any fictional text, there persists an urge for coherence, a unified subject and a relatively stable self. In contrast, Rule's work, whether fictional or autobiographical, reveals a passion for language and for multiple subjectivities; the invention and exploration of selves in language supersedes the illusion of a single, fixed prediscursive self.

Resisting Reason

Sexuality and Citizenship

"1954 was the last year I celebrated the 4th of July. I was not in a patriotic mood." So begins an essay, "The 4th of July, 1954," that Rule wrote thirty years after the event and which was included in the collection published in 1984 called *A Hot-Eyed Moderate*. The essay is a tight narrative knot in which Rule weaves reflections on history (1954 and 1984), place (England, the U.S., and Canada), and self-perception (the unpublished twenty-three-year-old and the outspoken fifty-three-year-old). Under the sign of celebratory patriotism, in a year noted for the rise of McCarthyism, Rule narrates a series of displacements that tell the reader a great deal about how cultural and personal meanings are made. To write "The 4th of July, 1954," in 1984 must have had both personal and political resonance for Jane Rule. The essay describes a party given in 1954 by Jessamyn West, who died in February 1984. Writing about the mid-1950s in the mid-1980s, Rule allied herself with other gay and lesbian writers and historians who were reexamining the postwar years in order to understand how sexual identities are produced, policed, resisted, and reclaimed in an intensely repressive era.

On the 4th of July in 1954, Rule tells us, she was invited to a party at Jessamyn West's house in Napa, California. West, a successful writer, best known for *The Friendly Persuasion,* had been Rule's writing teacher at Mills College a few years earlier. Napa, known now as the center of the California wine country, was known then for its state mental hospital. That particular summer Rule was frustrated in love and in writing. In 1952–53 she had lived in London with her first love, an English woman fifteen years her senior (though she hadn't told anyone that they were lovers) and she had written a number of manuscripts that remained un-published. Unable to remain in England, she returned home and en-rolled in the writing program at Stanford, but she found it to be too commercial and competitive for her tastes. She decided to take a teach-ing job in fall 1954 at the Concord Academy in Massachusetts, far from home and from her lover.

Feeling displaced and unproductive, Rule also felt vaguely menaced. In the essay she explains that she'd been in England when Senator Mc-Carthy started his witch hunts for subversives; she assumed the European press was exaggerating and couldn't imagine that anyone would take him seriously. After a few months back home in comfortable middle-class sur-roundings, she discovered that "most" people took the hunt for subver-sives seriously even if they were critical of some of McCarthy's tactics. Rule quickly understood the slippage between "homosexual" and "com-munist" in McCarthy's understanding of "subversive," and realized that just as she was preparing for her first teaching job, schools would be under close surveillance, and McCarthy's "activities gave a national focus to my personal discomforts" ("4th of July" 199).

In that frame of mind, Rule accepted West's invitation and took with her a young man from Harvard Law School whom she had met through a friend. He was more a convenience than a camouflage in a social group made of married couples in which heterosexuality was assumed and the men occupied positions of local authority: superintendent of schools, head of the mental hospital, high school principal, and funeral director. In her recollection of the day, Rule notes the "gallows humor" she found in voluntarily traveling to the site of the institution that already housed some of her "homosexual compatriots" (200). Another detail she recalls was Jessamyn West's recent acquisition of a television set. West cele-brated "television's power to expose . . . human mysteries to a large pub-lic" (201). The central event of the day recalled in the essay was a con-versation about McCarthy. In a fantasy of "poetic justice," West hoped that McCarthy himself would be charged with being a homosexual be-cause some of his aides were rumored to be homosexual. His sexual guilt by association would discredit him and put an end to his political influ-ence. Rule recalls intervening: "'He should be charged with the real crimes he's committing.' I held Jessamyn's eye and didn't glance at the psychiatrist" (202). Rule, conscious of her own powerlessness in this seemingly benign crowd that included the head of the Napa hospital, continues in a halting way to suggest that laws against homosexuality are bad law even when used against someone as repugnant as McCarthy. She recognizes that her teacher would exploit antihomosexual sentiment by applying antihomosexual laws in her fantasy of poetic justice—a fantasy neither poetic nor just from Rule's perspective. Pleading liberal tolerance for all forms of love, West defended herself, and the story goes on to say that she wrote a long letter to Rule to continue the argument. Looking back at her inability to respond to West's letter, Rule says that if she had defended her own point of view honestly, "as a homosexual," it would have seemed a case of special pleading. Her personal stakes in the issue would have undercut her position and simultaneously categorized her at best as "one of the sadder beauties of the human heart," to use one of West's phrases. Worse still, if Rule had elaborated a defense of homosexuality based on her own history, she could have lost the teaching job she hadn't yet begun in Massachusetts, and, according to the medical practices of the time, she would have been a candidate for incarceration at Napa.

Looking back in 1984 at that vexed political and personal moment in 1954, Rule extends the narrative by noting the persistence of McCarthy-like bigotry in U.S. politics in spite of McCarthy's ultimate demise. She recalls the election of Jessamyn West's adamant anti-Communist cousin, Richard Nixon; even though Nixon ultimately resigned, a victim of his own dishonest tactics, Rule wrote the essay as Reagan, "a leader in the Hollywood witch hunts of the 50s" (204), was seeking a second term. Rule ends the essay by separating herself from the moment and the patriotism (whether McCarthyism or complacent liberal tolerance) it celebrated: "I left the country, and for thirty years I have not marked the date" (204). Rule thus explains in retrospect her defection from U.S. citizenship and her disaffection with the values and norms the dominant culture upheld as reasonable or inevitable or tolerant.

In this brief essay, Rule encapsulates many of the main themes of the last twenty years of gay and lesbian history. She recovers or, more precisely, reconstructs a defining moment from the postwar period, examines the interplay of culture and subjectivity, privileges an engaged point of view rather than disqualifies it, and resists the multiple authorities that conspire to discredit and eliminate the degenerate anti-citizen. In the way she describes the party (the guest list, how the guests are identified, their place in the community), Rule reminds the reader that heterosexuality—like the Napa state mental hospital or the local high school—is a social institution. She also makes the reader understand the threat of social surveillance and sanction as experienced by the sexual nonconformist in her references to television as an instrument of exposure, loyalty oaths in public universities, and the silent presence of the head of the mental hospital at this private party. All of these gestures locate the essay in the ongoing conversation about the meanings of homosexuality in postwar America.

Just as significantly, important elements are missing from this essay. The young Rule yearns to return to England and the woman she loved, but there is no hint of internalized guilt or of even a momentary acceptance of a pathologized model of homosexuality. The essayist, at least in retrospect, realizes that her affair would limit her own credibility were she to talk about it openly, but the blame is put on the accusers rather than assumed by the accused. Equally missing—except for the brief mention of "homosexual compatriots"—is any trace of a gay and lesbian subculture providing at least a shadow community to counter the voices of authority and power in 1950s America. I don't mean to suggest that the essay should include the themes it omits, but I am suggesting that their absence is significant. For example, a lesbian subculture was literally unavailable to Rule (and to most lesbians) in 1954. She didn't frequent bars; the first lesbian homophile organization, the Daughters of Bilitis, wasn't formed until 1955; and *The Ladder* didn't begin publication until 1956. Rule could see quite plainly that homosexuals were victims (as indicated by her reference to the Napa hospital), but she couldn't yet imagine a viable resistance for homosexuals.

In the essay Rule negotiates her identity as a writer, a lesbian, and a citizen. By "identity" I don't mean a stable, internal "truth" that she "discovers"; rather, I understand "identity" as a site of mediation and negotiation. Thirty years after her actual conversation with West, Rule can call on the insights of gay and lesbian history and politics as they had developed by 1984, and she can speak from the confidence of her own success as a writer, to stage a resistance to the meanings of "writer," "homosexual," and "citizen" as defined by the regulatory regimes of 1950s U.S. culture. The regulatory regimes pertinent to her in 1954 are represented in the essay by the Stanford creative writing program, the Napa mental hospital, and Joe McCarthy. But it is her teacher Jessamyn West who provides a problematic mediating figure for negotiating these three aspects of her identity, especially from the perspective of 1984.

In the summer of 1954, Rule realized she was no longer "at home" in California and felt stifled as a writer and silenced as a lesbian. In the essay, Jessamyn West is the person with whom she has the closest personal connection. She embodies the successful writer Rule would like to become, she *is* "at home" in California and in her community, and she enjoys an apparently egalitarian marriage. Rule recalls West's identity as a writer several times within the essay. For example, she reminds us of West's family connection to Richard Nixon by saying: "Because [Nixon] was a cousin of Jessamyn's, I assumed he was something of a political embarrassment to her even before he was forced to resign, but in the tolerance of her heart she told of receiving a copy of his memoirs, inscribed, 'To the most famous author in the family from the most infamous.'"

More significantly, Rule represents West as a correspondent: "Jessamyn wrote me a long, affectionate letter on yellow foolscap further explaining her views of McCarthy, of the law, of love, which maintained the same views she had expressed at the party, inviting me to change mine" (203). The letter confirms that Rule's resistance at the party was ineffectual. And it further silences her, because, she says, "If I'd had the courage to answer as a homosexual, I would have made no headway in the argument. Instead I would have been excused from it, disqualified by my inability to be disinterested" (203). West, while seeming to invite Rule to write, continues to misread her and—unwittingly—tries to write her into a pathologized and pitied lesbian identity Rule disdains (to be a "sadder beauty of the human heart"). In 1954 Rule can't write her back. But as her papers at the University of British Columbia attest, Jane Rule always answers her letters, and this essay—dated as if it were a letter—finally completes the correspondence, though posthumously. Further, Rule inscribes this personal exchange into the larger political perspective that connects McCarthy to Nixon, Nixon to West, and the political repression of 1954 to the 1984 apotheosis of Ronald Reagan, who was himself implicated in the 1950s Hollywood purges and whose presidential victory brought back a reinvigorated anti-Communism and right-wing bigotry.

She ends the essay by writing "I left the country, and for thirty years I have not marked the date," again ascribing political meaning to her personal relocation. In 1954 West had given Rule a writing assignment she couldn't complete for thirty years. While Rule extends the discussion of national politics at the end of the essay to Reagan and the present moment, she doesn't explicitly acknowledge the feminist and gay/lesbian political movements that, in some ways, made it possible for her finally to answer West's letter. Rather, she *enacts* her own take on feminist and gay/lesbian politics by writing the essay and including it in her anthology of personal and political reflections, *A Hot-Eyed Moderate*. Here and elsewhere, Rule is allied with and stands apart from what have become the dominant narratives of gay and lesbian politics. In her essays and in her fictions, Rule resists not only pathological definitions of "lesbian" promoted by the dominant, heterosexual culture, but also political definitions of "lesbian" promoted by lesbian feminist and gay liberationist subcultures, definitions which she understands to be every bit as regulatory and confining as mainstream definitions. Her writing provides—as this essay does—a site for resisting the constraints of identity whether legislated by the state or a subculture.

Reading Fiction, Doing History

Rule's work—and her readers' reactions—provoke a reconsideration of the relation between fiction and history. Typically, historians consider fiction as a reflection of a particular moment or as an illustration of historical narratives derived from other sources. The historical record, whether straight or queer, is inevitably fragmentary. Historiography necessarily privileges publicly available documents (magazines, newspapers, written documents) or the testimony of men and women who are traceable by a group or community identity. We are fortunate to have, for example, the oral histories of the Buffalo, New York, lesbian bar culture made by Madeline Davis and Elizabeth Kennedy, and the story of Cherry Grove (a lesbian resort town on Long Island) told by Esther Newton. As revealing and enlightening as the emerging histories are, there is always more to be known, more to be imagined, more to be understood. As Martha Vicinus says: "The polymorphous, even amorphous sexuality of women is an invitation to multiple interpretive strategies. Discontinuity and reticence do not mean silence or absence. Many lesbian histories, contradictory, complicated and perhaps uncomfortable, can be told" (Abelove et al. 436). And yet, in the effort to create a coherent, legible narrative, gay and lesbian historians have privileged certain "defining events," such as the 1969 riots at the Stonewall Inn in New York City. Elizabeth Kennedy warns us that:

> By periodizing twentieth-century lesbian and gay life as pre- and post-Stonewall, we are creating a metanarrative, an overarching story, of lesbian and gay history, where we understand bar communities, resort communities, and homophile organizations as laying the groundwork for the development of gay liberation politics. By definition, seeing Stonewall as a major turning point in gay and lesbian life commits researchers to a certain vision of gay and lesbian history, one that makes central the creation of a fixed, monolithic gay and lesbian identity, most often understood as white and male. A pernicious effect of this metanarrative of Stonewall is that it tends to camouflage women's voices and make racial/ethnic groups and cultures invisible. ("Telling Tales" 73)

Among the lesbian histories that remain largely invisible are the stories of middle- and working-class women who, by choice or by circumstance, were not involved in political organizations or in the bar scene. Lesbians who worked in sensitive jobs or had custody of their children or who had a private network of friends that provided them with the sense of community that the bar scene did for other women were, nonetheless, trying to sort through the contradictory lessons about female sexuality available to them in mid-century America and fashion for themselves a positive sense of their place in the world. Many women who loved women in the 1950s and 1960s were unaware of a burgeoning lesbian subculture; isolation—because of geography or class or circumstance—kept them from any knowledge at all about lesbian possibilities. Barbara Gittings's story illustrates that one means for women to break their isolation and understand that their feelings were neither unique nor crazy was fiction; stories provided narrative form and coherence that available social scripts denied. Rule's fictions provide a means for us to complicate and add to the narratives of lesbian history available to us through the more orthodox documents of social history. The sexual subjects Rule imagines and the intense reactions of her readers provide one more interpretive strategy for bringing our history to light. These fictions are more than reflections of the moment in which they were written. Rule's narratives of sexual subjectivities were both produced and consumed as counternarratives at the time they were written and continue to serve as complicating narratives about lesbian history and possibilities today.

Defining Histories

Historians of sexuality have challenged deeply held assumptions about the relation of nature and culture, personal and social, private and public. Histories of sexuality demonstrate that whether or not we think of sex or desire as "natural," its meanings and effects are culturally defined. It is impossible to imagine desire apart from historical context, apart from its representations, apart from the ways its meanings are transmitted and controlled. Richard Parker and John Gagnon summarize recent discussions of sexual desire as follows:

> In the most recent discussions of sexual desire the focus moves from inside the individual to the external environment. . . . Rather than asking what internal forces create desire, the questions are, how is desire elicited, organized and interpreted as a social activity? How is desire produced and how is desire consumed? . . . Desire . . . becomes a social rather than an individual phenomenon. (*Conceiving Sexuality* 12–13)

Gay and lesbian histories, like feminist history, have demonstrated that sexual identities are woven together with other, inseparable identity categories such as gender, race, class, nationality. All of these strands of identity are constituted, policed, and maintained by the dominant culture in a constantly shifting relation to power. Jeffrey Weeks has suggested that we think of sexual identities as fictions, in the root sense of a shaping together of different elements into a recognizable and, therefore, legible composition. Weeks says: "A fictional view of identity does two things. First of all it offers a critical view of all identities, demonstrating their historicity and arbitrariness. It denaturalizes them, revealing the coils of power that entangle them. It returns identities to the world of human beings, revealing their openness and contingency. Secondly . . . it makes human agency not only possible but necessary. For if sexual identities are made in history, and in relations of power, they can also be re-made" ("History, Desire and Identities" 44).

Henry Abelove (1995) identifies two moments in les/bi/gay politics and history. The politics of the first moment (beginning roughly with the Stonewall Riot in 1969) resist invisibility and marginalization; he identifies this moment with the slogan, "We are everywhere." The tactic of gays and lesbians at this political and historical moment is to make their presence known, to recover lost histories, to claim their own sexuality so that mainstream, heterosexual society as well as gays and lesbians will recognize that we have always existed and exist throughout society today. The politics of the second moment (beginning roughly with AIDS activism in the 1990s) takes an "in your face" attitude; he identifies this moment with the slogan, "We are here." The tactic that typifies this moment is confrontational rather than educational. The gesture requires straight society to "deal with" gays, lesbians, queers, sexual outlaws of all sorts. Sexual identities seem to multiply and, consequently, the stability of the categories is undermined. Clearly these two moments are not neatly sequential. While the second depends in some measure on the first, they also coexist in politics, scholarship, and individual lives.

The moments Abelove identifies correspond to a change in the conceptual basis of gay and lesbian history from an *empirical* search for sexual subjects to a *discursive analysis* of sexual subjectivities. In North America, the first moment in the making of histories of sexuality was made possible by the coincidence of the Stonewall Riot in 1969 and the emergence of social history, specifically social history informed by feminist scholarship. Stonewall gave public voice (and public notice) to the presence of a gay and lesbian subculture that refused to be contained and policed by the anxious heterosexual majority. Like other oppressed groups, gays and lesbians were eager to uncover historical antecedents as a way of affirming their legitimacy as political actors. Until the early 1970s, questions of sexuality had been relegated to the private sphere and disciplines like psychology. Jonathan Katz says of his groundbreaking 1976 work, *Gay American History: Lesbians and Gay Men in the U.S.A.*: "I will be pleased if this book helps to revolutionize the traditional concept of homosexuality. This concept is so profoundly ahistorical that the very existence of Gay history may be met with disbelief. The common image of the homosexual has been a figure divorced from any temporal-social context. The concept of homosexuality must be historicized" (6). Gay and lesbian history looked at the ways that public authorities (the military, elected officials, schools, and other social institutions) policed homosexuality and then identified resistance to those authorities by the growing gay and lesbian subculture, visible in the early homophile movement and in gay and lesbian social institutions such as bars.

The narratives of the first moment in gay and lesbian history as articulated by scholars such as Allan Bérubé, John D'Emilio, Michael Bronski, Martha Vicinus, Elizabeth Kennedy and Madeline Davis, Esther Newton, and Lillian Faderman, for example, account for the conditions for gays and lesbians in the military during World War II and the beginnings of resistance in the period after the war.

The narratives of the first moment of sexual histories highlight the relative tolerance toward homosexuals during the Second World War and the dramatic geographical dislocations that laid the groundwork for the gay and lesbian subcultures of the postwar period. They also show how abruptly and completely public attitudes about sexuality and gender can shift as the highly politicized perceptions of national need change. Yet they also show that even in the context of the Cold War 1950s in the U.S., when homosexuality was stigmatized as sinful, criminal, treasonous, and sick, there were the beginnings of resistance in gay and lesbian social institutions, the early homophile movement, and homophile publications.

In the second moment of gay and lesbian history, historians of sexuality are moving beyond the recovery of sexual subjects; they are asking new questions of historical documents to try to understand how sexual identities are produced. Elizabeth Kennedy and Jonathan Katz, two of the pioneers of the first "we are everywhere" moment of gay and lesbian history, have moved their own work into the second "we are here" moment of queer history. Reconsidering her own work in the Buffalo study of lesbian bar culture, Elizabeth Kennedy wrote recently: "While gay and lesbian historians need to continue the 'empirical' uses of oral history—of adding social facts to the historical record—we also need to expand our understanding of what can be learned from oral sources" ("Telling Tales" 60). She argues that storytelling styles and attention to the constructed nature of oral histories provide information that extends and complicates the empirical uses of oral history. Oral histories are not un-mediated, raw documents of lesbian life but fictions that can tell us more than their most obvious content. Kennedy doesn't jettison the earlier re-trieval work, but returns to it with new methods of interpretation. In-formed by the work of Michel Foucault and of queer theorists, sexual historians like Kennedy are moving from the recovery of historical sex-ual subjects to an analysis of sexual subjectivities; from questions about *causes* of sexual orientation to questions about the *meanings* of sexual be-haviors and the *policing* of sexual identities. Briefly put, to quote Fou-cault:

> It is in discourse that power and knowledge are joined together . . . we must conceive discourse as a series of discontinuous segments whose tac-tical function is neither uniform nor stable. To be more precise, we must not imagine a world of discourse divided between the dominant discourse and the dominated one; but as a multiplicity of discursive elements that can come into play in various strategies. It is this distribution that we must reconstruct, with the things said and those concealed, the enunciations re-quired and those forbidden, that it comprises; with the variants and dif-ferent effects—according to who is speaking, his position of power, the in-stitutional context in which he happens to be situated—that it implies; and with the shifts and reutilizations of identical formulas for contrary objec-tives that it also includes. (*The History of Sexuality* 100)

The study of subjectivities depends on the prior, empirical discovery of sexual subjects, but shifts the focus from the historical product to forms of cultural production and control. To borrow Foucault's formulation, the history of sexuality examines "the historical relationships of power and the discourse on sex" (90).

Another way in which Foucault's thinking has become available to historians of sexuality is in the work of literary theorists and, now, queer theorists whose work is usually interdisciplinary. An important essay in the development of queer theory and new methodologies for approach-ing the history of sexuality is Jennifer Terry's 1991 essay, "Theorizing Deviant Historiography." Using methods from the history of science and from literary criticism, Terry illustrates ways of rereading the historical record—in this case a study of lesbians in New York in the 1930s by med-ical and scientific experts—to identify within a text shaped by the terms of authoritative discourse, sites of resistance by lesbian participants, and resistance to the meanings that scientific authorities were attaching to their bodies and behaviors.

I don't mean to suggest that this change in the direction of sexual histories is inevitable, uncontested, or wholly productive. In her article, "The Discipline Problem: Queer Theory Meets Lesbian and Gay History," Lisa Duggan describes the obstacles to legitimacy that gay and lesbian historians continue to confront within academic history departments and the disdain or dismissiveness with which much of the early, archival work is treated by queer theorists not trained in history who have come into academic life after gay and lesbian studies had achieved at least minimal recognition in some fields. She argues persuasively that much more archival work needs to be done. She shows that the institutional exclusion or isolation experienced by most historians of sexuality, the lack of engagement of some historians with queer theory, and the simultaneous condescension toward gay and lesbian history by queer theorists must be replaced by genuine engagement on both sides with the materials and methods each brings to the study of the production, meanings, and organization of sexualities.

Looking at the narratives, sources, and methods of sexual historians helps to approach Jane Rule's work in three ways. First, the recovered material concerning the ways that female sexuality in general and homosexuality in particular were regulated during World War II and in the 1950s helps us to understand the period when she was coming to terms with her own sexuality. As an adolescent, Rule lived in a world dominated by women in which men, such as her father, were, for the moment, absent. Whether or not she was entirely conscious of the implications, women were being encouraged to take on occupations and social roles that ran counter to traditional norms of middle-class femininity. By the time Rule was beginning to write, in college, social authorities were unanimous in condemning women who resisted "gender appropriate" behavior and in valuing women who would embrace conventional roles as wives and mothers to restore normality after the war. At Mills in particular, the (male) president, Lynn White (in *Educating Our Daughters,* 1950), redefined the role of women's education as socializing women for their rightful place in the home. Not all of the faculty subscribed to his mission for women's education, but the curriculum after the war was partially redesigned to enforce that view. The contradictions about norms for femininity during and after the war might have suggested to a young woman like Rule that these norms were arbitrary, political, changeable, rather than natural or inevitable.

Second, Rule's fiction both reflects and contests assumptions about femininity, masculinity, and sexuality that were the mainstay of public discourse during and after the war. We can look at Rule's fictions as an experimental ground for imagining subjectivities not readily available in public discourse. The earliest manuscripts show her struggling with ways to represent sexuality (and gender), working with available narratives but resisting their meanings. As her work develops, we can trace the invention of multiple sexual subjectivities, not devoid of social context but interacting with powerful regimes of family, community, and culture.

Third, it is interesting to consider Rule's fictions as providing sites of resistance for readers. Readers, like historians, don't occupy neatly sequenced cultural moments in which the meaning of sexual practices and identities follow a discernible progression. Readers from secular urban settings in which there is a visible gay and lesbian subculture exist simultaneously with readers from suburban or rural towns in which they feel isolated as they struggle with sexual meanings. Texts written in the 1970s that stage diverse, even competing, models of sexual subjectivities read differently in the 1990s, but in their very polyvalence, continue to provide sites of resistance for readers entangled in sexual prohibitions. Like the oral histories gathered by Davis and Kennedy or homophile publications like *The Ladder*, Rule's fictions and how they have been read tell us a great deal about available sexual narratives and, just as importantly, about forms of resistance.

Rule's understanding of her own cultural location(s) as a writer provides a particularly interesting case. Unlike some lesbian writers of the 1970s and later, Rule has the same skepticism about subcultures as she has toward the dominant culture. A writer may be shaped by the cultures she lives in, but she is not obligated to conform to the discourses about sexuality (or anything else) currently endorsed by cultural institutions. Seeing herself as a part of "ordinary" society, marked by lesbian sexuality but resisting the "popular" meanings of the marker, Rule has firmly resisted separatism and pressure to subscribe to the norms of feminist or gay or lesbian or queer subcultures. In an essay called "I Am Alone

Here," written in 1969 or 1970, Rule described the struggle of living an ordinary life:

> The cause of being lesbian is love. The effect of being lesbian is hatred and fear. I have been expelled from school, from church, from sections of my family for loving another woman. I have been called . . . a pervert, in the public press, and my books have been banned from libraries, described as a world of corruption and death. Those are melodramas to be lived through often in high style with a sense of rebel courage and romance, and I think back on most of them as silly rather than tragic experiences. (Box 18, folder 1)

Rule anticipates in this essay what Judith Butler means in the following: "Identity categories tend to be instruments of regulatory regimes, whether as the normalizing categories of oppressive structures or as the rallying points for a liberatory contestation of that very oppression. This is not to say that I will not appear at political occasions under the sign of lesbian, but that I would like to have it permanently unclear what precisely that sign signifies" ("Imitation" 13–14). Positioned within and against the dominant culture, within and against gay and lesbian subculture, Rule's writing resists simple understandings of lesbian lives, whether promoted by so-called authorities or by political movements. Her stories are not the call to battle of Monique Wittig's *guérillères*, the outlaw triumphalism of Rita Mae Brown's *Rubyfruit Jungle*, or the postmodern playfulness of Jeanette Winterson's *Written on the Body*. Rather, Rule transforms conventional, realist forms to create a place for lesbian subjectivities. Her fictions help the reader to see that the relation of power and knowledge that masquerades as the truth is itself a fiction susceptible to change.

Defining Fictions

A persistent question for me is: How was Rule able to invent lesbian narratives that didn't conform to the available models, whether those models were medical or literary? First, I want to consider what a "lesbian narrative" means in this context. Even though Rule is read (and ignored) largely because she is a lesbian writer, her work is far from monomaniacal. A quick census of her fictions reveals that about 20 percent of her female characters are definable as lesbians: more than the Kinsey prediction of 10 percent of the population, but far from a majority of her fictional universe which includes heterosexual and bisexual women, gay and straight men, asexual characters and characters for whom sexuality is not a defining issue. Rule does not privilege sexuality in her fictions; rather she shows the ways in which desire inflects changing understandings of the self, intimacy and domesticity, family, and community, to name a few of her narrative concerns. Even when lesbian characters are not the central protagonists of her fictions, however, lesbians are taken seriously and given defining points of view.

Rule's relocation as a citizen recalled in "The 4th of July, 1954," is consistent with her efforts to relocate herself within the literary and social discourses available to her in midcentury North America. Her education was shaped by the great canonical texts of the British tradition; Milton, Shakespeare, Donne, Yeats, Hopkins, and Auden, for example, were particularly important to her. As she tried to adapt the literary discourse she admired to her own stories, she uncovered its regulatory effects on gender and sexuality. Her dilemma, conscious or not, was to find a way to appropriate the power of an esthetic she valued without succumbing to its politics.

Rule restages the dilemma of the lesbian writer with some irony in one of her later novels, *Contract with the World* (1981), written twenty years after *Desert of the Heart*. Alma—the only one of six central characters in the novel who is narrated in the first person—tries to realize her wish to become a writer at the same time that she leaves her marriage to love a woman. Becoming a writer and becoming a lesbian are fundamentally joined, and her task is to give a textual reality to her sexual discoveries. Her chapter in *Contract* traces that double quest and is deeply ironic. In the end Alma fails at both; she is neither a successful writer nor a successful lesbian. Had she succeeded at one expression of herself, she might have succeeded at the other. Her failure is precipitated by her need for acceptance in conventional terms. Rejection slips accumulate and (heterosexual) male approval diminishes. She finally gives up writing, gets pregnant again, forsaking books for babies, to resume her place as a mother, albeit a single mother, in her middle-class home. Her quest is framed by her (ex) husband Mike. When they separate he gives her the blank notebook that she will use for her first writing efforts; when she is ready to admit failure, she visits him and returns pregnant, secure again in her body and how it will be read by her parents, her sons, her middle-class neighbors.

At the beginning of her failed quest, faced with the blank pages of her notebook, considering the new forms of her desire for her lover, Roxanne, Alma writes: "The problem is that I have no language at all for my body or Roxanne's body that isn't either derisive or embarrassing. . . . We make love without nouns. I didn't miss a language with Mike, only felt assaulted by his" (*Contract* 131). She looks for literary models— Gertrude Stein, Kate Millett, Rita Mae Brown; she tries to write about her affair with Roxanne by changing names and genders, disguising lesbian desire in heterosexual terms. The models prove inadequate for her story; heterosexual disguise leads to absurdities of plot and characterization. She realizes in her failures that the meanings of gender and sexuality are deeply embedded in narrative forms; surface changes in language are insufficient to tell the story of lesbian sexuality. Alma has neither the creative imagination nor the social courage to persevere.

Alma's story is a parody of the lesbian who would write, but the dilemma her character faces is deadly serious: how to find a language for telling a legible lesbian story? How to speak to readers who are conditioned by what they have read, who are both male and female, straight and gay, old and young? As Marilyn Farwell puts it in *Heterosexual Plots and Lesbian Narratives* (1996), how is it possible to write lesbian narratives in a language determined by heterosexual plots?

Marilyn Farwell's project is "to develop a textual theory of narrative in order to uncover the potentially disruptive elements in traditional plot lines and to underscore the traditional aspects of experimental writing" (14). She goes beyond the reductive oppositions that have characterized much of the work on sexuality and literature: traditional lesbian feminist criticism versus queer theory; Anglo-American critical practice versus continental theory, 1970s alleged asexual politics versus 1990s performative sexuality, narrative versus anti-narrativity, literary realism versus experimental writing. The paradox that motivates much of her analysis is that narrative is an ideological system that seems to foreclose the possibility of a lesbian subject, and yet as lesbians "we live and are constructed by linguistic categories and, most profoundly, by narrative itself" (18). Our ability to be lesbian is tied up with our ability to write lesbian, as

Alma's failure in *Contract* illustrates. Farwell maintains that while narrative is determined by paradigms that inscribe masculine and heterosexual centrality, narrative is itself, nonetheless, historical and subject to disruption. She argues that the lesbian subject realigns the "power-inflected boundaries of gender and sexuality" (18). The effort to bring Anglo-American materialist analysis and postmodern discursive analysis together is crucial because, as Farwell insists,

> while each element—narrative as a system and lesbian as a discursive construction—is primarily textual, I will also insist that each, at the same time, is profoundly political and related to experience. Narrative is the way we give meaning to life, the way we order the chaos of events. . . . Postmodernism's tendency to divorce textuality from experience, its denial of identity in theories whether of cultural construction or the textual free play of the signifier, and its refusal of agency, thus its refusal of feminism, ignore the real people who are oppressed by textual constructions. (19)

Farwell points to the ways that the basic elements of narrative can be (and have been) realigned by the lesbian subject to disrupt masculine centrality and heterosexual inevitability and to appropriate the authoritative function of narrative in Western tradition. The narrator as owner of language, the narratee as the figure who is addressed, the point of view that orients the narrative perspective, characters as sites of subjectivity, readerly expectations that plot will set events in logical or chronological relation to one another, and closure as "the ultimate place in which subjects are positioned in relationship to one another and to power" (48), are among the elements of narrative that Farwell proposes are subject to realignment and appropriation. Recognizing that the appropriation of discourse carries with it the possibility of absorption by the system of values and power that defines discourse, Farwell says, "When a woman occupies the space of the hero or lover she is differently aligned to power but not necessarily either devoid of it nor necessarily absorbed by the maleness of the binary structure" (59). The lesbian subject, by refusing "the gendered mechanics" of conventional narrative, creates a different space for the elaboration of subjectivity. She displaces the male bonding at the center of conventional narrative, revises patterns of activity and passivity with regard to language, gender, and desire, and inscribes counterplots that disrupt the conventional deployment of power.

The consequences of Farwell's linking of material and discursive analysis and her refusal to divorce the lesbian subject from the power dynamics of gender are developed further in her detailed discussion of three key moments in theorizing the lesbian subject. The three moments she analyzes are (1) the late nineteenth- and early twentieth-century sexologists' image of the congenital invert engaged by Hall in *The Well of Loneliness*; (2) the woman-identified-woman of 1970s lesbian feminists, a site of sameness; and (3) the postmodernist, queer figure of the lesbian as beyond phallocentric categories of gender, a site of difference. The originality of Farwell's analysis of the lesbian subject is her refusal to see these moments as a progressive history in which each step triumphs over its predecessor and replaces it with a more adequate model. Rather, she asserts that these insights play off rather than displace one another: "The mannish lesbian, the woman-as-lesbian/lesbian-as-woman, and the performative body/desire of the queer theory's lesbian subject are all responses to the initial negative narratives of the sexologists" (68).

Farwell not only refuses to uncouple the lesbian subject from gender, she insists that the lesbian subject is grounded in the female body. Her materialist analysis does not simply reinstate an ontology of lesbian identity, however. Citing the work of Linda Alcoff, she clarifies that she understands gender not as a quality or essence, but as a positionality; not as ontological but as directional. Farwell argues further that "while positionality is essential to the definition of the lesbian subject, and that positionality is determined in relationship to the gendered positionality of woman, the female body is the ground rather than the surface of these positionings. While males can, in different ways, occupy a female position, they do so differently and with different results from females. When I speak of lesbians, then, I speak of women" (67).

Farwell's work reclaims the power of narrative for the deployment of lesbian subjectivity and recognizes the continuing power of storytelling in daily life. Her efforts to move beyond seemingly irreconcilable theoretical antagonisms may not be wholly convincing to some; her bias is clearly weighted toward Anglo-American materialism and she equates continental theory more with early French feminists than with Foucault. Nonetheless, the analytical moves she develops are extremely useful for rereading lesbian fiction from the 1960s through the 1980s, particularly fiction written in popular, accessible, and apparently traditional modes

such as Jane Rule's work. Rule's work, in fact, is poised between popular fiction (her work, like Ann Bannon's, is now available through Naiad
Press) and "literature." In a somewhat snide aside in an article about lesbian romance, Joke Hermes compared Ann Bannon and Jane Rule as follows: "Novels of the 1950s and 1960s are generally called 'pulps,' although some of them are considered literary works. Ann Bannon, for example . . . is considered a pulp writer but Jane Rule's *Desert of the Heart*
is considered 'literature.' The lay reader may become aware of this last
fact by the numerous poetry citations" ("Sexuality in Lesbian Romance
Fiction" 50). In the same article, Hermes defines a "good romance" as
escapist, keeping the world at a distance. She condemns romances that
try to be "political treatises," and she especially rejects romances that
have ambiguous or open endings. Hermes rather naïvely assumes that
popular romance can retain its conventions and naturalize lesbian sexuality; she fails to understand the politics *of* narrative, seeing only political
argument *in* narrative and disparaging such argument as inappropriate
because it interferes with escapist pleasure. *Desert of the Heart* is literary,
not because there are numerous references to poetry, but because it engages the politics of narrative in the ways that Farwell discusses. Rule recognizes both the power and the treachery of canonical texts for the lesbian writer, but her stance is neither oppositional nor fully transgressive.
She engages the male-centered and heterosexual paradigms of traditional
narrative to speak to a readership formed by the expectations of traditional narrative and to realign the power relations that subtend conventional narrative paradigms. The pleasures of Rule's narratives are not escapist; they are, rather, the pleasures of engagement, the possibility of
identification with a fictional world restructured by lesbian subjectivity.

Defining Theories

In *The Apparitional Lesbian: Female Homosexuality and Modern Culture*
(1993), Terry Castle argues, as Farwell does, that for lesbian desire to
emerge in narrative, male homosocial desire must be absent. In her effort to theorize lesbian fiction, Castle turns to queer theory and reworks
Eve Sedgwick's powerful paradigm of male homosociality; she also turns
to feminist theory and tries to adapt Nancy K. Miller's classification of
plots available to fictional heroines to lesbian fiction. Each of these

moves—while very useful and suggestive—unwittingly demonstrates, on the one hand, the persistent asymmetry of genders in relation to power and, on the other, the incommensurability of lesbian fictions and heterosexual plots.

Eve Sedgwick's formulation of homosocial desire in *Between Men* (1985) has become a foundational concept for queer theory, making the structure of the male homosocial bond (male-female-male) legible throughout the European and American literary canon. Because Sedgwick is fascinated by relationships of power and desire "between men," her work has, inadvertently perhaps, deferred or even disavowed recognition of power and desire "between women." As a result, her work has contributed to the tendency of "queer" to redefine "gay and lesbian" by excluding rather than merely subsuming "lesbian." Castle's discussion of Sedgwick deftly illustrates the degree to which Sedgwick's work is stunningly useful for reading the power relations (literary and social) structured by the male-female-male homosocial paradigm while it fails to account at all for female bonding, especially sexualized female bonding. As Castle says, "If the subject of female bonding sets up a kind of intellectual or emotional 'blockage' in Sedgwick's argument, the specialized form of female bonding represented by lesbianism seems to provoke in her, interestingly enough, even deeper resistance" (*The Apparitional Lesbian* 70).

Castle proposes a way to use Sedgwick's paradigm against itself, so to speak, to arrive at a paradigm of female bonding. Castle's argument is extremely useful to the reader of lesbian texts because it brings to light literary power relations that confront lesbian writers. I have two reservations about Castle's reading of Sedgwick and her subsequent reformulation. First, Castle's critique is still bound up in the terms of Sedgwick's model and, therefore, doesn't go far enough. Second, Castle doesn't address fully the consequences of the assumptions underlying Sedgwick's argument, more explicit in *Epistemology of the Closet*, where Sedgwick clarifies that her focus is "on sexuality rather than (sometimes, even, as opposed to) gender" (*Epistemology of the Closet* 15). Because sexuality and gender are differently imbricated for men and women, an analysis that privileges sexuality without simultaneously examining the (asymmetrical and discontinuous) meanings of femininity and masculinity is likely, once again, to obscure the particularity of lesbian desire and representation by falsely universalizing a male model. In a rather lengthy pleading in the introduction of *Epistemology of the Closet*, Sedgwick herself recognizes the danger of limiting a project about sexuality to a gay-male-centered analysis even as she hopes that others will find her work useful for lesbian theory. Recognizing her debts to feminist and lesbian theorists even as she reiterates the gay male focus of her theoretical project, Sedgwick says: "That limitation seems a damaging one chiefly insofar as it echoes and prolongs an already scandalously extended eclipse: the extent to which women's sexual, and specifically homosexual, experience and definition tend to be subsumed by men's during the turn-of-the-century period most focused on in my discussion, and are liable once again to be subsumed *in* such discussion" (39, emphasis hers).

Sedgwick argues that the persistent subject of English literature is the "erotic triangle" of male homosocial desire. By this she means male bonding that is mediated through a woman. Male domination, Sedgwick argues, depends on attachments between men, but to maintain the distinction between men and women fundamental to male dominance and modern patriarchy, those attachments must not be overtly erotic. Castle exposes how Sedgwick's paradigm reinforces the patriarchal script as the only script: "The triangular male-female-male figure returns at the conclusion of each story—triumphantly reinstalled—as a sign both of normative (namely heterosexual) male bonding and of a remobilization of patriarchal control" (*The Apparitional Lesbian* 69). As Castle points out, Sedgwick goes much further, to assert the definitional interdependency of homosociality and canonicity: "Literature canonizes the subject of male homosociality; in return, it would seem, the subject of male homosociality canonizes the work of literature" (70). In Sedgwick's formulation, the proper place for a woman is determined exclusively by her relation to men, her ability to mediate male desire; no direct relation between women is imaginable. The power to be a subject, to signify as a narrating or desiring presence in the text is unavailable to female characters. A text that would stage female desire, or female homosociality would not, by definition, qualify as "literature."

Facing that impasse, Castle argues that to account for female-female desire, one would have to undo the triangular figure of male bonding that Sedgwick's project proposes as foundational. But rather than "undo" the male-female-male triangle, Castle substitutes a female-male-female triangle to articulate a *female* homosocial structure. In this substitution, male bonding is, necessarily, suppressed. The male term is isolated by the presence of the two female terms, taken out of relationship with another male term. Further, if the (female) homosocial triangle is replaced by a (destabilizing) female homosexual dyad, the male term is eliminated altogether, again repeating the shifts and effects Sedgwick discusses concerning male bonding and the threat male homosociality poses to patriarchal stability if it isn't contained by the triangular bond, mediated by a woman. In Castle's analysis of nineteenth- and twentieth-century novels that undo the "seemingly compulsory plot of male homosocial desire" (74), she argues that "for female bonding to 'take' . . . to metamorphose into explicit sexual desire, male bonding must be suppressed" (84). Male homosexual characters can coexist easily with lesbian characters, but male homosocial bonds (in which a woman mediates) must be eliminated. She concludes, "To put it axiomatically: in the absence of male homosocial desire, lesbian desire emerges" (85). The problem with Castle's substitution, even though she uses Sylvia Townsend Warner's *Summer Will Show* to illustrate it, is that it fails to take into account the pervasive power effects of patriarchy that make such a substitution imaginable only in a diagram in which gender is abstracted from its social meanings.

Castle maintains that the two contexts in realistic writing in which lesbian desire is most frequently represented are those in which male homosociality is marginal or absent: the premarital world of schooling and adolescence and the postmarital world of divorce, widowhood, and separation. In this context, Castle discusses lesbian counterplots to conventional narrative that shift paradigms of gender and desire so that lesbian desire can take a central, signifying place. She adapts Nancy K. Miller's terms for two plots historically available to heroines: the *euphoric* plot ending in marriage and integration into family and society, and the *dysphoric* plot ending in the heroine's physical or social death (*The Heroine's Text* 1980). In Castle's analysis the assumed heterosexuality of Miller's plots emerges, since for the lesbian both marriage (and other forms of heterosexual recuperation) *and* death would be dysphoric. Male homosociality reasserts itself in the euphoric marriage plot to eliminate a central lesbian bond, to place the woman in her "proper" place as a mediating presence between two men.

Among the schoolgirl fictions that Castle analyzes as examples of dysphoric counterplots are Colette's *Claudine à l'école* and Winterson's *Oranges Are Not the Only Fruit*; the first ends in the integration of the lesbian girl into heterosexual society and the second ends in the marriage of the beloved. She maintains that the lesbian novel of adolescence is almost always dysphoric, lesbian bonding merely a temporary phase within a larger heterosexual script. Perhaps because she is considering primarily English and American novels (with an aside to Colette), Castle fails to notice that Monique Wittig's *L'Opoponax* (1964) is a flagrant exception to the rule. Her novelistic portrait of the artist as a young lesbian has the lesbian heroines triumphant at the end of adolescence, having appropriated and reworked canonical texts (Baudelaire, Scève, Charles d'Orléans, and others) to speak their desire for each other.[1]

Castle's effort to adapt a model drawn from fiction shaped by heterosexuality to lesbian fiction fails in the same way as her effort to substitute a female homosocial triangle for the male paradigm elaborated by Sedgwick. The power asymmetry in gender relations makes direct substitution of female for male impossible: a female homosocial triangle (and, consequently, a desiring female dyad) in realist fiction would be unimaginable. Recognizing the centrality of male bonding to social power relations, Castle proposes that the *euphoric* lesbian counterplot is necessarily comic or utopian; it imagines a world in which male bonding has no place. Typically a heterosexual (often married) heroine is converted to homosexual desire when a heterosexual bond fails. Castle identifies *Desert of the Heart* as an example of a euphoric counterplot. This typology, however, obscures as much as it reveals. The lesbian "counterplot" is constrained by the heterosexual assumptions of the original plots. Castle finally has to conclude that the dysphoric/euphoric endings Miller discusses don't work for lesbian stories.

Castle's typology obscures the narrative complexities of *Desert of the Heart*. Rule's novel does begin with a failed, heterosexual marriage and includes the homosexual conversion of one of the heroines, Evelyn, but that is only part of the story. The originality of *Desert of the Heart* is that

---

1. "Women Reading Woman: Duras and Wittig," unpublished paper by the author given at the International Colloquium in Twentieth-Century French Studies, Duke University, March 12–14, 1987.

there are two, not just one, narrating characters. Ann's story tells a "plot" entirely different from Evelyn's. The failure of marriage—and more specifically the trip to Reno to get a divorce—that opens the book and Evelyn's story is as much about state regulation of intimacy as it is about private homosocial bonds. At the end, the state apparatus that clearly works to sustain a male-centered, heterosexual social order is not overcome in a utopian, narrative gesture but continues to define the world in which Evelyn and Ann will try to survive. Female bonding and desire exist within male-dominated heterosexual social order in an uneasy, unstable position. Rule has devised a narrative form that permits the use of a realistic genre to tell a euphoric lesbian romance.

Rule's second published novel, *This Is Not for You*, in contrast to her first, reads from the very beginning as dysphoric, in the sense of a lesbian subject trying to impose a heterosexual story on her (absent) interlocutor. The narrating lesbian subject assumes homophobic meanings of lesbian for herself and remains alone at the end of the novel. In many ways, *This Is Not for You* can be read as an ironic rewriting of *The Well of Loneliness*; Rule doesn't make her narrating subject into a heroine the way that Hall does, but she shows, through the perspective of a pathological lesbian subject, the consequences of that stance. Rule goes one step further: there is no triumph of heterosexuality and male desire for the beloved at the end of the novel. The beloved of the title, to whom the narrative is addressed and from whom it is withheld, is unable to consummate her marriage at the end because of her husband's impotence and his unwillingness to accept her sexual agency. She leaves her husband to join a silent, religious community of women, reclaiming control of the silence the narrator tries to impose on her. By becoming a nun, she asserts a primary affectional and spiritual bond with other women, sanctioned by the Church and apparently desexualized.

Rule's narratives expose the limitations of Castle's counterplots. Rooted in realism, her narratives realign gender and sexual paradigms by deploying lesbian subjects in multiple ways, more as Farwell suggests. Gaps in an otherwise closed narrative invite an ironic reading of the pathological lesbian subject-as-narrator in *This Is Not for You*; dual narrating lesbian voices that engage different values and meanings in *Desert of the Heart* create a space for lesbian desire without denying the heterosexual injunction of social institutions and the force of their role in daily life. Later novels will develop other ways of redefining fiction and, in the process, redefining sexuality both within and against recognizable narrative patterns. Rule's fictions exceed the paradigms of desire in which the male homosocial bond is central. In her fictions the male homosocial bond is not suppressed so much as displaced. To assert that the absence of the male homosocial bond is a prerequisite for the emergence of lesbian desire assumes an exclusionary, hierarchical and agonistic understanding of gender and sexuality that continues to be defined by male bonding. Rule goes beyond this understanding to create narratives of multiple bondings and polymorphous desire that are neither utopian nor dysphoric. Rule's fictions demonstrate Farwell's argument that the narrativized lesbian is a trope that functions in literal and nonliteral ways. The lesbian subject "can function as a single character, as a couple, or as a community" (*Heterosexual Plots and Lesbian Narratives* 61). Lesbian subjectivity, as she suggests, can also function as a nonliteral point of view that orients the narrative perspective. The ironic use of a single narrating voice in *This Is Not for You* (1970), the dual narrative of *Desert of the Heart* (1964), narrative shifts in *Against the Season* (1971), and multiple narrative voices in *Contract with the World* (1981) are just some of the ways that Rule inscribes lesbian subjectivity in her narratives.

How did the young writer in the 1950s (when both *Desert of the Heart* and early versions of *This Is Not for You* were written) imagine a site of resistance to authorizing narratives of female (and especially lesbian) sexuality? Part of the answer, I suspect, can be found in two stories about her adolescence that Rule has told and retold in different forms over the years. I call these "defining stories" rather than "defining events" or "defining moments" because the telling (how the narratives are shaped and reshaped) is as important as the events that prompted the stories. While the original events may be irretrievable, the urge to explore their meanings is revealed by the existence of multiple narratives about them. In these stories Rule defines and redefines the relations between power and desire, social institutions and sexuality, literary discourse and lesbian subjectivity. Each story also exposes the mechanics of social surveillance in reference to a school setting and explores the disciplinary function of narrative. By resignifying schoolgirl fiction, Rule's stories suggest that the school may unwittingly produce a resisting lesbian subject rather than achieve its intended recuperation of the lesbian girl into adult heterofemininity. I mean to echo here Judith Fetterley's analysis of a resisting (feminist) reader who engages a (conventional) text while resisting its assumed meanings.

Defining Stories

Rule has observed that her fiction includes many children, adults, and old people, but few adolescents between the ages of thirteen and fifteen. She explains in her unfinished manuscript for an autobiography (*Taking My Life*): "What has put me off, I think, is the odd . . . line between emotional ignorance and dishonesty which characterized those years for me and misshaped my understanding for much longer" (65). Two stories from that period of her life, however, have found their way into numerous interviews, unpublished texts, private papers, and—occasionally—into print, notably in *Lesbian Images* (1975). One story involves a confrontation with the headmistress when Rule was a senior at the Castilleja School in Palo Alto, California. This event is narrated in some detail in *Taking My Life* and has made its way into print several times; each of Rule's tellings stresses different details and is told with indignation or humor, according to the context and audience. The second story involves a passionate friendship between an adolescent schoolgirl and an older, married woman, marked by multiple emotional, intellectual, and moral contradictions. References to this friendship have made their way into print as well, but usually in veiled or very abbreviated form. The intense feelings and confusing contradictions of this friendship are explored in Rule's first, unpublished manuscript for a novel, called *Who Are Penitent* (box 11, folder 1), written during her year in London in 1952–53.

That Rule reworked these stories over at least a thirty-year period, from her first unpublished novel to her unfinished autobiography, and that traces of each find their way into her major novels attest to the centrality of the problems they raise to her writing. As I mentioned in chapter 1, Rule says in the unpublished essay, "I Am Alone Here," written in 1969 or 1970 (box 18, folder 1): "My characters are not veiled portraits of me or the people I know. They are ideas embodied in metaphors of personality living in a world I invent for them to show as clearly as I can what I understand of human experience." This is the most useful perspective for reading her multiple versions of these two stories. They are rooted in her experience of herself, other people, and the world, but storytelling (whether it is called autobiography or fiction or interview) is not veiled confession, but the embodiment of ideas in narrative form, a way to explore the meanings of human experience.

Story #1: The Headmistress

To summarize the first story I will draw on several interviews, the introduction to *Lesbian Images,* and passages from the unfinished autobiography *Taking My Life.* During her senior year at the Castilleja School, a private school for girls in Palo Alto, Rule, nicknamed "Jinx" by her family and close friends, wrote a regular column for the school newspaper. In high school Jinx stood out in many ways; for one thing, she was over six feet tall. She had developed a reputation for high spirits among her friends and on several occasions challenged school authority when she thought it was being abused. At the same time, she took her education—including athletics—seriously. Jinx was a day student at a school where most were boarders. As was the case at most private schools for girls at that time, Castilleja students were required to wear drab uniforms and were forbidden to wear makeup. During senior year the students were supposed to learn how to dress and how to prepare themselves to appear as proper ladies after their schoolgirl years in uniform. In Rule's unfinished autobiography, the headmistress hires a woman "from a charm school in San Francisco," using funds from the student treasury, "to give us lessons in make up, wardrobe, and deportment . . . in the gym, we were instructed to imitate our instructor—as tall as I in her stocking feet and wearing four inch platform shoes—as she walked to music. I threw myself into that exercise with an abandon that made [the headmistress]—ever watchful—hiss me off the floor" (86).

Rule remembers that, outraged, she wrote an attack on the exercise in enforced femininity for the school paper, arguing that instead of learning to walk in heels, they should be learning to "walk to the nearest college." The headmistress called Jinx in to chastise her for the article and sent her "home to think." A week later, the headmistress outlined the conditions for Jinx's reinstatement at the school: "That I give up all extracurricular activities, the paper, clubs, sports, that I leave the school grounds promptly when my classes were over, that I voice no criticisms of the school myself and report to her anyone doing so" (87). In some versions of this event, Rule recounts this as an expulsion; in others, she vehemently maintains that she quit, walked out of the headmistress's office, and marched directly to Palo Alto High School, where she enrolled by the end of that very day. Her parents supported her decision and to this day her mother gets angry at what she continues to count as an abuse of authority on the part of the school.[2]

Later, when Jinx's application to Stanford was rejected, even though students from Castilleja with lesser records were admitted, she discovered that a letter from the headmistress had been appended to her high school file saying that her academic record should be discounted because she was of "unfit moral character." Adding this last innuendo to several comments made secretly by the headmistress to schoolmates and their mothers, Rule realized in retrospect that she was being accused of lesbianism.

Story #2: The Married Woman

The basic elements of the second story are as follows. An adolescent girl of fourteen or fifteen strikes up a friendship with a young and married woman artist. In some versions of the story, the artist and her husband, a graduate student, rent an apartment across the street from the girl's school. The artist is commissioned to do portraits of the girl and her siblings, and becomes friendly with the girl during the sittings for her portrait. The artist comes from an unusual family that has lived in many parts of the world; she had an incestuous relationship with her brother, and she is interested in the sexual awakening of the girl; she asks her questions about boys, encouraging her to show an interest in them. At one point, the artist says that her landlady (and friend) has suggested that the girl has a crush on her. The artist says that the landlady was once in love with a woman and perhaps that is why she sees it in their friendship; this is the first time the girl is aware that sometimes women do love each other. The girl hotly denies the landlady's accusation, but the idea has been planted in her mind. The artist is surprised by the girl's sexual

2. Conversation between the author and Mrs. Rule, February 1997.

naïveté, teaches her about masturbation, and gives her both *Lady Chatterley's Lover* and *The Well of Loneliness* to read. The artist includes, as part of her sexual instruction, the developmental imperative that a woman has to make love first with a man or she risks becoming a lesbian. A woman's life can accommodate occasional lesbian affairs, she teaches, but the first obligation is to heterosexuality because a woman should want first and foremost to marry and have children. This hypothetical lesson is taught within an increasingly passionate friendship in which the girl first experiences desire through the artist's kisses and constant attention. Eventually, the artist and her husband move away and have several children. The girl continues to know and visit them, is friendly with the husband as well as the wife. The artist is increasingly restless with her domestic role, becomes suicidal, seeks psychiatric help, and eventually reintegrates into her marriage, but at the expense of her art, her energy, and her friendship with the girl.

The most extensive fictional treatment of the story of the married artist as sexual mentor is the 1953 novel manuscript, *Who Are Penitent*. In *Who Are Penitent*, Rule encases the story in a narrative heavy with references to religion (liturgy, metaphysical poetry, definitions of sin) and literature (Donne, Hopkins). In this telling, the artist (Jane Crown) and her young family have moved from California to a town near New York where the girl (Linsey) visits. Several narrative elements shift the meaning of the story in interesting ways. First, the girl stays with an uncle in Greenwich Village through whom she has a glimpse of a gay and lesbian subculture. She meets a couple worthy of Beebo Brinker's world: Jackie and Mike, "batching it" in an apartment near her uncle's.

The Mike and Jackie couple repeat and replace the married artist/girl couple in a reworking of meanings about religion, creativity, and sexuality. Jackie, too, is an artist, and Mike is a butch figure who has run away from home to make a life in the Village. Significantly, Mike is marked as "ethnic" in the same way she is marked as "lesbian": she uses the derogatory term "Wop" to refer to herself in the same way she internalizes homophobia. The association of ethnic or racial bias with sexual bias, internalized racism with internalized homophobia, will be developed further in later texts by Rule.

Jackie doubles the artist in her profession, even as she replaces her as a teacher of art and sexuality. The girl asks Jackie to do her portrait just as the married artist had done before. Recounting Mike's story during the sittings for the portrait, Jackie reveals the social costs of lesbian desire. Mike was driven out of her small town and came to the city.

After a series of punishing, melodramatic events, the girl watches the married artist and her family reintegrate into mainstream, middle-class life as they walk into a new house in suburban Connecticut. The married artist has successfully withheld her love from the girl ("the one wise thing I've done," 181) but has abandoned her talent as an artist, the price for marital order.

In "I am Alone Here," written about sixteen years later, Rule returns again to this second story, telling it in an autobiographical mode. The essay is a meditation on fear: fear of speaking in public, alone before an audience; fear of speaking for herself; fear of how she is read, particularly by critics who reduce her love stories to stories of perversion. In this essay, unlike some of the other versions of the story, she says "I did not know the word 'lesbian' when I first loved a woman. I, therefore, had no idea that what I felt was wicked or perverse." About her first love she says:

> The woman I first loved was ten years older than I, married and expecting a child. From the safety of her accomplished womanhood, she thought she could risk loving me. At fifteen, I was no threat to her husband, a kind and perceptive man, and I loved her child when she was born. Without conventions to confuse me, caring about the people she cared about seemed natural, but her guilt grew until for my sexual sake she sent me away so that I would not grow up perverted as she was, unable to enjoy vaginal orgasm, always regressing to the desire for another woman. . . . Over the years, with the help of many doctors, she's been cured of melancholia. She was cured of loving women, too, and of painting and singing. (Box 18, folder 1, pages 4–5)

Elements of both stories find their way into at least nine unpublished manuscripts and three published essays and interviews.[3] Traces of the stories can be found in many more of Rule's published stories and novels.

---

3. Versions of the stories are found in at least nine unpublished stories and interviews and three published essays and interviews including: a story written for a college English course in April 1948 called "The Story of a Portrait" (box 13, folder 1); an undated college story

Reading the Stories: A Resisting Lesbian Subject

While presented as separate stories, the stories of the headmistress and the married woman are deeply entangled. In the unfinished manuscript for an autobiography, the friendship with the artist leads to rumors (before the fact) of lesbianism that are a whispered background to Jinx's expulsion from school. But because the punishment precedes the "crime," perception substitutes for fact, and stories anticipate experience, the storyteller sees an entirely different set of meanings in the stories than she is supposed to see. What should be cautionary tales warning against perverse sexuality become cautionary tales warning against the perverse exercise of power.

The two stories, precisely because there is no original, no authorized version, and no final draft, establish an open-ended exploration of the meanings of gender and sexuality in language. The moments of silence or muted language in each story—and in the coupling of the stories together—dramatize the mutual reinforcement of gender and sexuality for women within the regulatory regimes that constitute and serve the white, middle-class nuclear family in mid-century America. The multiple versions delineate an emerging lesbian subjectivity formed by (and in resistance to) the authorizing discourses of school, family, marriage, and medicine. The contradictions and breaches in those discourses destabilize dominant models of gender and sexuality, unveiling them as malignant effects of power rather than as vital expressions of nature. Judith Butler's arguments in "Imitation and Gender Insubordination" (1991) are particularly useful as an interpretive frame for considering the meanings these stories continue to generate.

In the first story, in the female-centered world of the private girls' school, a site since Colette in which lesbian desire precedes heterosexual

---

called "Benediction" (box 12, folder 2); the unpublished manuscript for a novel, *Who Are Penitent,* written in 1952–53 (box 11, folder 1); a letter to E.K. dated 11/3/53 (box 19 folder 2); an unpublished story probably written in 1956 called "Gift Grotesque" (box 12, folder 7); "I am Alone Here" written in 1969 or 1970 (box 18, folder 1); *Lesbian Images* (1975), 3–5; a profile by Paul Grescoe in *The Canadian,* 12/4/76 (box 14, folder 5); an interview in 1981 with Michele Kort; *Taking My Life* (box 13); an unpublished 1993 interview with Lynne Fernie and Aerlyn Weissman as background for making the documentary *Fiction and Other Truths.*

recuperation, students are gathered to learn femininity. A professional is hired to model femininity under the surveillance of the headmistress. Recognizing that what they are being taught is drag, the young, pre-lesbian student, in an act of overt gender insubordination, actively parodies the movements she is being taught to imitate. Her transgression is her recognition that what is being presented as authentic femininity is actually impersonation. In some of the versions Rule, referring to her own six-foot frame, underscores the draglike appearance of the femininity teacher "as tall as I in her stocking feet and wearing four-inch platform shoes." In *Lesbian Images* Rule talks about the "gendering" of physical stature: her brother's height had been considered an asset, her own an awkward liability. As Butler argues, "Drag constitutes the mundane way in which genders are appropriated, theatricalized, worn, and done; it implies that all gendering is a kind of impersonation and approximation" (21). Having parodied the teacher in the gym, the young student compounds her transgression by denouncing the hypocrisy of the school in the semiofficial public discourse of the school paper. The school pretends to be developing the intellect but instead is socializing students for appropriate gender behavior. Jinx's place in the school was already somewhat precarious. As a nonboarder, she moved back and forth between the school and home. For boarders, the school acts consistently in loco parentis, teaching and reinforcing appropriate behaviors. When the headmistress sends Jinx "home to think," she assumes a continuity of authority between school and family. Instead, Jinx finds allies in her parents, a breach in the continuity of authority against which she is testing herself. The terms of her reinstatement in the school serve only to confirm her new perception that the school is hypocritical about its explicit mission to develop minds, that it is primarily an instrument of social (and gender) control. To be reinstated, she would have to give up most of the activities she found useful for her education and she would have to be complicitous with the headmistress, she would have to be an informer, to name names, to become part of the surveillance apparatus. She rejects those terms and breaks with the school.

Challenged, the school asserts its power as social authority more emphatically, though more covertly. Not only does the headmistress continue to exercise power over the adolescent's education and social integration, she shows that for women, gender-appropriate behavior and sexual orientation are inextricably linked. In a silent move that can be discerned by the narrator only in retrospect, the headmistress interprets gender insubordination as sexual nonconformity. To parody femininity is to undermine the logic of inevitable heterosexuality. The panicked reaction of the headmistress who reaches out beyond her institutional tie to the girl, to "protect" future schools against the girl's disruption of gender and sexual norms proves the fragility of the myths that sustain femininity and heterosexuality in the middle-class world the school serves, at the same time that it shows how potent insubordination can be. The headmistress's gesture simultaneously reveals that the school participates in a much wider network of policing; the headmistress's power and the stakes of female gender and sexual conformity are much greater than the rebel student could have known.

In the second story, which is entirely bound up with the first, the very object of nascent lesbian desire becomes the enforcer of the heterosexual norm. Having invested in a social order that can tolerate occasional, silenced, hidden expressions of lesbian desire, the older married woman needs the young, unformed girl to subscribe to a system in which heterosexuality is affirmed as prior, permanent, and definitive; lesbianism must be recuperated as occasional, temporary, and contained. The married woman is presented as an already transgressive sexualized subject for whom marriage should replace incestuous desire and keep lesbian desire in its place. Like a Foucauldian confessor, she incites discussion about sexuality; she provides the young girl with the standard, popular narratives of heterosexual desire and lesbian inversion with *Lady Chatterley's Lover* and *The Well of Loneliness*. But the girl is already a canny reader. *Lady Chatterley's Lover*, as a narrative of heterosexual initiation, would enforce female passivity dependent on male initiative leading to further female degradation. Such a story provides little incentive for an independent young girl. *The Well of Loneliness* is offered as a cautionary tale about the meanings attached to "lesbian." But the girl doesn't see herself reflected in the mannish Stephen Gordon, so it doesn't work. Either the sign "lesbian" has been incorrectly defined, or the desire she feels isn't "lesbian." In this way a founding narrative of lesbian fiction destabilizes the meaning of the sign, lesbian, for the young girl.

In *Who Are Penitent*, despair marks both the married artist (who represses her lesbian desire within a seemingly safer heterosexual marriage) and the butch Mike (who has internalized the homophobia she learned from the town she left behind). Somehow the girl and Jackie, the lesbian artist, reach a silent understanding that a more hopeful sexual ontology (acceptance of what is) can replace the more conventional, despairing ethics of sexuality (what ought to be). Their understanding, however, remains prediscursive, it has not yet found a language. That Rule named the married artist "Jane" in this novel suggests that the boundary between the married woman and the girl is blurred: both participate in the same social power structure whether they resist or succumb to its injunctions; the means for speaking otherwise are just out of reach.

Through the persistent retellings and internal contradictions of these two stories, the reader can see how gender (marked feminine) and (hetero)sexuality are institutionalized: propped up and policed by a pedagogy of imitation and repetition. The multiple revisions of the second story, to use Judith Butler's formulation, expose heterosexuality "as an incessant and *panicked* imitation of its own naturalized idealization" ("Imitation and Gender Subordination" 23). Whether enforced by social institutions like the girls' school or maintained by the medical profession, gender and sexual norms are revealed as fragile, easily disrupted by a more pervasive, disruptive desire that will always prevail if not contained. Butler protests speaking "as a lesbian" because "identity categories tend to be instruments of regulatory regimes, whether as the normalizing categories of oppressive structures or as the rallying points for a liberatory contestation of that very oppression" (13–14). She recognizes that to "be" a lesbian is sometimes politically necessary as a rallying point of resistance in a homophobic society, but she resists replacing the homophobic definition of lesbian with another liberatory, but still normative, definition of lesbian that seems to be transparent, clear, determinant: "Can sexuality even remain sexuality once it submits to a criterion of transparency and disclosure, or does it perhaps cease to be sexuality precisely when the semblance of full explicitness is achieved? Is sexuality of any kind even possible without that opacity designated by the unconscious, which means simply that the conscious 'I' who would reveal its sexuality is perhaps the last to know the meaning of what it says" (15)? The multiple attempts to narrate and interpret these two stories of Rule's adolescence unmask identity categories (woman, lesbian) as instruments of regulatory regimes.

Silences (whether the veiled language of the headmistress, the articulate silence of Jackie and the girl, the gap between the headmistress's discourse and the parents', or the gaps between the different versions of the stories) create fissures in the discourses of power that allow the young writer to imagine different narratives with different meanings. The singular and punitive meaning of "lesbian" has been exposed as an effect of power; it has been replaced not with another, clear, but positive meaning, but with multiple possibilities. Unlike the married artist who achieves a fixed clarity (and stagnation) in a suburban landscape at the end of *Who Are Penitent*, the girl is left at the end of the novel in a changing landscape (the felling of a venerable redwood on property that had belonged to her childhood and that must be sacrificed to progress) whose meanings are in flux. The girl's situation is unstable, unclear (in the way Butler uses the term), and undefined. Narratively, the girl is not removed from literary realism and a social matrix in which gender insubordination is punished and lesbianism is pathologized; rather, she is positioned differently. The social and discursive positions that these stories define provide the young lesbian who would be a writer with a way to write realist narrative without succumbing to the seeming inevitability of heterosexual plots. Rule eschews utopian narratives that remove characters and situations from struggle with the regimes of power that define the societies in which she has lived. At the same time, she resists (and will continue to do so throughout her career) a reverse discourse that promotes a clear, counter signification for the sign, lesbian. Rule's critics position her as a lesbian writer in order to contain and control the meaning of her work; Rule's work positions her as a lesbian writer who disrupts conventional meanings while remaining stubbornly unclear about the meaning of "lesbian writer."

| THREE |

Revising Fictions

Early Experiments

"Trapped in the Hope of Real Articularity"

Jane Rule wrote her first published story, "If There Is No Gate," in 1959; *The San Francisco Review* published it the following year. She also included it in her first collection of short stories, *Theme for Diverse Instruments*, published by Talonbooks in Canada in 1975. The story stages the resistance of the unconscious to representation and, therefore, to conscious examination. At the same time, the story invites the reader to examine the dreams and images the narrator finds it impossible to represent. The story explores the dilemma of a narrator wounded by her failures as a woman. Turning on the hypothetical situation defined by the title, the story also explores the role of social institutions in shoring up psychic stability. The narrative brings together, in a new configuration of meaning, traces of the stories about the headmistress and the artist discussed in chapter 2. It also returns to a number of other stories Rule had already written in letters and notebooks, such as the account of her stay in a mental home in England in the summer of 1955 after a physical and emotional breakdown. In a letter to a friend written months afterward, Rule says she had stayed in the home for a month and then left against the advice of doctors who said she'd have to stay a year to recover fully. In a notebook she kept with story ideas, Rule first called this "the mad story" (box 18, folder 17). She conceived of it as telling the story of a "woman brought up to value control as a means of sanity," who increasingly recognizes chaos in the external world as she denies it in herself.

The very dense, suggestive narrative begins as the narrator, a middle-aged woman speaking in the first person, is about to leave "a kind

of rest home, settled against the gentle Devon hills" (135). As she prepares to go back into the world, she remembers the first time she
thought she was losing her mind, when she was twenty. On that earlier
occasion, she caught "a touch of paranoia as one does a cold in the
early spring" when her mother enlisted her to deliver a load of clothes
and books to a mental hospital. The mother chose her daughter, as
"the first of her children to reach the age of immunity." At the top of
the box of clothes is her old school uniform. She tries to train her eyes
on it ("shroud of my innocence, my anonymity, like a charmed relic of
another life") as she enters the institution, but she is assaulted by the
sights and sounds of this "gigantic aviary of madness." The school
uniform, now smelling of camphor, might be read as the costume of
prepubescent adolescence, before the young girl puts on the costume
and makeup of sexualized femininity. It is also the costume of one social institution, the school, claimed here as a defense against being
swallowed up by another, the asylum.

All the inmates she remembers from her visit to the mental hospital
are women performing exaggerated gestures of femininity: those who
were "unmated," as she puts it, wailed at the sky, others repeated obsessively the gestures of child tending, some were in surprising pairs "bold
and impersonal as doves under the eaves." She focuses on one pair who
merge the image of mother-and-child with the image of lovers: "One
woman, holding another, rocked and sang a vacant lullaby, as pure as any
bird song, as inhuman." The image of female failure and madness contained by the walls of the madhouse remains as a "touchstone of sanity"
in the mind of the narrator; social and mental disorders can be safely
walled off, the vulnerable individual is protected by the solid, social institution. And yet, she finds it hard to recall the meaning of the touchstone, the sense of it: "Perhaps the experience no longer becomes me,
fits too smugly over my middle-aged humility, like a confirmation dress
or a wedding gown." The costumes of feminine rites of passage are discarded as outgrown signifiers for the middle-aged woman even as the
image of the institution that would contain madness and wall in gender
failure loses its talismanic ability to reassure. The narrator can no longer
displace her own uncertainties on those institutionalized women whose
feminine gestures are repeated endlessly in an empty rehearsal of loss.
She is resolute in her determination to overcome her feelings of vulner-

ability rather than seek to understand them. The narrator retreats to the conclusion that "recovery, not discovery, is the way back to health."

After invoking the memory of her visit to a mental hospital, whose sense and comfort now elude her, the narrator returns to the present moment in which she is a "guest" at a more benign institution in which she is urged to explore the unconscious and set aside her conscious memory: "I am to enter the world of dreams and visions." The rest home prescribes discovery as the means to recovery, but we have already learned that the narrator is defending against that road to health. Contrasting the two institutions, she remembers the mental hospital as a place where "dressed in someone else's clothes, absent-minded, it would be so much simpler to be mad." Here, in this home, her mind is "more decorous and lucid than ever"; it's her body that suffers attacks of fear.

Her doctor, the guide to her unconscious, is a woman who had been a guest in the home, then entered a silent religious order before discovering that psychiatric rather than religious discourse was the language of her vocation. She now uses silence, not as a medium in which to seek the divine, but as a screen to help patients project and explore their inner worlds. Just as the narrator described the female inmates she'd seen at the mental institution when she was twenty, she describes in the present moment several female and male guests of the rest home, all of whom seem to have an easier job of using therapeutic media—talk, dance, sculpture, and paint—to explore their inner secrets and terrors. The narrator chooses images of exposure rather than exploration to characterize the activities of the other guests. As if to school herself, she recites what she does when she encounters behaviors she'd rather ignore. She explains, for example, that if she comes across "a girl dancing naked" she averts her eyes, though her gaze then falls on awkwardly copulating swans. A woman next to her in the painting studio paints a series of images with "mindless accuracy" even as the narrator fails to represent her own dreams on canvas. Another guest she describes is a young boy who exposes himself to a bird, a flower, or to her.

The narrator claims that she might learn to value her nightmares, but not her inadequate representations of them: "I am still trapped in the hope of real articularity" (136), she says, inventing a word even as she fails at articulation. She recalls the conditions that led her to the home: a period of hard work and exhaustion had made her subject to "sudden, unreasoning fears." At the beginning of her stay, she was in a dazed, dreamless state, heavily sedated, deep in the darkness of sleep. The conditions of numb, emotional vagueness and ignorance resemble the confusion of adolescence. The narrator rejects grief or shame as factors that might have precipitated her breakdown. Grief she had experienced when "the only child I could have was born dead." Shame followed as her husband turned to another woman to meet his emotional needs. She was able to bear both of these failures of her femininity, seeing them as local, particular, rather than as fundamental assaults on physical and mental order: "It is something vaguer, deeper than these very personal, very limited experiences that challenges stability—or maintains it." The doctor gradually teaches her to dream and to examine the dreams in her waking life. The narrator says: "Dreams did seem to replace memory." Her dreams reconstitute memory, prying open the walls she had constructed to repress or ward off the significance of the memories of stillbirth and conjugal rejection.

The first dream that she recounts reworks the grief and shame of losing her baby and her husband that she had dismissed in her first analysis of her breakdown. Because the events are transformed by dream, we can begin to understand that they *do* participate in a "vaguer, deeper" meaning that challenges or maintains order. In an image that anticipates the description Rule made of herself as a young woman at Jessamyn West's party in "The 4th of July, 1954," the narrator recounts her dream as follows: "I stood on a great raft in a violent sea. All around me friends drank cocktails and chatted, unaware of danger for themselves or of the desperate struggle I was involved in." The image of her mother sending her off with discarded clothes to the mental hospital is transformed in the dream. The daughter is forced by her mother to canvas the neighborhood, ringing the bell at strange houses to "ask for donations of eyes, arms, teeth, genitals." Recycled costumes are replaced here by recycled body parts, obliquely suggesting recycled sexual identity. The narrator tries to contain and tame the meanings of these dreams even as she had tried to contain the meanings of memories by "sifting the simple facts from the irrelevant desires." The reader, however, can discern that facts are never simple, nor desires irrelevant. It is precisely the relevance of desires that the "guest" at the rest home is being asked to discover. The narrator's resistance increases, and she claims to have submitted the unconscious to rational, conscious control: "The unconscious once recognized, however, will not continue to accommodate the moral intellect with fables." Not surprisingly, repressed desires return in the narrative in the most fantastic (and unexamined) dream images of the story:

> One night I dreamt of a gangster standing in the road, having his portrait painted by a dozen middle-aged women while he made a speech about the evils of suicide. He carried and waved two old frontier pistols to illustrate his talk, then suddenly dropped dead, his hair changing from black to red as he lay in the dust.

The narrator gives up trying to represent this dream in her therapeutic painting class even as the writer gives it to the reader to examine. The image is irresistibly suggestive of Rule's story of the artist and the young girl. Elements of the artist and the girl recombine in the narrator's character and replay their significance in her dream. Here the girl is gangster, an outlaw sexuality in far-west drag. The artist has been multiplied into a dozen middle-aged women who here resemble the narrator in their age and effort to paint. The phallic frontier pistols will be taken up in the décor of the casino in *Desert of the Heart*, which Rule was writing at the time she wrote this story. As Ann, in that novel, looks at the guns on the wall, we are reminded that they are highly suggestive images, deeply ingrained in the culture:

> In themselves [guns hung on the wall] they did not interest her except as shapes, but through other people, who so often studied them, she had discovered nostalgia, possessiveness, fear, and [Ann] had sketched these attitudes into stances of the body in its alien clothes. Sometimes she overheard and remembered remarks of Freudian embarrassment between a tourist husband and wife. (*Desert* 33)

In the dream in "If There Is No Gate," the dreamer kills the gangster off, but his appearance and possible meaning continue to shift as his hair changes from black to red, suggesting a roulette wheel or a move from credit to debit or a shift from evil to desire.

When the narrator in the short story turns from her empty canvas, where she is unable to translate the dream into an image, she goes to see her doctor, the guide to her unconscious. The narrator minimizes the significance of her dreams, insisting that what she has seen in the world is more nightmarish than the visions of her unconscious. She externalizes chaos and disorder and with it madness as she says to the (silent) psychiatrist: "It's the world outside myself and my control, the public catastrophes I cannot be held responsible for. It's other people's nightmares that live in my back garden." The narrator insists that she has "no vocation" for madness. The psychiatrist's only intervention is to say: "Nothing keeps you here. . . . There are no walls. There is no gate." The story ends as the narrator packs up her clothes in her little room under the eaves that recalls in its institutional location the image of two women as mother-and-child and/or as lovers in the mental institution she observed at twenty. But the narrator has failed as a mother and she is alone; there is no other woman with her as daughter, no man or woman with her as lover. The question of her sexuality (an irrelevant desire) hasn't been asked by the narrator in the story. Looking out on the rituals of the rest home, she sees again the characters who had caught her eye earlier in the story: the boy who had exposed himself, now seated quietly; her painting companion, now in conversation with the doctor. One character is missing from her narrative: the naked, dancing girl. What does this ellipsis signify?

At the end of the story the narrator thinks about a last question that remains doubly foreclosed: first because she won't utter it; second, because she imagines the doctor would not have had an answer. The foreclosed question is: if there are no walls, if there is no gate, what kept her *out*? This question is more important to her than asking what kept her *in*. The unasked question that can't be answered returns to the (false) touchstone of sanity that opened the story. If the institutions that monitor and contain chaos in order to assure social and psychic stability are porous or illusory or optional, how does a person know who she is, what she means, and where she belongs? It's easier to fall into chaos and madness than to stay away from it; the lucidity of the conscious mind barely walls off the disturbed and disturbing unconscious. The hope of "real articularity" is a trap because it is predicated on clear boundaries, a definitive inside and outside. The story suggests in the images of cells, inside and out, little rooms tucked away in the attic under the eaves, a logic of the closet—recovery being preferable to discovery, conscious containment being preferable, more reassuring than irruptions of the unconscious, exposure of "irrelevant desires" to the gaze of others. Similarly, to dismiss failure at mothering and marriage as local and containable, as personal failings, is far less frightening than seeing them as signs of a deeper failure—not of one person's adaptation to convention but of the conventions themselves.

What the narrator leaves out at the end is as revealing as what she leaves in. The boy, exposed in his nascent virility, can be understood through a sympathetic physical response as a sign of the narrator's barrenness: "I felt one violent shudder of wings in my own passive womb, then the familiar, terrible vacancy." Interestingly, the narrator sees the boy as a sign of her reproductive failure rather than as a sign of the desiring male. But the meaning of the naked, dancing girl can't be so easily recuperated into a discrete, personal failing. The exposed female body, in its nascent sexuality, evoked within the story a gesture of shame (averted eyes) that merely brought the narrator to a more explicitly sexual image (copulating swans). The meanings of that vision are repressed at the end of the story. Desire expressed through the young girl's dancing body is potentially too disruptive to be addressed, it resists recuperation into a story that would be recognizable to the narrator, like the story of reproductive failure which may be terrible, but is, nonetheless, legible and clear. The confusion of the mother-and-child/lovers and the potency of exposed female desire in the image of the naked, dancing girl are repressed. To function, to reenter the outside world, the narrator must disavow these unrecuperated traces of female sexuality, leave them behind on the institutional grounds.

Another detail in the story that remains opaque to the narrator reinforces this interpretation. Faced with another indecipherable dream in the sequence that ends with the gangster and the portrait painter, the narrator asks herself (and the reader): "What was I to do with rules like 'Change I to you and add e-s' which I seemed to be teaching to strange natives" (137–38)? The new grammar suggests the self-reflective, interchangeable sameness of the mirrored self and other in conventional representations of lesbian lovers. To add "e" feminizes nouns and adjectives in some languages, while "s" pluralizes beyond a single or singular example. The grammar of her dreams inscribes a lesbian subject and culture (strange natives) foreign to her, a language that, on a deeply unconscious level, she longs to master. She can dream a language she can't yet speak, at once desiring and denying "a real articularity."

Institutions in this story—like the school in the story of the head-mistress or the Napa mental hospital in the 4th of July story—regulate and contain gender and sexuality. Their very existence, however, suggests that outlaw desire exceeds the categories that would confine it. Outlaw desire that is here repressed, has the potential to destabilize meanings—the assumption, for example, that motherhood and marriage define feminine maturity. The narrator longs for permanent guideposts to living, whatever her own individual failings might be. Instead, these markers of femininity are revealed as provisional and contingent. The meanings of femininity beyond motherhood and desire, outside hetero-sexual marriage, remain unavailable to the narrator even as the images of the story generate possibilities for new meanings for the reader. The narrator moves from a dreamless, drugged state to a provisional, falsifying lucidity that continues to repress dream images that escape conscious representation and signification. Outlaw sexuality remains hypothetical in "If There Is No Gate." If there is no gate, if there are no walls, what then? What would be "in," and what would be "out," what would happen to the logic and clarity of the closet? The seemingly more benign "rest home" is actually more threatening to the narrator than the mental hospital because the terms of sanity are less clear, the boundaries are more pervious. The presenting issue of the narrator in "If There Is No Gate" is gender failure; undefined by her child or husband, the narrator has failed in her social roles. But the deeper question of the story is sexual definition. The desiring female subject (the dancing girl) is repressed at the end, and the narrator can't (yet) decipher a grammar predicated on the exchange of "you" and "I" in a discursive field marked by the feminine plural. Gender and sexual crises are not the same, but gender crisis may mask a crisis of sexuality, the failing grammar of gender may give way to an emerging grammar of sexuality.

An earlier, less successful, but suggestive story that Rule wrote as a college student in 1951 examines gender, sexuality, and desire in a masculine context. "Between Darkness and the Sun" (box 12, folder 2) is a lyrical piece about a male homosexual character and is fairly typical of much of Rule's early writing in that she chooses a young man through whom to stage a crisis of gender or sexuality. She marks her main character as a recognizable trope of the homosexual male: "This is the blond boy, the one who is always too weak and too young, but nevertheless there in all the books." She gives him the same name, David, she gave to her fantasy lover in high school, the one she invented to ward off her fear of failure at heterosexual love. As David is introduced in "Between Darkness and the Sun," "he has just come from his minor role in a minor play," anticipating in this image of a minor actor another character named David, in *Memory Board*, written thirty-six years later. In the story, David "pretends at first to have forgotten to remove his makeup, or perhaps he is an older woman's lover but really belongs to her husband." Seeming to leave his "performance" behind, "pretending" to forget that he is in drag, the young boy might seem to belong, sexually, to a woman but "really" belongs to a man. In this exchange, the character embodies the erotic triangle of male homosocial desire delineated by Sedgwick. In the male-female-male triangle, attachments between men are paramount, but must be mediated through a woman in order to sustain the distinction between men and women essential to maintain patriarchal control. The costume and makeup of the boy already begin to break down the triangle even as the narrator speculates that he "seems" to belong to a woman, but "really" belongs to her husband.

Although the story begins with a recognizable literary trope of the homosexual male (further emphasized by the traces of makeup that mark the cross-dresser), Rule uses this figure to question the gender conventions that define male homosexuality in a homophobic, misogynist context. In so doing she further destabilizes the gender conventions that sustain the male homosocial triangle and patriarchal clarity.

When David makes love to men he doesn't have the reactions he is "supposed" to have, he "could not feel obscenity, could not be wicked because he was in love. David was a hero worshiper and love making to him was only another part of the ritual. . . . When he was alone, he did not quite believe in his own potency. Gray-haired men cried out to be women, begged him to be a woman in the dark, but the blond boy did not want either. He liked the strength, the familiarity of men. David admired manhood and made love to it" (3). For David, homosexual desire is not a transgression of masculinity, but a fuller expression of it. Homosexuality is not an imitation of heterosexuality in which men play the role of women, it is a potent, bonding force between men that reconfirms manhood. In the story David dreams that a woman might teach him despair, and the rhetoric of the story is heavy with images of Good Friday death and Easter resurrection. But he doesn't learn heterosexual despair and the religious discourse doesn't work. Perhaps the most original and interesting aspect of the story is the young writer's use of a stock homosexual figure, but her refusal to reinscribe clichés about gender or about homosexuality through him. Masculinity is not propped up by a mediating (and subordinate) femininity. These stories, typical of Rule's early efforts, explore conventions of gender and of sexuality through substitution, reversal, and disguise. Gender crisis is a screen for sexual crisis, male characters stand in for female, characters assume costumes and roles and in so doing undermine the conventions they mimic. Rule shifts back and forth between disciplinary social institutions (schools, mental hospitals, convents) and unruly subjectivities, examining how subjectivities are institutionalized, given coherence and apparent stability by seemingly impersonal forces. The tensions that underlie these narratives mark the struggle of a lesbian writer to create narratives that valorize lesbian subjectivity within the constraints of heterosexual plots, as Farwell put it.

Rule's second unpublished novel, written in 1957 and called alternately *This Not Quite Promised Land* and *Not for Myself Exactly*, was never published in anything like its original form. Yet this novel (together with her first novel, *Who Are Penitent*, written during Rule's year in London, 1952–53) was reworked and revised repeatedly. The early novels and their revisions present a particularly revealing case study of the obstacles to lesbian narrative created by the conventions of Western fiction. Rule's early negotiations with narrative conventions in these manuscripts ramified in two different but closely related directions: one toward a seemingly heterosexual narrative that barely disguises lesbian subjectivity, the other toward an overtly lesbian narrative shaped by the conventions of anxious, heterosexual subjectivity. The first, a surfacely heterosexual narrative, is illustrated in an unpublished 1970 novella that retains the title, characters, and many other elements from *This Not Quite Promised Land*. Rule explores this direction further in a number of short stories written in the 1960s for mainstream women's magazines like *Redbook*. "House," published in *Redbook* in 1967, is a good example. The second direction, a narrative with a lesbian protagonist whose identity is shaped by homophobic, heterosexual values, is most fully realized in Rule's second published novel, *This Is Not for You* (1970). Rule also explores this direction in other short stories written primarily for lesbian periodicals in the 1960s, such as "My Country Wrong," published in *The Ladder* in 1968. In *Desert of the Heart* (1964), which I take to be a later novel than *This Is Not for You*, notwithstanding the dates of publication, Rule is able to create a different sort of narrative that articulates lesbian desire in a realist mode, beyond the limitations of homophobic containment, without entirely suppressing the male homosocial bond as constitutive of social order.

Disguising Desire: Not for Myself Exactly

In a letter to her college friend Ellen Kay, written from Vancouver on August 2, 1957, Rule says that she is fifty pages into a novel. She is struggling with narrative form because she wants to write the novel in the first person, from the point of view of a male character who talks about events he can't have participated in or witnessed. She titles the novel *This Not Quite Promised Land* and then retitles it: *Not for Myself Exactly*. Barely four months later, on November 25, she writes again to Ellen Kay, announcing,

> Yes, the book is finished, it lies somewhere between novella and novel, but, as I finished it, more novel to me, not only because it grew to 230 pages but because it seems to me the space of a novel. I have sent a copy to [her English lover from 1952 to 1953]. It is dedicated to her, because the world it creates is somehow even more hers than mine, not in fact, not perhaps even in mood, but in a way deeper, vaguer than I can name. I call the book NOT FOR MYSELF EXACTLY, which makes the dedication rather nice and is privately a good title . . . I am quietly pleased with it. (Box 19, folder 3)

The convolutions required by the choice of a male first-person narrator to tell a story he can't have witnessed and the recognition that the novel is about the world of the lover she lived with in England in "a way deeper, vaguer that I can name," illustrate very well the challenge of writing a lesbian love story in a tradition in which narrative is marked masculine and heterosexual. As her letter indicates, this novel is not autobiographical in the sense of recounting the facts of the relationship she lived in England in the early 1950s. The connection is, however, important to the meaning of the book, and details of the draft confirm this. The parents of the (male) English lover in the novel live at the same address as the parents of Rule's (female) English lover; the English man and the (much younger) American woman whose story is told by the novel share a flat at the address where Rule and her (older, English) lover lived.

The connection between Rule's year in England and this novel is, as she says, both "vaguer and deeper" than a transposition of biographical facts into fiction. The manuscript shows Rule trying to create in narrative a world shaped by her early, lesbian relationship but not limited to it. The novel investigates differences in cultures (Derek is English; Page is American), in ages (Derek was old enough to have fought in World War II, Page [the central character] and Peter Sargent [the narrator and Page's eventual husband] were young enough to have been spectators rather than participants but old enough to have been wounded by it), and in temperament (Derek is fatalistic and worn down, Page is optimistic and energetic). But fundamentally, through a complicated relay of secrets and substitutions (lovers standing in for earlier loves, men playing the role of father to children conceived by their wives with other men), the novel investigates (female) sexual initiation and forbidden love. There is, however, no convincing reason within the plotting of the novel why the love between Derek Good and Page Benjamin should be forbidden. If we imagine that Derek's character is a disguise for an older, woman lover, a covert, guilty affair makes more sense as the chief obstacle in the plot.

The improbable narrator, as well as the improbable plot, in the first version of this story illustrate the difficulty of narrating a woman's story. Rule uses a narrative form that unwittingly reproduces Sedgwick's male homosocial paradigm. The triangle formed by Peter-Page-Derek sustains the narrative: Peter (now married to Page and thinking back to the first year they knew each other, seven years before the narrative frame) tries to re-create the story of Derek and Page. Even before generating Derek's story with Page, Peter has assumed Derek's role as father of Page's child, conceived during her affair with Derek but born after his death and after her marriage to Peter. This substitution repeats an earlier substitution of one man for another through the medium of a woman's body: Derek had assumed the role of father to Jackie, his (dead) wife's son who was the result of a wartime affair with another man. In other words, first Derek and then Peter legitimate and contain a woman's sexual excesses by naming the woman (Mrs. Good, Mrs. Sargent) and claiming her son. Outlaw female sexuality is redeemed by heterosexual marriage. It takes a man to tell a woman's story; in telling it, he bonds with another man, whom he replaces as lover and as father. The male narrator legitimates the woman's sexuality and the other man's progeny, containing female desire and assuring the perpetuation of patriarchy.

Thirteen years later, in 1970, Rule turned the novel into a novella and returned to the original title, *This Not Quite Promised Land* (box 11, folder 3). She deleted about half of the novel and made Page more clearly the narrative center. In the novella Rule displaces Peter as narrator and disrupts to a certain degree the dynamics of the Derek-Page-Peter triangle of the first draft. The story begins in August 1971 in Vancouver as Page receives a letter from her son, Ben, from London. He writes her from the Senate House cafeteria in London where twenty years earlier she had met Derek Good. Ben is unaware of that meeting and knows only that the man he takes to be his father, Peter Sargent, met Page at the same spot nineteen years earlier. The relay of substitutions continues to underlie the narrative: Page replaces Derek's dead wife, Peter replaces Derek in Page's life. Ben takes the physical place first Derek and then Peter had occupied in the cafeteria. As in the first version, the substitutions are also allied to secrets; only some of the characters are aware of substitutions that are vital to their own self-knowledge.

Most of the text of this novella comes directly from the earlier, unpublished novel. Some of the problems, as I have suggested, are resolved, but some persist. The most interesting problems concern the apprentice writer's continuing experimentation with narrative form and her efforts to represent female sexuality, particularly in a context that is presented as "forbidden." Here Rule puts problems of narrativity and knowledge at the center of the novella. For example, she includes a correspondence between Derek and Page within the narrative itself. Their letters thematize the difficulties of representation and interpretation, reminding the reader of the power of language to withhold knowledge as well as reveal.

After Derek and Page first make love (which I'll return to in a moment) Page goes to Edinburgh and they exchange letters. Derek's letters are filled with conventions that serve to screen his identity, to defer or deny any knowledge of who he is or what he feels:

In Edinburgh, Page received the first of Derek's many letters, a tidy, quiet note, enquiring about her trip, the weather, the theatre, her health. She could find nowhere in it the man she loved. Even the handwriting was strange. Who was this Derek Good, who signed his full name as if the letter were a legal document? Page tried to answer it and could not. Two days before she left Edinburgh she managed to write to him, a very different kind of letter from the one he had suggested by his own. (Box 11, folder 3, pages 22–23)

Page's response to sexual constraint is the same as her response to narrative constraint: she defies the limits Derek seems to set, she transgresses the conventions. Her own letter is described as follows: "In it she smashed Derek's hope of establishing a vague, friendly correspondence, out of which, after a number of months, they could drift into silence without grief" (23). His response is to replace the distancing conventions of his previous letters with a different sort of convention. He sends flowers to Page's ship at the first port of call in Ireland with a note, "I love you. D." The vague questions about the weather are replaced by an expression of love that could be seen as a ritual, conventional gesture except that it is the first time he has addressed it to Page. He replaces his legalistic full name with his initial—at once a gesture of intimacy and a disguise.

Significantly, when Rule composed her unfinished autobiography nearly twenty years later, she wrote that her English lover sent flowers to her boat that she, Rule, received in Ireland. In that context, the flowers are also a substitution, one in which a real lover replaces the appearance of a lover: her grandfather had in the past sent her flowers to give the impression to others that she had a mysterious romance. She writes in the autobiography: "I no longer needed a grandfather to make romantic gestures, but when a cabin mate asked who they were from, I hesitated before I said simply, 'Someone I met in England'" (154–55).

In the novella, letters develop and prolong the intimacy between Derek and Page when they are separated by "a continent and an ocean." The narrator suggests that if Derek and Page had faced "the daily fears" their relationship would have faced in everyday life, the intimacy they developed by letter would have ended quickly. Distance and the written word tempt them to articulate a love "they would otherwise not have risked" (23). Eventually Page arranges to return to the University of London on a Fulbright scholarship. When her return is certain, Derek stops writing to her. She returns to their original meeting place in the Senate House cafeteria, and although Derek isn't there, Peter is. He notices her and for several days observes her as an anonymous spectator or voyeur: "He chose a place to sit where he could watch her without being discovered" (34). When after three days Derek has still failed to materialize, Peter approaches Page, and the substitution is explicit in Page's response: "She looked at him for a moment as if she were looking through him into another August, another face" (35). Even as the relationship between Peter and Page begins, Page tracks down Derek by using information from his letters. She goes to his parents' house in Horsham and the landscape looks familiar because she has read about it in his letters: "The names suddenly became places" (40). As she walks through the town she seems to rediscover details she is seeing for the first time. Reaching his parents' house, she recognizes it: "She hesitated, then moved toward it, watching her own figure walk in a landscape with the double vision of a dream" (40). Letters, then, serve to withhold and to reveal, to mislead and to guide the reader into previously unknown landscapes, providing a knowledge that is double, like a dream, or like fiction. When Page does move toward the house she sees Jackie, Derek's stepson, who invites her into the house and leads her to Derek.

The most awkward obstacle in the narrative form Rule had chosen for the first version of the story, the 1957 novel—using Peter to narrate a story that belongs to his wife and that he witnessed secondhand and after the fact—is overcome in the novella by displacing Peter as the narrator. In the novella, the homosocial triangle is destabilized by introducing what at first seems to be a conservative narrative device: a third person narrator removed from the story. The effect, though, is to shatter the power of the homosocial triangle to signify, opening up the possibility of making a woman the center of the narrative as a subject rather than as a mediator between men.

The reconfigured narrative form has the further effect of making the dynamic of substitutions an explicit component of the narrative structure. Substitution, alluded to in the 1957 novel, is a central theme in the 1970 novella. When Peter learns (from the academic adviser, Elizabeth Lucas, who directs Page's work as well as his) that Derek exists and that

Page is unaware of Peter's feelings for her, he becomes angry because ignorance has caused him to misread Page and to let himself become vulnerable. When he takes her on a date to the theater to see *Porgy and Bess,* he begins to take Derek's place at her side. As stand-in he becomes spectacle rather than spectator and resents the way he imagines that others are interpreting his role. Elizabeth Lucas and her husband are sitting two rows behind Peter and Page: "Peter had the sensation that he was watching the performance through their eyes rather than his own (60)." He imagines that they are viewing the spectacle of his suffering through the spectacle on stage. The multiple viewing positions and layered interpretations that characterize the scene in the theater repeat the structure of double vision that Page experienced through Derek's letters and her visit to the landscape of his home. In other words, representation in this novella, whether through letters or theater or the narrative itself, is built on substitutions, invites multiple interpretations, and disguises even as it reveals emotional and sexual discoveries. In an interesting coincidence, the name that Peter and Page invent for Elizabeth Lucas's husband, who works in artificial intelligence, is the "Tin Man of Oz," a "friend of Dorothy" who would signal in a queer reading that the surface heterosexual story is a disguise for an underlying homosexual narrative. It is also through him that Peter and Page get to Vancouver, not quite Oz, "this not quite promised land." In the terms of the novel, Vancouver is presented as a "familiar foreign landscape," a not quite English city, not quite a new Jerusalem, but a young city built on elements of old world culture in a new landscape.

In the 1970 novella, Rule revises the sexual initiation scene she had enjoined herself to rewrite in the margins of the earlier novel. The novella more clearly focuses on Page's efforts to read her sexuality against the available narratives of female desire: legitimate containment in marriage or the outlaw desire of the street prostitute. In the first chapter, I discussed the way in which Rule wrote the sexual initiation scene in the 1957 novel. Erotic violence merged pleasure and disgust, masculine aggression and female masochism. In the 1970 novella, the gender roles are not as conventionally assigned. Assuming the role of a married couple (Derek puts his wedding ring on Page's finger for the benefit of the hotel clerk), they spend a night in a Brighton hotel, as they did in the first version. This time the night is described as follows:

Anywhere else Derek and Page might have known their night would have its tomorrow, consequential as any day in either of their lives; but they were in a hotel room, whose walls seemed to define the space of their world. Time was no more than the rhythm of their appetites, Page wild and erratic with what she had never known of her body before, Derek obsessed with the need to make her come to him totally. When they finally slept their exhausted brief hour, they lay separate as bodies flung apart by explosion. When they woke, they had no more need of each other than strangers. (13)

Having discovered her body, Page attempts to read it. The only terms available to her outside of the conventions of marriage are excessive, outlaw, but she can't feel the shame that is supposed to follow. When she returns to her own hotel room in London, she rediscovers the ring on her finger. She then thinks to herself:

> "I'm nothing but a whore," she moaned, tucking her knees up under her chin and rocking back and forth. "Page Benjamin of no fixed address . . ." like drunks, dope addicts, and all the other petty criminals who lived in the printed world of the newspaper. But no conventional tears of shame would come. "And I asked for it. I begged for it. I loved it." (13–14)

Certain that any stranger on the street would surely recognize her as the whore she has become, Page attempts to disguise herself as a respectable woman.

Having broken the seemingly inevitable association of unleashed female desire and shame, however, Page wants to assume the role of prostitute. She wants to be "used like that," to meet Derek's needs and her own. To be a desiring woman is to be "without address," without a legitimate place in a social order determined by men, neither daughter nor wife.

Toward the end of the novella, Peter falls ill and definitively ends the affair saying: "You've given me a life worth losing, Page. Now let me go" (106). Faced with what she sees as her own failure to marry Derek and to bring him back to life, Page has an emotional breakdown that recalls the narrator in "If There Is No Gate." She is taken by Charles Lucas, the Tin Man, to a rest home at Tunbridge Wells. Like the narrator of "If There Is No Gate," she is heavily sedated at first and resists her insistent, recurrent dreams. In contrast to the narrator of the short story, Page

learns that she is pregnant, not barren, but in her case pregnancy is a social failure if unredeemed by a man. Peter assumes fully his role as substitution for Derek, legitimates Page's sexuality by marrying her, takes
her to Canada, and raises Derek's son as his own. The narrative shifts
back to the present moment and ends with the image of Ben writing in
the Senate House, asking to be let go by his parents.

This surfacely heterosexual narrative explores the injunction to
women to subordinate desire to the demands of heteropatriarchy. Female transgression risks being exposed through "illegitimate" pregnancy
for the heterosexual woman. The woman's own body betrays her secret.
The story shows, however, that this transgression can be redeemed by
male protection: Peter can give Derek's baby a name. But what of lesbian
transgression of patriarchal demands? The transgression may be easier to
conceal but redemption is unimaginable.

In the novella, a third-person narrator moves in and out of the consciousness of different characters in conjunction with the positioning of
Peter as spectator and voyeur; the mobility of perspective creates a way
within the narrative form to destabilize male centrality and heterosexual
plots in a realistic fictional genre. The novella reestablishes the masculine
power to name and to legitimate both female sexuality and the story of
a woman, but we can begin to see in the shifts in narrative form how a
heterosexual romance can be reshaped by a lesbian subjectivity, a direction that Rule will develop more successfully in some of her short stories.
Her second published novel, *This Is Not for You*, takes up the problems
of representing forbidden, female desire in another mode entirely. With
this novel she narrates the denial of a lesbian story through a lesbian narrator who defines herself as a sexual monster.

Denying Desire: *This Is Not for You*

This Is Not for You was published in 1970, the same year Rule returned
to her unpublished 1957 novel to write the novella *This Not Quite
Promised Land*. Like the novella, *This Is Not for You* revisits early material to rework it in new ways. The manuscript for *This Is Not for You* was
completed in 1965, the year that *Desert of the Heart* was published in the
United States, but Rule's agent couldn't interest a publisher in it for several years. *This Is Not for You* reads like a much earlier novel than *Desert*

of the Heart in style, narrative structure, and content; even the negative title echoes *This Not Quite Promised Land* and *Not for Myself Exactly*. The novel recalls unpublished manuscripts in several other ways as well. Rule returns to material from her college years. The story focuses on the unrealized affair between Kate George, the narrator, and a college friend, Esther Woolf. The small women's college in the Bay Area where they are students together is never identified, but it is a barely disguised Mills College. The narrative, like the 1970 novella *This Not Quite Promised Land*, is framed in the present moment (late 1960s) but is primarily focused on re-creating a story that begins in 1951 and extends over fifteen years, ending in the present. Most of the story, however, is located in the 1950s as is clear from the values and politics, particularly concerning gender, sexuality, ethnicity, and nationalism.

The second of the five sections of the book is located in London during the same year, 1952–53, that is represented in *This Not Quite Promised Land* and contains material that Rule had developed in another, early unpublished manuscript, "The London Year." The other three parts are located in California, Washington, D.C., and New York; in the New York section particularly, there are faint echoes of Greenwich Village as the site of a gay subculture that was also alluded to in her first unpublished manuscript for a novel, *Who Are Penitent*. At several moments in the novel the narrator explicitly reminds the reader that events she is describing—a drug bust, for example—would be viewed much differently "now" than at the moment represented in the novel. The narrator also admits grudgingly and dismissively that a gay and lesbian movement has changed the way some people view sexual orientation "now" as opposed to "then." The reminders are necessary because for the most part the story not only represents the fifties but could very well have been written then. Kate George continues to define herself and her world through the values of the 1950s American, white middle-class into which she was adopted as a child and which she, in turn, works to maintain.

Another way in which *This Is Not for You* recalls earlier, unpublished manuscripts is in the use of religious language, particularly in long discussions about morality. Esther Woolf, who is a nonobservant Jew, converts to Christianity and enters a silent order of nuns at the end of the novel. Toward the end of the college section of the novel, Kate gives a sermon in the college chapel about Cain and Abel, betrayer and betrayed, as part of her senior project. This too reworks early, unpublished material. When she was a senior at Mills, Rule wrote a sermon entitled "Judas or Christ" in which she asks: "Judas or Christ—how can one tell? We are Judas and Christ; we are the betrayer and the betrayed, gaining with an awareness of our double nature, humility and salvation" (box 17, folder 6). Rule quotes this part of the sermon verbatim in the novel, adding only "perhaps" before "salvation" (60). Her college friend Ellen Kay was Rule's reader and moral support for the college service; it was she who suggested the question. Ellen Kay later did enter a silent order of nuns for a time before changing her vocation to another—active rather than contemplative—religious order. Also, according to the unpublished manuscript for an autobiography, *Taking My Life*, Rule and Ellen Kay took a trip together to Mallorca that resembles one of the episodes in the 1970 novel. *This Is Not for You* is dedicated to "E.K." I don't mean to suggest that *This Is Not for You* is a fictionalized retelling of Rule's relationship with that college friend. For one thing, the narrator, Kate George, except for that fragment of a college sermon, in no way resembles Rule. It is not biography but a history of (re)writing that is interesting here. The novel takes up issues and problems that Rule had already written about in one context that she chooses to reexamine in a different narrative context, uncovering or generating new meanings.

This Is Not for You recalls earlier work in its packed layering of plots and subplots, major and minor characters, landscapes from California to England to Greece to the East Coast of the United States and its lack of narrative focus. There is, however, another kind of nearly obsessive focus: the use of a single, first-person narrator who is a lesbian.

Rule's use of point of view and her implied response to a lesbian fictional lineage, in *This Is Not for You*, are the most original aspects of the novel. Although Kate George appears to control the narrative in the first person, Rule creates a less obvious narrative frame shaped by what I will call a resisting lesbian subjectivity, again echoing Fetterley. The second, less visible frame is detectable through certain gaps, contradictions, and involuntary associations in Kate's story. Kate is a closeted, controlling lesbian who had internalized the pathological model of lesbianism promoted by the repressive heterosexuality of the 1950s. The resisting lesbian subjectivity of the larger narrative frame exposes the origins and effects of Kate's values. The resisting lesbian subjectivity creates an ironic commentary on Kate's story, revealing her apparent lucidity, generosity, and self-sacrifice to be delusional, egocentric, and destructive of the very person she claims to protect.

The novel is presented as a (dead) letter from Kate to Esther that she will never send and Esther will never read. The choice of narrative form was a risky one because the unreliable narrator is the reader's only explicit guide to interpretation; the reader needs to be alert to ironies that escape the narrator's notice. Many of the reviews of the book—in both the straight and the gay press—illustrated how risky a choice it was. Rule complained in a 1975 interview with the Toronto gay newspaper, *The Body Politic*, that gay readers condemned the book as promoting a homophobic view of lesbian identity and that straight reviewers praised the book for the realistic portrait of Kate as a sad, tortured lesbian.

More attentive readers recognized that the implied author's perspective provided a searing critique of Kate's. One such reviewer was "Isabel Miller" (Alma Routsong) in *The Ladder* (June–July 1970) whose own, positive lesbian novel, *A Place for Us*, had been published privately in 1969 and was later published commercially as *Patience and Sarah* (Zimmerman xi–xii). Miller concludes her review of the novel by saying:

> [Rule has] given us this tragic admonitory tale of what happens when you make moral decisions for other people without consulting them, when you despise love, when your emotions are inaccessible to you, when you're closed and cold and self-righteous and condescending—when you're a prude: you drive your girl to sick men and drugs and doomed marriages and divorce. (*The Ladder* 12)

"Gene Damon" (Barbara Grier) in her annual list of lesbian titles for *The Ladder* wrote in the April–May 1971 issue: "1970's best lesbian novel is Jane Rule's THIS IS NOT FOR YOU, N.Y., McCall's, 1970, though it requires an attentive and serious reader" (28).

This Is Not for You, though written earlier, was published during the first, energetic wave of gay and lesbian pride engendered by the nascent gay rights movement. Between Miller's review and Damon's praise, for example, the foundational lesbian-feminist essay "Woman-Identified-Woman," attributed to Rita Mae Brown, was published in the pages of *The Ladder*. Lesbian readers were hungry for affirmation, an affirmation they felt they had already found in *Desert of the Heart*.

It is not surprising that many readers didn't have the patience or the attentiveness of Alma Routsong and Barbara Grier and, hence, didn't recognize the originality (and the politics) of Rule's second novel.

The lesbian fictional lineage of *This Is Not for You* is not *Desert of the Heart* but *The Well of Loneliness*. *This Is Not for You* can be read as a counternarrative of *The Well of Loneliness*; Rule's central figure is a lesbian who, like Stephen Gordon, accepts without question the negative definition of the lesbian as deviant upheld by the dominant culture. The difference is that the implied author of *This Is Not for You* invites the reader to see that Kate George has deluded herself. Rule exposes the consequences of internalized oppression not only for the central character but for those around her. Just as Radclyffe Hall tells through Stephen Gordon a "narrative of damnation," as Stimpson calls it, Rule has Kate George invent a narrative of damnation to explain herself and to give her choices meaning. There are, as Terry Castle and others have suggested, hints of alternatives to the dysphoric story that is Stephen Gordon's even within *The Well of Loneliness*, but readers have traditionally read the novel as the story of the lesbian as congenital invert doomed by her monstrous sexuality. The novel nonetheless gained cult status because it took lesbians seriously and gave a fictional face and voice to a lesbian subject. Rule, however, adapts narrative convention in such a way that the dysphoric narrative that Kate naturalizes is exposed as the product of the model of lesbian sexuality she has adopted for herself and against which she wants to protect Esther. Radclyffe Hall accepts sexual inversion as biologically determined; Jane Rule exposes the pathological model of lesbian sex as an effect of power maintained by regulatory fictions.

Kate George in *This Is Not for You*, like Stephen Gordon, considers herself to be fixed in the terms of lesbian identity promoted by the dominant culture of her time—the United States in the 1950s, rather than Britain in the 1920s. Just as *The Well of Loneliness* is about the world of the "congenital invert," *This Is Not for You* is about the lesbian as grotesque and about the morality of the closet. To function in straight society and satisfy her forbidden desires, Kate has fashioned a double life corresponding to the "double nature" of humanity that she preached about in her Cain and Abel sermon. Her sexuality is introduced from the beginning as a source of shame, a sign of sickness that risks exposure. Her sexual initiation is with a swimming coach in Carmel the night before a meet. They have too much to drink and in what begins as a comforting gesture, the coach takes her to bed. Her initiation resembles the initiation scene in the 1957 novel version of *This Not Quite Promised Land* in that taboo sexuality is named by insults "words I had read on fences and in literature but had never heard pronounced before" (15). She takes this to be the language of desire and she wants to learn it well: "I wanted to listen for stress, for accurate pronunciation just as I did in German class, and I wanted to go on trying to feel what I had begun to feel" (15).

Significantly, sexual insult is linked to ethnic slur in the language she is hearing and wants to imitate. Kate is presented in the novel as the (illegitimate) daughter of an American Indian woman and a white man; she repeatedly uses racial slurs to identify herself as a "half breed" throughout the book. Adopted by an older, white middle-class couple—an Episcopal minister and his wife—she has herself adopted what she takes to be their values and maintains a willful ignorance about her heritage and her biological parents. The sexual and ethnic hate speech with which the swimming coach assaults her becomes for Kate the language of desire: "Give a little clootch whiskey, and what you've got is nothing but a piece of fucking tail, a little redskin cunt" (15). The next day Kate sets a record at the meet but even that becomes a source of humiliation because she vomits as she exits the pool: "The lead item on the sports page the next day would be NEW NATIONAL RECORD SET under a picture of me retching up the whole of the night before" (16). The nexus of shame and pleasure, humiliation and triumph, secret sickness and public exposure that characterize the logic of the closet are the very terms of the language she learns to name lesbian desire and to name herself.

The linking of ethnic and sexual insult has a double effect in the novel. First, by equating ethnic slurs and sexual insults, the writer shows that both are contemptible. It is one of the ways the writer sets up her ironic use of Kate's point of view. More important, the link suggests a deeper connection between ethnic and sexual "otherness." Kate loathes her ethnic identity every bit as much as she loathes her sexuality. Both are a source of shame in a society that demeans difference; the only appropriate response is denial. At the same time, she can't change either the conditions of her birth or the expression of her desire. Consequently she must maintain a double life; any breach of the separation between what she shows and what she hides would undermine the whole structure. She can reveal the fact of her double life to some people, but she must believe in the rightness of the separation between her social self and her sexual self, or the very terms of her identity would be challenged. Like the narrator in "If There Is No Gate," Kate needs clear walls to separate inside and outside, madness and sanity, the unconscious and the conscious mind. The double life that she develops corresponds to her double family history: the hidden, but "real" origins as an "illegitimate" "half-breed," and the public "adopted" origins as the daughter of wealthy representatives of social legitimacy—a minister and his wife. She believes her sexuality is innate, indelible but illegitimate; her public self is adopted, provisional, promoting the values of those privileged by class and skin color. Her hidden (sexual) relationships are shadowy, anonymous, divorced from her feelings and from her daily life; her public (emotional) relationships are open, personal, and integrated into her daily life.

In *A Lure of Knowledge* (1991), Judith Roof argues that Kate's "anonymous and illegitimate" background is not relevant to her sexual behavior (110). While this may be true to a certain degree within the character's consciousness, the connection between her "illegitimate" origins and her sexuality is just one of the aspects of herself that the character can't see but that Rule encourages the reader to see. The deeper link between her family and ethnic origins and her sexuality is in language, specifically the meanings ascribed to "otherness" by the dominant culture. Throughout the novel, desire and ethnicity are presented as effects of language. The names that secure Kate's identity as ethnic "other" in white, middle-class society are tangled up with the names that make her a sexual "other" in a heterosexual world. Ethnic otherness and sexual otherness are both effects of language and are both invented to sustain the racial and sexual privilege of the majority culture. Kate's character is an example of how a self identified as white, middle class, and heterosexual is propped up by a hidden "other" who is a lesbian of uncertain ethnic and class origins. The respectable self depends on the despised other (and on a carefully maintained gap between them) for its definition and clarity. The seemingly secure public self is, in fact, constantly threatened by the exposure of the hidden other.

A scene in the college section of the novel recalls Kate's sexual initiation but places her in the position of sexual and narrative control. Kate is making love to Sandy, a lesbian college classmate, who is relatively open about her sexuality. Kate realizes that Sandy is, in fact, less experienced, less expert than she is. In a scene of sexual bravado, Kate thinks as she makes love:

> In the dark, particularly, words are important, as graphic and repetitive as the body's rhythm, but anticipating it so that nothing is uncertain or clumsy. While touch is gentle, exploring, let words invade, startle so that crude touch does not. Then speak gently so that breasts do not forget what thighs open for now. Talk to desire, call to it, make it come to you all together. Now.
>   "There," I said. "That's something worth feeling guilty about, anyway." (54)

The merging of crude assault and desire that marked her initiation continues to shape her desire and behavior.

Another revealing sequence illustrates the fragility of respectability and the public self and the ever-lurking threat of hidden desires. Kate returns to California to nurse her adoptive mother who has suffered a stroke. One of the effects of the stroke is that it has shattered the wall of the superego, releasing her mother's unconscious, leading her to hallucinate forbidden obscenities. Esther comes to Kate's aid and helps Kate contain her mother's imaginings, which include fantasies of a relationship between Esther and Kate, the very relationship that Kate is trying to deny. Kate tries to tame her mother's obscene outbursts by framing them with innocuous clichés. At the same time, however, this uncontrolled language exposes her own desire:

> As we sat with Mother playing therapeutic games, I had rested in your immunity to her sudden sexual references, cats copulating on her dresser, the mailman naked at the door, our own night adventures. I could let them seem as natural a part of the conversation as references to travel, friends, the garden, and the weather. When we weren't with her, we could talk of other things, but I wasn't immune to such a permissive limbo. My mind and body ached with obscenities of their own. (136)

Kate gives in to her hidden desire in a world apart from the life her friends and family know about. She spends summers in London, frequenting lesbian and gay bars. She can give full expression to her desire only in this anonymous, nocturnal, urban world. In one of the few descriptions of Kate's night life, racist slurs and violence are again associated with lesbian sexuality:

> I often was not sure through the first pint of beer whether a companion was male or female. That doubt one night made me reticent with a tall Negro for longer than pleased her. Later, when I was certain and friendly, she accused me of prejudice. "Look, if you're a nigger, I'm a—" clootch, squaw, I would have gone on to say, if my nose hadn't been broken in the middle of the sentence and my two front teeth knocked out shortly after that. Yes, grotesque. That part of my living was. Spoken of at all. I had to speak of this, lie about it, because I was in the hospital for a week with those and other painful but fortunately not serious injuries. (112)

Kate's characterization of her sexuality as grotesque is linked not only to racist speech and violence but to gender ambiguity. Gender clarity is a strict requirement for the ordering of Kate's world and public identity. Gender ambiguity is associated with gay and lesbian bars because lesbians are not "really" women, they are closer to the "third sex" that Radclyffe Hall represents in her novel. Gender clarity is required in the daytime world of straight, public life. Kate is threatened by any public displays of gender ambiguity, in part because she fears that her own uncertain status will be exposed; she will be guilty by association. One scene that is particularly telling (especially because it is unnecessary to advance her story about Esther) occurs in London as she goes to meet Andrew. Andrew, who is conventionally handsome, the very model of masculinity in the way he presents himself to the world, undergoes a sustained crisis of masculinity later in the novel and is, therefore, an especially interesting choice for the following scene:

> I caught a bus along Oxford Street and sat down, by mistake, next to a woman with pale red hair and a neatly trimmed red beard and mustache. No one looked at either of us which, under the circumstances, was unnerving because it left me isolated with what seemed after a time to be my own fantasy. When I got up to get off at Marble Arch, she followed me down the sidewalk and right into the hotel lobby. I saw Andrew standing by the counter at the theater ticket agency. As I hesitated, she did, too, just at my elbow. Andrew looked up, saw us and hesitated. I ran to him. (80)

Significantly, she sits down next to this person "by mistake" rather than "by chance." She understands the public spectacle that follows as the result of her own lapse of judgment or attention to dangerous associations that might expose her hidden self to the public eye. Is this person in drag "part of a circus" as Andrew tries to tell her, or her own fears materialized beside her in a public place? Does her hidden, lesbian identity marked in this figure by masculinity (beard and mustache) follow her around like a shadow, isolate her from others who only pretend not to see? The grotesque belongs to her nocturnal, anonymous world but risks erupting into the streets in broad daylight, just as her mother's obscene imaginings break into speech when conscious control is shattered by a stroke.

The choice of Andrew as male savior of gender clarity in this scene is further significant because he is introduced in the book initially as the sometime sexual partner of Peter. Esther and Kate meet Andrew and Peter while traveling through Spain and Portugal; later Andrew goes through a crisis of masculinity that mirrors in some ways Kate's crisis of sexuality, though she is blind to the similarities. Andrew is presented as a heterosexual man who goes along with Peter's sexual needs even though their sexual relationship doesn't mean anything to him and he claims he doesn't really like it. Why he agrees to this arrangement is never explained. Peter, on the other hand, is presented as a "true" homosexual who is often tortured by his own desire and who eventually kills himself, returning to the very site where he and Andrew spent a seemingly carefree few days with Kate and Esther in Mallorca. Looking back on a conversation with Andrew during their time on Mallorca, Kate frames it in a way that could lead her to make an analysis of racism and homophobia as the products of white, heterosexual privilege. But Kate falls just short of seeing the implication of her own indignant reaction and instead reconfirms racist, homophobic "othering" that sustains class and race privilege in a litany of ethnic and sexual stereotyping. Kate recalls a conversation in which Andrew asks:

"Why does a man want another man on top of him, Kate? I don't want to be a prude. I want to understand, but I just don't. I had a friend once in the Army. He wasn't anything like Pete. He was tough. There was nothing too tough for him, but he'd go down on his belly for any pansy he could find. He wanted to be humiliated. . . . It's different for a woman."

"Jill goes down on her back," I said, but he didn't hear me.

. . . Don't blame the Indian at the bootlegger's, the Negro with the switchblade, the Jew in his brother's pocket, the woman in her sister's bed. Morality is a luxury which only the Anglo-Saxon male can afford. Being able to afford it, he must buy it, judge others who can and don't, excuse the rest of the world with condescending kindness. (36–37)

Unlike David in Rule's early story, "Between Darkness and the Sun," Andrew can only read sexuality in stereotyped gender terms. Not surprisingly, he maintains throughout the novel an unexamined, clear, but outmoded and inadequate class-based understanding of masculinity as well.

Much later in the novel Andrew, who is the son of an oil-wealthy Alberta family, marries a college friend of Kate's who comes from a relatively poor background. He goes through a melodramatic crisis of masculinity because he can't seem to make enough money to afford the things his family of origin considers necessities (a live-in nurse for their infant, a wife who stays at home) but that other people recognize as luxuries. Kate recognizes both his pain and his myopia about the nature of his crisis, but fails to see that her own crisis of sexuality (or rather, her refusal to see it as a crisis) is as much a product of artificial and mutable class-based values as Andrew's.

The one consistent threat to the closet lesbian identity—and clarity—that Kate works laboriously to maintain is Esther, whom she both desires and loves. Her need to keep her public and private worlds strictly separate and Esther's threat to her carefully orchestrated life are summarized early in the novel when Kate says:

Since I could not [cut myself in half], I came upon a way to cut my life in half. Not quite, for winter, whatever the weather, is longer than summer. I wintered in California in the mild, academic climate with you. I went to Europe in the summer for a very different sort of life, which I never spoke of, from which I only gradually recovered each fall in your company and in work. But I had a recurring nightmare that a path through a narrow wood and across a shallow stream was all that separated those two worlds. And in that dream you were always about to discover it. (8)

Her response to the threat that Esther poses, similar to Andrew's response to his wife, is to infantilize Esther, to try to contain her within the terms of the falsely clear morality she has fashioned for herself. Kate's morality seems to require selfless sacrifice on her part but in fact she sacrifices Esther in order to maintain the double life that justifies her own sexual identity in her eyes. Kate can't allow Esther to have a mature, independent view of herself and the world because her view might compete with Kate's, she might seriously challenge Kate's "superior" analysis by loosening up the categories. Throughout the novel they have arguments about morality that echo the conflict between what "is" and what "ought to be" in *Who Are Penitent*. Esther bases her judgment on practical consequences while Kate bases hers on abstract ethics. In thinking back on their disagreements, Kate recognizes that she needed then, as she does now, to maintain the gap between abstract ethics and the exigencies of lived experience. Esther threatens to collapse that difference and must remain outside of Kate's world, innocent of her desire; Esther must not be allowed to unsettle the architecture of denial Kate has constructed for her world.

As the scene in the London bus illustrates, the rigidity of Kate's sexual identity is shored up by rigid gender identity. Esther, on the other hand, is capable of a more flexible understanding of femininity; she takes what Kate would consider risks:

> There is, at a women's college, always some emancipating encouragement for those with masculine tastes for such things as mathematics, philosophy, and friendship. You had to model it. I could not. I knew better, which forced me to be occasionally condescending, protective, inadequate. (7)

Rule's narrative experimentation in *This Is Not for You* plays on and disrupts the conventions of gender and desire in narrative form discussed by Marilyn Farwell in *Heterosexual Plots and Lesbian Narratives*. Farwell's analysis is aligned with postmodern critics who point to the inadequacies of master narratives (historical, philosophical, scientific) to account fully for human experience. That is, the master narratives present the illusion of comprehensive coherence, a seemingly seamless screen that covers over or marginalizes groups that don't fit the terms that make the narratives meaningful. Farwell shows that narrative categories reflect and reinscribe dominant gender and sexual ideology. Using Gerald

Prince's definitions of the narrator and the narratee, Farwell argues that narrative categories are simultaneously sites of ideology and sites of potential disruption:

> It is in the subject or protagonist, the object of the protagonist's attentions, the narrator, the narratee, and the figure who sees the events or action—the focalizer—that the magnitude of the Western narrative as a power-inflected system is apparent. Each of these categories is encoded with power and desire before a specific character enters the picture; at the same time . . . the character who moves the story along, who narrates it, the character who sees, and the one who is seen can challenge these codes. (*Heterosexual Plots and Lesbian Narratives* 31)

Traditionally the narrator is the active, speaking subject and occupies a masculine space. The narratee, addressed by the narrator, occupies an immobilized, silent, receptive, and feminized space. In love sonnets, for example, the narrator is the lover/speaker and the narratee is the (silent) beloved who is addressed. Traditionally the narrator and the "focalizer" (Farwell's term for the character whose point of view orients meaning in a text) are the same or closely allied.

Viewed through Farwell's critical perspective, Rule's narrative choices in *This Is Not for You* take on a particularly sharp edge. Rule's ironic use of the narrator, narratee, and point of view in this novel exploit and expose the conventions of gender and sexuality embedded in traditional narrative. Rule's use of irony aligns the reader with an implied lesbian subjectivity that disrupts the reader's conventional expectations while providing a counternarrative to Kate's story of denial. Mainstream readers who were locked into narrative conventions praised the novel for its bleak portrayal of lesbian identity; lesbians conditioned by narrative conventions condemned it for the same reason. More canny readers could see that Rule was exposing and disrupting the values inscribed by conventional narrative. The novel includes an ironic metanarrative that looks critically at how a story is told even as it tells a different story.

Rule disrupts narrative conventions by pushing them to the limit. The novel is a truncated epistolary novel; there is no exchange, no multiplicity of voices and views; there is only Kate's letter that also refuses to be a letter. As the opening sentences indicate, Kate is writing for herself, not for Esther: "This is not a letter. I wrote you for the last time over a year ago to offer the little understanding I had, to say good-bye. I could have written again, but somehow your forsaking the world for the sake of the world left me nothing to say" (3). Throughout the novel, Kate repeatedly interpellates an absent narratee, "you," creating an "other" that she at once denies and requires to consolidate her own identity. Esther will never receive Kate's text, having, literally, taken herself out of circulation. In many ways the novel is about the power to name. Kate wants to contain Esther within the names she gives her; she criticizes Esther's changing of her last name for a husband and then of her whole name for God. Kate's explicit goal in the novel is to assume the full power of narrator, to write Esther's story in her terms, to invent Esther in her own image of her. Consequently, the "Esther" of Kate's narrative is a projection of Kate's desire (and her denial of desire) rather than the object of her desire.

Kate and Esther occupy the conventional positions of narrator and narratee, and yet they also disrupt the gendered meanings associated with those positions. For example, Rule plays on the conventional masculinity of the narrator's role. In an early scene, Sandy approaches Kate and engages in a sort of traffic in women with regard to Esther. Sandy asks if Kate wants Esther or not; if she doesn't, Sandy will take her. Esther, the absent, silent object of exchange, a commodity to be bartered, is, in Sandy's terms, "going to waste" (52). On the face of it, this is an exaggerated version of the male homosocial triangle, in which a woman (here the "feminized" woman) mediates the social bond between two men (here the "masculine" lesbians). Kate makes the terms of the exchange explicit by asking if Sandy is looking for "a wife," if she wants to find a woman to play that sexual and social role for her. Even as she asks the question, Kate claims to detest even the vocabulary of that kind of arrangement between women; so named, such an arrangement might become real. Sandy resolves the exchange she initiated by offering a bargain: if Kate will give herself to Sandy, she'll stay away from Esther. Kate accepts the sexual exchange, but not the role of "wife." A scene that begins by mimicking the dynamic of the male homosocial triangle ends with a lesbian dyad that has eliminated the "feminine" third term. But the Kate-Sandy dyad is a temporary expedient meant, in Kate's mind, to protect Esther from becoming the arbiter of her own desire.

Kate's position as narrator plays on her fear of gender ambiguity, her terror that she will be exposed if gender clarity isn't maintained in recognizable terms. Esther is in the feminized, passive narratee position, and yet it is her character that disrupts conventional boundaries of femininity even as Kate tries to reimpose them, contain her, infantilize her, and keep her in a passive, "defined" role in her narrative. Esther's final gesture, entering a silent community of women, ironically confirms the passive (contemplative) hyperfeminine position even as she rejects Kate's narrative of her. Her silence is far from passive; she is unavailable rather than denied. Esther's choice of the convent pushes Kate's logic of the closet to its extreme conclusion and reverses the values it upholds. The convent encloses a silent community of women for whom the inside and outside are clearly delineated. But in contrast to Kate's shadowy urban underworld of *femmes damnées*, Esther's community works toward its own and the world's salvation.

Rule places the narrative and sexual exchange (or lack of it) between Kate and Esther within the larger, ironic frame, mediated by an implied narrator, or, I would say, an implied resisting lesbian subjectivity. The resisting lesbian destabilizes the self-loathing, controlling lesbian represented by Kate. The implied narrator exposes Kate's identity as a performance, a desperate effort to maintain by artificial means a social order that presents itself as natural. The implied narrator provides a standpoint for the reader from which to consider Kate's narrative. The ironic countertext Rule invents in *This Is Not for You* shows Kate's blind spots and exposes her abuse of narrative and sexual power. Kate doesn't tell Esther's story, she invents a story of Esther that justifies herself. She doesn't protect Esther from sexual harm, she pushes her into wounding relationships with men and away from integrated relationships with women. Above all, the implied narrator exposes the model of lesbian identity that Kate embodies as the anxious projection of heterosexual, white, middle-class values. Kate, and the world that has adopted her, requires clear gender boundaries, a heterosexual norm, and pathologized homosexuality. Her narrative maintains these values. But certain openings in her narrative (the London bus scene, her mother's unleashed imagination, for example), unexamined links (sexual insults and ethnic slurs), and characters who resist her efforts to contain their meanings (Esther, Sandy, and others) suggest a larger frame through which to reinterpret her story. In this frame, Kate's generosity is exposed as an elaborate defense, her understanding of lesbian desire is unveiled as outmoded, the product of homophobia. The very act of writing this nonletter, which is written for herself rather than for Esther, reveals that her lesbian identity is precarious, needs to be rearticulated, not to protect Esther (who is now beyond the reach of her words) but to protect herself from the challenge that Esther poses. The novel anticipates the concept of the lesbian subject as performance that Judith Butler elaborates more than twenty years later in "Imitation and Gender Subordination":

> This is not a performance from which I can take radical distance, for this is deep-seated play, psychically entrenched play, *and this "I" does not play its lesbianism as a role*. Rather, it is through the repeated play of this sexuality that the "I" is insistently reconstituted as a lesbian "I"; paradoxically, it is precisely the *repetition* of that play that establishes as well the *instability* of the very category that it constitutes. For if the "I" is a site of repetition, that is, if the "I" only achieves the semblance of identity through a certain repetition of itself, then the I is always displaced by the very repetition that sustains it. . . . What "performs" does not exhaust the "I." (*Imitation* 18)

In *This Is Not for You*, Rule exposes the delusional inadequacy of a lesbian identity that hates itself and, consequently, wounds others. She shows how this pathological lesbian subject is the product (and support) of an anxious and threatened social system that requires white privilege and a walling off of the "other." Rule suggests through the ironic frame the possibility of a lesbian subjectivity that is not contained by the terms Kate represents. She simultaneously implies a resisting lesbian subjectivity and the instability of sexual categories per se.

Once freed from the pathological model that Kate represents, lesbian subjectivity becomes a destabilizing narrative element, unsettling conventions of gender, sexuality, narrative, and, in some cases explicitly, ethnicity. Lesbian subjectivity in Rule's work is not a stable category but, precisely disruptive of categorical systems, a precursor to queer subjectivity as it has been developed in the 1990s, but with a difference. Gender and sexuality (and their imbrication with race, ethnicity, class, and generation) continue to signify in conflicting but coexisting systems in Rule's work. Working within realist genres, Rule does not provide a revolutionary vision that looks beyond the social categories of the dominant culture, but rather dramatizes the struggles engendered by the persistent, defining power of those categories. However inadequate, demeaning, and destructive the dominant culture may be, it continues to exercise power. Rule's work explores how power operates in both intimate spaces (subjectivities and homes) and public spaces (communities and nations) and, consequently, how the intimate and the public define each other. Just as important, her work focuses on sites of resistance within both intimate and public spaces.

Unsettling Women

For two years after she completed *This Is Not for You* in 1965, Rule stopped writing, perhaps because she was discouraged by publishers' lack of interest in her manuscript. In 1967 she started an immensely productive period and by the end of 1968 she had finished at least sixteen short stories and had sold six of them to *Redbook, Chatelaine,* and *The Ladder.* In the summer of 1968 a publisher expressed interest in both *This Is Not for You* and her next project for a novel, which would become *Against the Season.* This encouragement and a two-year grant from the Canada Council spurred continued productivity so that by the time *This Is Not for You* was published in 1970, *Against the Season* was nearly completed and she was well on the way in her preparation of short stories for her first anthology, *Theme for Diverse Instruments.*

The consequences of the narrative experiments in *This Not Quite Promised Land* and *This Is Not for You* are explored further in the short stories Rule wrote during that period. As I suggested at the beginning of this chapter, Rule's early narrative experiments ramified in two different but closely related directions: one toward a domestic, heterosexual narrative that is informed by a lesbian subjectivity; the other toward an overtly lesbian narrative nonetheless shaped by the conventions of heteronormative subjectivity. When Rule collected stories for *Theme for Diverse Instruments* she included both strains; her choice of stories written for *Redbook* as well as for *The Ladder* (in addition to previously unpublished stories) is an indication that she found both important.

Both of these narrative strands combine conventions of gender and sexuality and resistance to conventions in volatile, suggestive ways. These stories from the 1960s provide an interesting corrective to some directions in queer theory three decades later. In her 1992 essay, "Sex without Gender and Other Queer Topics," Biddy Martin expresses her concern about "a tendency . . . to construct 'queerness' as a vanguard position that announces its newness and advance over against an apparently superseded and now anachronistic feminism with its emphasis on gender" (*Femininity* 71) She argues that queer theory stunts its own potential for rethinking identity and social relations when it "at least implicitly conceives gender in negative terms, in the terms of fixity, miring, or subjection to the indicatively female body" (73). This tendency, perhaps unwittingly, returns to a prefeminist position according to which the feminine is marked as gendered and the masculine is neutral. As Martin points out, the queer vanguard, as a consequence, asserts itself through gestures of escape from gender (marked feminine) such as forms of disembodiment and gender crossings. She says: "I am particularly interested, here, in a resistance to something called 'the feminine,' played straight, and in a tendency to assume that when it is not camped up or disavowed, it constitutes a capitulation, a swamp, something maternal, ensnared and ensnaring" (73). Martin further points out that the opposition between gender and sexuality found, for example, in Sedgwick's work, tends to remove discussions of sexuality for men from consideration of gender and even from consideration of the body. Recent work on masculinity and race have begun to answer Martin's concern, but the tendency continues to be evident in much queer theory. As Martin says, the consequences of conflating gender with femininity and most specifically with the female body are that "lesbians, or women in general, become interesting by making a cross-gender identification or an identification with sexuality, now implicitly (though, I think, not intentionally) associated with men, over against gender, and by extension feminism and women" (77).

The two narrative strands I've identified in Rule's early stories illustrate in different modes the inseparability of gender and sexuality and provide a way out of the theoretical impasse Martin identifies. The first strand (the domestic, heterosexual narratives mediated by a resisting lesbian subjectivity) take heterosexual femininity as the site of resistance to conventions of gender marked feminine or masculine. The second strand builds on the narrative form of *This Is Not for You*, staging a lesbian narrator like Kate George who is caught in a pathological model of lesbian identity, but using the fissures and contradictions of the narrative to rethink the formation of lesbian identity. These narratives refuse to scapegoat femininity "played straight" in the way Martin has identified and at the same time they show the constant imbrication of gender and sexuality. Two such stories are "House," first published as "Not an Ordinary Wife" in *Redbook* (1967), and "My Country Wrong," first published in *The Ladder* (1968). "House" challenges the norms of domesticity through an unorthodox (but heterosexual) female subjectivity. "My Country Wrong" takes up the story of a lesbian expatriate caught in the conventions of her class and generation even as she watches them disintegrate.

"House" is part of a series of stories for mainstream women's magazines that Rule called the "Harry and Anna stories." Harry and Anna are a white, middle-class married couple with two children (a boy and a girl) living in a young, Canadian city on the ocean that is clearly Vancouver. The landscape, and the family, recall the 1970 novella *This Not Quite Promised Land*. Harry and Anna are marked as "middle aged," which in "House" means in their thirties. They are, in other words, potential readers of magazines like *Chatelaine* and *Redbook*. They are not quite, however, the model consumers who purchase respectability and class values along with the products advertised in those magazines. In "House," Harry wants the family to purchase a house with a lawn and a mortgage, like all their friends of the same age and standing. Anna, however, resists, preferring the apartment they live in which is shabby but has a view and allows them to own a boat and stay out of debt. Her dream is to move to an island, to resist being swallowed up in the bland, bored sameness that marks the lives of their friends. Harry, in contrast, longs to be "ordinary."

Significantly, the conflict between Harry and Anna is presented from the beginning as a refusal of Anna to "grow up," to act like "other women," in other words, to adapt to the dominant model of feminine maturity. Marriage and motherhood are not enough; Anna must also consume goods and acquire debt to prove her maturity. In the story, Harry eventually prevails. They sell the boat and their old car, buy a house and an Austin that is just like everyone else's, take on a mortgage and abandon Anna's dream. Once they have moved, however, the children feel alienated and lonely in their separate, small rooms; Harry feels trapped and bored and dreads recrimination from Anna. Returning home one afternoon he hears loud thuds and crashing plaster. Anna has gotten a wrecking bar and, with the help of the children, is tearing down walls between rooms and opening up windows, oblivious to the danger that she might be destroying supporting walls. After a moment of terror, Harry joins the wrecking party.

Tearing down the house provides a metaphor for reconstructing heterosexual domesticity. The external architecture is the same, but the living spaces, the intimate recesses are rebuilt to accommodate another kind of living. Neither Harry's initial yearning for ordinary middle-class routine nor Anna's dream of an island life apart from the city prevails; instead, the family changes the architecture of domesticity from within. Anna acts as the agent for change in this scenario. She has both the imagination and the courage to take the risks necessary even if she might, in the process, tear down a supporting wall. While this may seem tame accommodationist compromise from the perspective of the 1990s, the story provides a provocative site of resistance to the ideology of mainstream women's magazines in the 1960s, especially because it is presented at the beginning as a challenge to norms of feminine maturity. Rule manages to write a story legible to the readership of *Redbook* while resisting the values it promotes.

"My Country Wrong" takes a different narrative tack to create a site for rethinking lesbian identity. Written, like *This Is Not for You*, in the first person, from the point of view of a lesbian narrator, the story begins with a series of negatives and a sense of loss that underscore the aloneness and alienation of the narrator.

There should always be a reason for going somewhere: a death in the family, a lover, a need for sun, at least a simple curiosity. Even a business trip provides excuse for discomfort, focuses discontent. To explain why I arrived in San Francisco on the twenty-third of December, instead of on the twenty-sixth when I was expected, would be nothing but a list of nonreasons. I did not want anything. It was the least distasteful of the alternatives that occurred to me to fill the hole in a blasted schedule. I don't want to talk about the death of friends, failures of domestic courage, the negative guilt of an ex-patriot. It is probably better to be grieving, tired and guilty in a familiar place. (149)

The particular "hole in a blasted schedule" the narrator needs to fill—Christmas eve and Christmas day—would beg for interpretation in any narrative context, but especially in Rule's work. Christmas as a family-centered event in a culture and an economy shaped by the traces of a Christian calendar plays a role in nearly all of Rule's novels and many of her short stories. It provides an obvious narrative means for bringing people together who might normally (or by preference) be apart; or it provides a means for underscoring the marginalization of people who are not or will not be defined by the Christian calendar.

The meanings Rule attaches to Christmas vary from text to text, but it is a holiday she often incorporates in her stories. For this narrator, Christmas serves to delineate the emptiness in the narrator's calendar and her life. The story thus begins with a gap, a negative space created by a conventional calendar the narrator doesn't observe but that continues to shape her plans. The whole story, in fact, explores gaps left by fragmenting systems of meaning that once created coherence but are no longer adequate. The narrator's alienation from her family is not angry, but is well established. She had avoided Christmas day at home for fifteen years. She has given up United States citizenship as well, not out of anger at the United States but out of a desire to vote where she lives. The narrator is presented as a perpetual traveler in a world in a constant state of change. Conventional markers of identity (family, nationality) that had seemed indelible are shown to be mutable. The narrator has chosen against some ways of defining who she is, but she can't shed all the trappings of her class and background; as a result she sends confusing signals to people around her and, finally, to herself. The title of the story is an ironic rephrasing of a once unquestioned certainty. The men in the narrator's family through her father's generation were military men. Born into a family that stood for "my country right or wrong," the narrator is left with "my country wrong." The ellipsis is, like so much in the story, left as a lacuna for the reader to interpret. Does the title mean that she thinks her country of origin is wrong or that it would be wrong to think that the U.S. is her country?

The location of the story—San Francisco—provokes a series of reflections and encounters that prompt the narrator to consider the erosion of the (apparent) certainties of her childhood and youth. One of the strengths of the story is Rule's use of suggestion, her refusal to fill in gaps to create a fully articulated, coherent story. The reader catches glimpses of the narrator's story, but the narrative is fractured, important connections are left unexplained. We are never told how the narrator knew friends she visits, what "nonreasons" have led to her empty holiday, what losses, guilt and failures in courage have brought her to an anonymous (if extravagant) hotel room in San Francisco "home city as much as I ever had one, growing up American" (149). The fragmentation and gaps in the narrator's story correspond to the failure of any master narrative to give a coherent or redemptive meaning to the larger world in which she moves. The story is about discontinuity, the breaking apart of systems that give meaning to individuals and to the cultures they live in. In the process, the older systems are shown to be inadequate. The patriotism of an earlier generation, for example, legitimated some people at the expense of others. Citizenship is exclusionary, marginalizing some in order to sustain others.

In the opening pages of the story, the narrator thinks back to her childhood during World War II, a war in which her father served willingly, but which promoted racism against Japanese Americans at home in California. She thinks back through several generations of the maternal family tree in San Francisco, remembering some women who succeeded at marriage and family and others who failed. The city becomes the narrative site where private and public histories are played out, the domestic and the national are joined. The implied present moment of the narrative is 1968 and the city is again full of uniforms at the height of the Vietnam War. This time, though, the uniforms fit less comfortably and her friends are going to jail in protest rather than to war. She picks up recent books to read which remind her of persistent racial and generational conflict that undermine her last "irrational liberal hopes" (151).

The story is framed by two visits to homes. The first visit is to heterosexual friends who are renovating a Victorian house in a deteriorating neighborhood, creating a home for their two children but also for war resisters and other people who seem to drift in—part of a voluntary family that doesn't conform to the manners that the narrator was taught. This familylike group communicates primarily through the clichés of the day (jokes about people over thirty, the jargon of meditation), but these phrases are used as a means to express real affection, to make contact. Like the house in "House," this Victorian has been gutted and is being rebuilt to meet the needs of a reconfigured family. The narrator perceives it as a provisional "stage set" in which the inhabitants play out their lives; they make art, give shelter, raise children.

The second visit is her return to her parents' house a hundred miles south of the city at the end of the story; contrary to habit, she joins them for Christmas dinner. Here manners are maintained, but communication is reduced to comforting clichés that fail to connect. During this visit the narrator learns that her brother is about to be sent to Vietnam. The older generation assumes that class privilege will keep him from harm. Rule represents the deterioration of the traditional family and its values in a passage that begins "Christmas dinner at home." A series of disembodied fragments of conversation circulates around the table achieving what the French novelist Marguerite Duras called, in a similar dinner scene in *Moderato Cantabile*, a conversation that is generally partisan and particularly neutral, connoting a vague set of shared values (here: white, upper middle class, heterosexual, Republican, and patriotic) but expressing no individuality or detail that might risk disagreement, a break in the surface harmony. The unconnected bits of conversation include opinions such as: "They give them estrogen, that's all. When they're about eight or nine. They stop growing and start developing. And if it's a matter of having to wear a bra in the fifth grade or go through life six feet tall"; "Aren't you proud of your brother going off to Vietnam? They'll only send him where it's safe, of course, just where the President goes"; "Friends of ours won't even take a plane that flies *over* France."; "People with long hair want to go to jail" (167). Significantly, the first fragment concerns hormonal engineering, the effort to keep girls within the norm of acceptable feminine growth even if it means artificially accelerating their sexual maturity.

Between the two home visits, the narrator spends Christmas eve with a younger friend, Lynn, who is also a discreet lesbian. We learn about Lynn's sexuality through its political effects. She can't get work in the war industry because she can't get security clearance. Lynn takes the narrator to a lesbian bar in the Haight-Ashbury. The theme of border crossing takes on a different meaning in this sequence. At the bar the narrator is again not quite a tourist, but no longer a citizen; here, as elsewhere in the story, she belongs partially to different worlds in which conventions, manners, language, and costumes are not quite congruent. In this world she sees herself marked as different by her costume and her age: "I was not properly dressed, being properly dressed, in navy silk with a green silk coat. I have other kinds of clothes, even a pair of modest boots, which I would have been glad of, but in whatever costume I would have to carry my age" (159). As the narrator peruses the women in the bar, she notes the variety of costumes, including some women "in earnest drag." Lynn introduces her to Ann, a much younger woman who is attracted to her. When Ann asks if the narrator is a tourist, the narrator says "not really," and thinks: "I hadn't been in this kind of bar since my own college days when I was a tourist, but not simply in this world—in all worlds of social definition" (160).

The narrator's unwillingness (or inability) to fit available definitions except in a provisional or approximate way is extended to sexuality in the following exchange, Ann asks:

> "You aren't gay, are you?"
> It's an unanswerable question from my point of view, but I am more often than not doubtful about my point of view.
> "Yes," I said, regretting it.
> "Then why are we sitting here?"
> Why? . . . Because I had on the wrong clothes. I was also wearing the wrong manners, heterosexual, middle-class manners which involve so many frankly empty gestures. (163)

The answer she gives Ann is that she doesn't know what else to do. Eventually they return to her hotel room and make love.

Like many of the readers of *The Ladder*, the narrator belongs to a class and generation that were, in the late 1960s, in a definitional limbo. The costumes and conventions they were brought up with no longer fit or were acknowledged as "frankly empty." But the codes of the bar scene don't fit much better, sexual definition is still an unanswerable question. When Ann tries to seduce the narrator by saying that she finds older women wildly attractive, the narrator responds that she does, too: "But not in bars . . . I like them in their own living rooms or on lecture platforms or in offices. I've never danced with one" (164).

The narrator, adrift between the certainties of her parents' generation and the rebellion of her younger friends, provides an opening in the narrative for self-redefinition. At the same time, she illustrates the entanglement of the public within the intimate, of cultural values within personal self-definition. The narrator in "My Country Wrong" embodies a floating signifier, unmoored from the empty signifiers of the heterosexual middle class but not fully secured within the apparently clear codes of the gay bar scene. Old narrative certainties have fragmented and a new multilayered narrative is yet to be realized, but the story provides a point of recognition for lesbians struggling to redefine themselves and their place in a world that includes both private and public spaces, bedrooms, and lecture halls. Just as Anna and Harry are uncertain about what their newly configured domesticity will look like once the walls have been knocked down, the narrator in "My Country Wrong" hasn't yet defined what her "right" country might be. In another set of narratives, some written before these stories, some after, Rule experiments with new narrative forms that suggest ways of rewriting sexuality and gender. What is interesting is that she tries out different forms simultaneously. After *This Is Not for You*, however, she will no longer write a sustained narrative in the first person. The vantage point provided by the ironic frame of that novel, expressed through what I have called the implied, resisting lesbian narrator, is played out more explicitly in the narrative forms of her later fictions.

FOUR

Composing Selves

Dueling Narratives

"Home Movie": Projecting a Lesbian Subject

In "My Country Wrong," the narrative is prompted by a gap, a "hole in the schedule." The narrator herself represents a lapse in meaning; she is presented as a lesbian caught between conflicting systems of meaning, clothed in the manners and conventions of an upbringing that no longer fits, an outsider to the new domesticity of her heterosexual friends, a tourist in the bar scene to which her lesbian friend takes her. As the scene at her parents' Christmas dinner illustrates, though, the narrator is not just an empty place at her family's table; for the reader, the narrator provides a site for destabilizing narratives of gender, sexuality, and the self that had seemed immutable, that had passed for true. The shift from reading the lesbian subject as a gap in the dominant narrative to staging the lesbian subject as a site for reimagining sexuality and gender is apparent in many of Rule's fictions. She often moves back and forth among competing understandings of what a lesbian self might mean: a fixed identity, a changing subjectivity, a category to be discovered, a challenge to definitions of gender and sexuality.

In a writer's notebook from 1967, Jane Rule wrote: "Problem about short stories: I don't want to write thin magazine stories. That's why I start out without a story, just a tension or circumstance. Then I can catch a language, but without a direction I can't write a story. But impatience to get something on paper produces dutiful, dull totally discovered ideas or moments, suggestive scenes without point. I've got to get the 2 together, be willing to sit with a note book until I am ready out of a rich world to say something" (box 18, folder 14, June 14, 1967). Rule's desire to make discursive exploration the heart of her project rather than repeat "dutiful, dull . . . discovered ideas" prefigures current thinking about lesbian subjectivity. As I have argued in previous chapters, Rule's work illustrates the struggle of a writer to create lesbian narratives against the conventions of heterosexual plots, as Farwell puts it in her work; Rule's work further bears out Monique Wittig's contention that when the lesbian writer enters language, she unwittingly reveals the unspoken heterosexual contract that shapes meaning in language and exerts material power in society. Wittig and Farwell are aligned with lesbian critics and feminist queer theorists who have moved away from "identity" and toward "subjectivity" and "positionality" as conceptual categories for discussing gender and sexuality. The shift in conceptual categories is, to be sure, informed by Foucault's work on discourse, but the theoretical move in a North American context has important political implications that are worth reviewing.

Bonnie Zimmerman noted in 1992 that much lesbian theorizing has continued the work of 1970s lesbian feminists (Bunch, Frye, Rich) who figured lesbianism as an attack on the patriarchy and male-defined heterosexuality. In a ground-breaking article in 1993, Shane Phelan demonstrated the ways in which this form of lesbian feminist opposition, by continuing to focus on patriarchy and heterosexuality, risks bearing out the lessons of Lyotard and Foucault that "being in opposition is one of the modes of participation within a system" ("(Be)coming Out" 776).

Phelan argues further that recent lesbian theorists who retain "lesbian as a meaningful category" have begun to imagine a way out of this critical and political impasse. Citing Gloria Anzaldúa, Diana Fuss, Judith Butler, and Teresa de Lauretis, Phelan shows that these diverse theorists are moving "toward views of lesbianism as a critical site of gender deconstruction" (766). Two important aspects of Phelan's argument are useful for considering lesbian fiction, particularly Jane Rule's work. First, the move from thinking of "lesbian" as a fixed category, to be discovered, toward thinking of "lesbian" as a subjectivity, a position within multiple discursive fields to be explored, claimed as a site for resistance, retains the distinctiveness of lesbian as a meaningful category but removes it from the meanings assigned by patriarchy and heterosexuality. Second, Phelan is clear that "lesbian" is a gendered as well as a sexualized term. In her spirited discussion of the lesbian subject that I referred to in chapter 2, Marilyn Farwell similarly reclaims the centrality of gender to any analysis of the sexual subject, a link often elided by queer theory. Like Phelan, Farwell says: "The lesbian subject . . . has been created . . . in relation to 'woman' and must be analyzed not as an escape from gender but as a challenge to this traditional category of gender" (*Heterosexual Plots* 67).

The significance of the shift from identity to subject, from a fixed "being" to a shifting position is explored in Teresa de Lauretis's landmark article from 1990, "Eccentric Subjects: Feminist Theory and Historical Consciousness." De Lauretis elaborates her concept of an "eccentric subject" as a "remapping of boundaries between bodies and discourses, identities and communities" (138), developed primarily by feminists of color and lesbian feminists. She says "such an eccentric point of view is necessary for feminist theory at this time, in order to sustain the subject's capacity for movement and displacement. . . . It is a position of resistance and agency, conceptually and experientially apprehended outside or in excess of the sociocultural apparatuses of heterosexuality, through a process . . . that is not only personal and political but also textual, a practice of language in the larger sense" (139).

De Lauretis prefaces her discussion of the eccentric subject with a reading of a text that leads to the knowledge that stable notions of self and identity rooted in the past, in "home," are "'based on exclusion and secured by terror'" (136). Home must eventually be given up, replaced with an unstable but more dynamic notion of "community." In Rule's fiction, fixed notions of "home" are often contested along with stable notions of "family" and "self." As I argued in chapter 3, both "House" and "My Country Wrong" suggest that seemingly fixed meanings are subject to change. Rule has tried from her earliest work to create a poetics of possibility that contests a fixed lesbian identity, whether demeaning or celebratory. Language, as the passage from her notebooks I quoted above demonstrates, is her testing ground; her goal is "to catch a language" rather than "tell" an already determined story.

"Home Movie," a short story first published in *Sinister Wisdom* in 1980 and then reprinted in the collection *Outlander,* published by Naiad Press in 1981, provides a good point of departure for discussing Rule's effort "to catch a language" to create a lesbian subject formed within language but also in tension with it. Situated in Greece, often marked as an originary site for lesbian subjectivity, the story centers on a North American woman, Alysoun, who is an artist and an outsider like many of Rule's characters. As a musician she interprets musical scores, "repeating" the music she is given, but "interpreting" it through her own talent and sensibility. As a visiting foreigner (on tour as a soloist, a clarinetist), she observes a society whose rules are familiar and yet different from the ones that formed her. She also looks back on her own formation with the perspective that distance and displacement allow. Through an act of literal and figurative "translation," she imagines her own desire for a Greek woman.

A series of projected images in which Alysoun is both spectator and spectacle articulate the formation of a lesbian subject. The projections begin with home movies glimpsed through an open window in Greece that trigger uncomfortable memories of home movies from her childhood in America. Home movies she accidentally witnesses and then remembers capture images that are distorted, exaggerated, repeated, reversed, fragmented, and reassembled; the relatively crude apparatus of the hand-held camera, the repeated rituals of family holidays, and the games families play by reversing the projector, zooming in to exaggerated close-ups, speeding up and slowing down, all underscore the arbitrary, cliché character of the medium and, by extension, the limits and conventions of growing up middle class, white, and female in mid-twentieth-century America. The story ends with a televised performance that carries Alysoun's adult face back "home" while publishing her features throughout the world.

The story follows a trajectory in which Alysoun moves from embarrassed passive spectator of herself as a child (framed in her father's home movies) to the confident active image of a successful artist beamed around the world. The primitive technology of home movies and the sophisticated high tech of satellite transmission each signal in different modes the ways in which a lesbian subject negotiates the languages of "home" and of the street, of family and culture, of the intimate and the performative. In the first paragraph, Alysoun, far from home, sits in a café and is an inadvertent spectator of the intimate lives of strangers:

Alysoun Carr sat at a table in a street café in Athens drinking ouzo. Directly across from her, through an open window and onto a far wall, a home movie was being projected. A young couple grew larger on the wall. Suddenly the enormous head of a baby filled the whole window, as if it were going to be born into the street. Alysoun, careful in a foreign country never to make so melodramatic a gesture as to cover her eyes if she could help it, looked away. She added water to the ouzo and watched what had been clear, thick liquid thin and turn milky. She did not like the licorice aftertaste, but she liked the effect, which was a gentling of her senses so that she could receive things otherwise too bright or loud or pungent at a level of tolerance, even pleasure. In another ten minutes, if the movie lasted so long, she could watch it without dismay. (3)

Isolated in a public place, Alysoun is portrayed as a fascinated if embarrassed voyeur. The fantastic image of a baby in a home movie (who risks being born into the street) becomes a reflection/reminder of her own overexposed childhood; her first gesture is to look away, to numb or "gentle" her senses hoping to tolerate the spectacle/memory or even take pleasure in it. Significantly, the "ten minutes" needed for the ouzo (clear turned to murky) to take effect take the reader into Alysoun's reverie about her own childhood, and though we return only briefly to the spectacle on the far wall of the stranger's home, we do watch the home movies of Alysoun's memory, an internalized projection. The "young couple" of the first paragraph has been reduced to "her father" in the second, the mother eclipsed by the father's framing of Alysoun's childhood.

The technology of home movies (capturing holidays, creating an illusion of reversed action as the projector seems to pull a diver up through the water and back to the diving board) is understood as reactionary by Alysoun. The moment of unbearable intimacy and exposure she turned away from in the first paragraph takes her to the most dreaded moment in the childhood viewings—"when her own baby face would fill the frame."

Alysoun is her father's favorite ("Alysoun was the prettiest baby I ever saw"), perceived as beautiful in the family films even as she offers up a "silent snort" instead of a smile, but she knows she has disappointed her father by growing up into an adult who, unlike her siblings, has "failed" to reproduce. Her siblings took pleasure in tricks that turned visual expectations inside out in the father's home movie, but Alysoun creates disappointment by living against paternal expectations as an adult. Reversing the action (or the viewer's expectations) may be a game for her siblings, but Alysoun knows by the ways she has disappointed her father in adult life that one doesn't counter paternal expectations with impunity. The split between the cherished, paternal image of herself as a baby and her perplexed adult self is unsettling. "Only the camera could give him back that pretty baby who, snorting out at her adult self, made Alysoun feel as disoriented as if she had been physically dragged by the camera back up out of the water and onto the spring board." In the story, Alysoun has learned that only by reproducing the heterosexual parents' scenario is the child allowed to become an adult, to move beyond the frame of the family of origin into a family of her own that reproduces the home movie in a new generation.

In the present moment, a glimpse back at the Greek home movie across the way shows Alysoun a remarkably bad representation of a flower garden. She is led to remark that cliché is more universal than great art. "People talked about the universality of great art, but far more universal is the mark of the amateur, trapping all he loves in the cage of his unpracticed seeing." It is the clichés of family photos, the conventions of middle-class life that repeat themselves endlessly across cultures and borders, capturing the loved one in the prison of the familiar. Alysoun would remain stymied by the language of cliché if it weren't for other languages she learns to use, gifts from other female characters: the languages of flowers, music, and desire. These female characters (an unstable but dynamic community of sorts) assist Alysoun to project a lesbian subject rather than avert her eyes from the image of a presexual, subjected child.

In a gesture that reverses the Lacanian model of the child moving into the Symbolic Order as he separates from the prelinguistic bond with the mother, Alysoun remembers when she learned to name the world around her as her mother taught her the language of flowers. In the story, Alysoun retrieves this language at the invitation of Constantina, a Greek translator who, like Alysoun, is thirty. Constantina, comfortable in her Greek homeland, rescues Alysoun from her awkward isolation and from overbearing male colleagues as she asks for Alysoun's help in translating a Eudora Welty story into Greek.

Constantina's invitation brings back dream memories to Alysoun. Alone in her hotel room, she remembers learning about flowers from her mother: "She had learned the names of flowers very early in her vocabulary, where they stayed certain and bright, a gift from her mother. . . . In memory no film had ever picked from her, Alysoun, not much more than flower-high, walked with her mother naming the last of the Daffodils—Carlton, King Alfred—and the early tulips—White Triumphator, General de Wet. . . . She was walking, nearly hidden in the rhododendrons, saying, 'Unique, Pink Pearl, Sappho . . .' when she slept. It was noon when she woke" (7). The flowers become real to Alysoun in language, signaling that nature itself is a product of discourse, or at least that nature becomes accessible through the mother tongue. In a state of dreamy half-sleep, Alysoun moves from early to late spring, from military masculine names to sexualized feminine names "pink pearl, Sappho." Her mother's garden thus leads her back to Sappho, giving her a world she can offer Constantina in language as well as a means to name herself.

Alysoun and Constantina spend the afternoon before Alysoun's concert walking among flower vendors, creating what they call a "Eudora Welty bouquet" as Alysoun identifies the flowers from the story Constantina is translating. With this exchange of words and flowers, their friendship is established and they walk arm in arm as Alysoun muses: "Accompanied by a man, [she] felt not so much protected as invisible, and she sometimes wondered if her need to vomit or scream was a fear not of the dangers of the street but of obliteration. With Constantina she had the odd, lighthearted sense of being conspicuous and safe" (11).

Three other moments in the story delineate Alysoun's newly created subject position in a language she at once remembers, offers up, and claims as her own. First, alone in her hotel room, arranging the magnificent bouquet they acquired, Alysoun imagines herself confessing another secret to Constantina: she had loved a woman long ago who has since become unreal to her. As she plays out a fantasy conversation with Constantina in her mind, "Fear woke in her womb, feeling so like desire that if someone very loving, very skillful had been there at that moment to hold her, to touch her, she would not have been resisted. Constantina" (13). A repressed memory that had turned to fear is transformed back into desire through her fantasy seduction by Constantina.

The second moment that marks Alysoun's new knowledge involves another fantasy exchange with a woman. She begins a letter to Eudora Welty. She knows she won't send the letter, but it is the gesture of writing, of putting words to her new knowledge that is important. After trying to explain the pleasure that thinking about her story has brought, Alysoun writes about what the story has taught her: "I've discovered that fear is desire, not shame or guilt or inadequacy or any of those other things. The question to ask about fear is not what are you afraid of but what do you want. If you know what you want and you can have it, then fear doesn't seem like fear at all" (13).

Finally, after a successful concert, Alysoun is taking her bow when she becomes aware of "the cameras." This time, her father is a mute spectator as her concert is beamed via satellite around the world. Transforming the confining childhood memories of the opening paragraph, Alysoun looks into the camera, "and for one dangerous second she was tempted to snort before, instead, she smiled her full . . . professional smile through a rain of flowers her mother had taught her to name" (14).

Languages learned and practiced in a shifting community of women allow Alysoun to break out of the infantilizing frame of unmet heterosexual expectations and to claim an articulate lesbian subjectivity. Significantly, Rule invents a character whose sexuality is defined less by the object of her desire than by the desiring subject. The seduction by Constantina is imagined but not realized, the letter to Welty is composed but never sent. Constantina is not so much the object of her desire as a means for her to name it, to become a desiring subject. The final image not only transforms the opening image of which Alysoun is an unwilling spectator into a triumphant projection in which Alysoun is a confident performer, it also signals the inevitable coexistence of the intimate and public, the personal and social aspects of sexual subjectivity. Alysoun's claiming of an adult, lesbian subjectivity is not just a private matter, a hidden hotel fantasy. It entails public scrutiny; whether or not her family of origin will "see" the full meaning of the image on their television screen, Alysoun is ready to project it.

"Home Movie" illustrates that subjectivity is dynamic and is formed in relationship: to other subjectivities, to multiple languages. One of the narrative forms that Rule develops to stage the drama of lesbian subject formation as negotiation is a dual narrative in which there are two narrative centers of interest. The story is told in the third person from a narrative perspective that stands outside the characters and yet moves in and out of their sensibilities. An implied narrating subjectivity orchestrates the double-voiced narrative, just as an implied subjectivity shapes Kate's first-person narrative in *This Is Not for You*. *Desert of the Heart* (1964) is the first such double narrative; *Memory Board* (1987) takes up the form again much later. In the first novel, the narrative form is used to rewrite sexuality by contesting received ideas about women and desire; in the second, Rule contests received ideas about gender, moving back and forth between fraternal twins whose different lives have been marked as much by gender as by sexuality.

Desert of the Heart: Resignifying Sexuality

Kate, the narrator in *This Is Not for You*, struggles to contain lesbian desire as a private, hidden secret, requiring anonymous, often punishing encounters. Kate strives, desperately, to keep the private walled off from public exposure. In *Desert of the Heart*, private desires are clearly entangled in social institutions. The state has a stake in regulating intimacies; lesbian sexuality and heterosexual marriage are shaped by the narratives of literature, popular culture, medicine, and the law; intimacy is subject to the regulatory gaze of authority. The genesis of the novel shows Rule working to develop a complex narrative form to interrogate competing configurations of femininity, maternity, intimacy and desire. In contrast to the anxious, controlling "I" and denied "you" of *This Is Not for You*, the narrative form in *Desert of the Heart* works toward a fragile "we" incorporating two very different (though apparently similar) female subjects. Evelyn, the older, married woman, is abject in relation to the system of gender, sexuality, class, and race into which she was born and schooled. Ann, younger by fifteen years, is paralyzed by rage and loss in relation to the same set of norms for femininity and sexuality. Stunned by failure, Evelyn begins the narrative grieving the loss of her marriage even as she precipitates its end. Ann has become melancholic because she suffers the ungrieved and unacknowledged loss of her mother, who abandoned her as a small child. In her first stage of loving Evelyn she acts out this unresolved anger and love.[1]

---

1. I am indebted to Judith Butler's discussion of melancholia here, especially in *Bodies that Matter*, 234–35.

The narrative of *Desert of the Heart* begins on July 27, 1958, as Evelyn Hall, a university literature professor, arrives in Reno to begin the six-week residency required for a "quick" divorce. She feels defeated by her failure at marriage, incapable of becoming "naturalized" as a citizen of what remains to her an alien territory. As the plane approaches the airport, the desert landscape looks familiar, not because Evelyn has ever been there, but because she has known it in its various representations: travel posters, advertisements, westerns, and as a ground for moral teachings in great texts of Western literature such as Dante's *Inferno*. Her mapping of familiar images on an alien landscape parallels her reading of herself as a woman. Her sense of self is mediated and determined by a learned ideal that creates an impression of familiarity and strangeness. The desert appears to her as sterile, harsh; in herself she only sees lack.

In the beginning of the book Rule brings the social and psychological together in a metaphor of language:

> Conventions, like clichés, have a way of surviving their usefulness. They are then excused or defended as the idioms of living. For everyone, foreign by birth or by nature, convention is a mark of fluency. That is why, for any woman, marriage is the idiom of life. And she does not give it up out of scorn or indifference but only when she is forced to admit that she has never been able to pronounce it properly and has committed continually its grossest grammatical errors. For such a woman marriage remains a foreign tongue, an alien landscape, and, since she cannot become naturalized, she finally chooses voluntary exile. (7)

Rule seems to say that the unconscious is not only structured like a language, in the Lacanian sense, but is structured by language. Evelyn is a woman for whom texts define both work and life; she reads herself and the world around her through the texts she has learned in the canon of Western literature. She measures herself against a standard of femininity that she doesn't question, grounded in literary and religious texts and reinforced in the commercial culture of midcentury America. She thinks to herself that "for any woman, marriage is the idiom of life." Her failure to learn the idiom is testimony to her own inadequacy, not the inadequacy of the institution. And yet, the opening sentence of the narrative suggests a different point of view: that the idiom itself may be lacking.

Rule struggled a long time with the opening paragraphs of this novel; the form and images of the final revision anticipate the central narrative concerns of the book. Written in the third person, the narrative is aligned with Evelyn's subjectivity without being restricted to it. Evelyn is trapped by her failure to live up to a middle-class, midcentury American model of female success as wife and mother. A different narrative perspective (pervasive but not embodied in any character) suggests that the model itself may be faulty. Throughout the novel, the desert is the literal and literary framework for Evelyn's struggle to redefine herself, joined very early on by Ann Child's parallel struggle. Ann, fifteen years younger than Evelyn, who is approaching forty, is a child of the desert, Reno is her home. She understands her femininity and her landscape through idioms that are different from the ones that Evelyn has internalized, but not necessarily any more enabling. The chapters alternate between Evelyn and Ann: the characters and landscape are seen through Evelyn's sensitivity and then through Ann's, with traces of a larger narrative vision orchestrating the duet, which is sometimes staged as a duel. The desert, like the female body, is heavily inscribed with competing meanings within each character and between them. The work of the double narrative is to resignify the meanings of both the desert and desire, displacing the power of master narratives to determine fully the meanings of a woman's life. In contrast to the singular narrating subject in *This Is Not for You*, locked in the terms of her own denial, two narrating subjectivities are put into relation with each other, to open up a poetics of possibility. In *This Is Not for You*, Kate interpellates an absent Esther who first can't and then won't talk back. In *Desert of the Heart*, Evelyn and Ann interrogate each other, not because they shore up each other's views but because they challenge each other to think beyond the categories that define and confine who they are.

From *Permanent Resident* to *Desert of the Heart*

Filed with correspondence between Rule, her agent, and publishers, who, between 1961 and 1963, repeatedly rejected the novel first called *Permanent Resident* and then *Desert of the Heart*, is a notebook page written in Rule's handwriting in which she tries to explain how she understood the novel as she wrote it:

The book is an exploration of a particular society's moral response to sterility, of landscape, of industry, of personal relationships. The desert landscape around Reno, so reminiscent of the landscape of Dante's seventh circle of Hell, called by the early pioneers "the valley of desolation," is naturally uninhabitable, and yet Reno is a thriving community. Not natural resources, but man's ingenuity provides a living for the population in industries such as gambling, marrying, and divorcing, an extraordinary purification of competitive free enterprise in which there is no longer any product. Reno exports advertising and imports customers.

The two main characters of the book are Evelyn Hall, a transient or "customer" who has arrived in Reno to get a divorce after sixteen years of marriage, and Ann Childs, a successful cartoonist and change girl at one of the clubs who has been raised in Reno. Their two points of view, each echoed or modified by various minor characters who are either transients like Evelyn or permanent residents like Ann, dominate the book: and the relationship which develops between the two women could be said to be the plot of the novel.

The book is not a moral allegory, for morality is its subject matter rather than its theme. There is no judgement of the characters except those judgements they make of themselves or each other. The book is a serious cartoon in which the author is neither for nor against, and certainly not impartial to, the subject matter. The tone is involved irony. (Box 19, folder 7)

Rule characterizes the novel at this particular moment (after she wrote it, before it was accepted for publication) in the tradition of the late eighteenth- or early nineteenth-century comedy of manners. She sees the book as a study of social values (rather than as a romance), exploring the problem of sterility in the landscape and business as well as personal relationships. Personal relationships include parents and children, husbands and wives, friends, people thrown together by chance (in the boardinghouse, for example) and lovers. The description clearly shows that Rule had in mind both the Nevada desert in its specific geography and history and literary deserts. Just as Evelyn sees the desert through her previous experience of its representations, the reader will approach this desert through previous readings in which the desert is a place of trial and punishment, quest and suffering, leading either to deeper insight or to defeat. Rule is very clear in this abstract that the book is not meant to bring judgment on the characters but to explore the way the characters make judgments of themselves and each other. Her characterization of the tone as "involved irony" suggests that there is at once engagement and distance from the two main characters.

Other documents show that Rule had been fascinated with Reno since her family had moved to Reno just as she was getting ready to go to college. Although she never lived there for any extensive period of time, she visited on vacations and was clearly fascinated by the moral and physical landscape she observed. In a paper called "So What?" that she wrote for a humanities course her first semester at Mills, she examines the morality of personal wealth that entails abuse of resources and a permanent underclass. She wrote: "Then there's always Harold Smith of Harold's Club in Reno. He gives his profits to the church and to the town only for the good of the people. Let me just ignore the copper roof on his new house and say that his stolen money is being distributed with the utmost care" (box 17, folder 4). The next semester she wrote a paper for an English course on the theme "Culture or Freedom." It begins:

> Reno, the home of Harold's Club, the six week's shelter for the gay divorcee, the midnight train stop, is my setting, and my subject lies beneath the cheap glitter in the soul of the city where I hope to find culture. . . . The beauty of this country is not man-made; it is found in the sage brush of the plains, in the lakes which are the greatest surprises of the desert, in the brilliant sunsets, in the great mountains bare or snow-covered. The drama is in the court rooms and in the gambling houses. The literature lies in the history of the deserted gold and silver mines, in the broken down mansions and in the great river valley pass through the mountains. (Box 17, folder 4)

In her early literary efforts after graduating from Mills, she turned to landscapes such as London, Vancouver, the East Coast of the United States, and San Francisco. She didn't return to the desert landscape until ten years later, when she began the manuscript for *Permanent Resident* early in 1960. Her notebooks and letters show that she decided early on the landscape and the time frame (July 17–September 8, 1958), the six weeks Evelyn would need to establish residency for her divorce. Some of the characters, like the novel itself, would change their names before the final version: Evelyn Hall was first Evelyn Cross; could this be a suggestive shift from bearing the weight of Christian imagery to refiguring

Radclyffe Hall, as Bonnie Zimmerman suggests? Harold's Club became Frank's Club for legal reasons. Rule had worked for a few days at Harold's Club to get an insider's perspective and the publisher wanted to avoid a possible libel suit. A few plot elements shifted as she developed the novel, but the most persistent problem she faced was narrative form. In a plan for the novel that Rule wrote after working on it for some time, she included a tentative opening for the book that is very close to the final version, except that it is written in the first person. The first paragraph reads, for example:

> Conventions, like clichés, have a way of surviving their own usefulness by becoming the idioms of living. For all of us, foreign by birth or by nature, convention is a mark of fluency. That is why, for a woman, marriage is the idiom of life. And she does not give it up, as I have, out of scorn or indifference, but only when she is forced to admit, as I was that, after sixteen years, I had not only never been able to pronounce it properly, but had committed continually its grossest grammatical errors. For me marriage remained a foreign tongue, an alien landscape, and, since I could not become naturalized, I chose voluntary exile. ("Plan for a Novel," box 18, folder 3, page 2)

Later in this six-page "Plan for a Novel," Rule cites many of the literary deserts that shape Evelyn's vision of Reno and inform her "moral despair." In her plans for the character that becomes Ann Child, Rule sees her right away as a "Lesbian cartoonist," but has trouble rescuing her, and other characters, from ridicule. The names she gives her (Joy, Ann, Fidelity, June, Clover) seem awkward; in her head she thinks of her as "the kid," a nickname that a veteran change apron at Harold's Club gave to Jane herself when she was doing research there. In a fit of fantasy she imagines calling her "July Forth." Rule thinks of the character as a kind of younger sister of Evelyn, young enough to have missed believing in the ideal of feminine domesticity that shaped Evelyn's sense of herself and of her failure. Ann is thoroughly skeptical about all institutions, whether her gambling casino or Evelyn's university, but there are no authorizing institutions that have taken their place.

Originally Rule imagined that Evelyn would work at Harold's Club, which would become the locus for the rest of the book. Evelyn's and Ann's conflicting views of the Club would provide grist for debate about society and values. In this early plan, Rule describes one of the images of the novel—the one-way ceiling mirrors through which players and employees are monitored for theft and fraud—as follows: "To see that the standards are maintained a series of catwalks have been built: the mirrors on the ceiling are the windows through which the secret watchers can check the floor; but the employees, when they look up, see only their own faces—lovely, obvious irony of conscience" (box 18, folder 3). In the final version of the novel, the Club is clearly one of the important spaces of the novel, but the desert is just as important. Ann and Evelyn explore its landscape and its history from Pyramid Lake to ghost towns, and learn from a wise old woman who has lived there all her life. Through these explorations Evelyn frees her vision from the literary metaphors that shaped her view in the beginning without losing the value of the desert as a place for testing the self. One character change that is hinted at in the early plan involves the character who would become Silver (Sil) in the final version. Sil is a tall white woman, a former prostitute and madam who has a loving and sometimes sexual relationship with Ann. In the final version, Sil's marriage to Joe is one of the rituals that brings the characters together. Sil's wedding is a vaudeville parody of a wedding and yet shows the continuing force of both the ritual and the institution. In her original conception of the novel, Ann's closest friend is April Brown, a "negress" who works in the ladies' room at the Club. Rule saw this character as a West Indian with training as a nurse and a social worker. This character disappears in the final draft, her role assumed by Sil.

Even after Rule had produced eighty pages of sketches and notes for the novel, she hadn't decided on point of view. She was considering a first-person narrative by Evelyn, a third-person narrative from Evelyn's point of view or "a more experimental form . . . a first-person narrative by the author, who is not involved in the story except as a consciousness." To describe this experimental form she gives the following example:

I ought to tell this story from Evelyn Hall's point of view. What happens to her is so obviously the point, but I haven't been able to get any closer to her than the third person, and even in the third person I find it difficult to call her by her first name. I want her tall, near-sighted, intelligent, and, by the end of the story, wise; but I also want people to like her. How can I show her suffering at the beginning without making her rather unpleasantly pathetic? If I give her dignity, which I am convinced she has, her bones jut out into other people's ribs and inferiority complexes. If I give her a wry morality, she becomes so cryptic that even I don't understand her. And so, instead of being able to see the story through her eyes, I get very little but a view of the back of her handsome, academic head. You see, though I have no place in the story, I am the third person. (Box 18, folder 3)

By the time she finished *Permanent Resident,* the third-person narrator had become an invisible choreographer, placing the characters in changing relationship to each other and to the landscape, both geographical and moral. This narrating "consciousness" is what I am calling the pervasive resisting lesbian sensibility that shapes Rule's mature fiction. Evelyn is no longer "the" point of the story but one point, equal in importance to Ann. The reader, like the invisible third person, gets more than a view of the back of Evelyn's head and then Ann's head; rather, the reader sees through Evelyn's consciousness and then Ann's without being limited to either one of them.

On July 16, 1961, Rule wrote to her college friend E.K. to announce that she had finished the novel she'd been working on for eighteen months (box 19, folder 4). She was pleased with it and had sent it to her agent in New York on July 14. In the letter, Rule explains that she has successfully combined "a clear narrative style" that she worked for in the last book (presumably the unpublished 1957 novel, *This Not Quite Promised Land/Not for Myself Exactly,* which she wrote after her move to Vancouver), and another "image clustered structure" that she considers richer, though, she admits, some people call it obscure. She says she used the "image clustered structure" in "If There Is No Gate" and her first novel, presumably *Who Are Penitent,* the novel she wrote during her year in London in 1952–53. As in "If There Is No Gate," dreams punctuate the narrative in *Desert of the Heart,* particularly Evelyn's dreams as she reworks inherited, learned meanings and imagines new ways of understanding herself and the world.

Rule says in the letter to E.K. that she tried to set the novel aside several times because the problems it raised were so difficult to write about, but finally she couldn't think of anything else. She writes:

I suppose both the landscape and the town were too strong to leave without making use of them. Their natural and symbolic meanings moved so well together. If I tell you the sources I've depended on, it will sound a book more heavily symbolic than it reads, for the narrative is clear and swift, the characters very much present in the actual world of the place, in daily activities of the town, in the ordinary problems of kitchen and bed. But Dante and Bunyan and Eliot and Yeats haunt the desert and the gambling casinos and the court. I have tried to cope with what I think is a basic issue in human experience, that rich inheritance of moral imagery which is often intellectually appreciated and philosophically rejected and emotionally experienced. I reach to touch a sense of guilt which comes out of a tradition of moral teaching that psychology has sought to limit, in some cases destroy. (Box 19, folder 4)

Rule needed to create a narrative form to stage the conflict within a character who can simultaneously appreciate intellectually, reject philosophically, and experience emotionally the "rich inheritance of moral imagery." Psychology in Rule's letter is seen as an inadequate corrective to traditional moral teaching. While resisting the guilt imposed by traditional morality, Rule is nostalgic for the rich cultural context associated with it. Psychology lacks such an esthetic. As a way of organizing the world, psychology in *Desert of the Heart* has other failings as well. Popularized Freudian explanations of lesbian desire, for example, control Evelyn's interpretation of the feelings she is having toward Ann in the beginning. Ann is the daughter she has always wanted to have; Ann is a narcissistic projection. Ann, too, is caught in a popularized Freudian paradigm, imagining that she wants to possess Evelyn as a mother figure, the better to dominate, defame, and then destroy her absent mother who betrayed her daughterly desire. Only through their dueling narratives can they work themselves free of these predetermined meanings in order to imagine another meaning for their desire.

Even though the novel was accepted fairly quickly by Macmillan in Canada, they wouldn't publish it until British and American publishers would also accept it, assuring a much bigger market. The title was ultimately changed at the suggestion of the British publisher because the term "permanent resident" had no meaning in an English context. The many rejections Rule received echo the pervasive homophobia of the early 1960s. To include lesbianism as a theme was seen as sensationalistic, exploitative, the stuff of "paper books of a certain sort" (box 18, folder 17). The reviews of the book when it came out continue the misreadings of publishers; some can only see it as a tragic, sordid story, others dismiss it as a theme that has already been done to death in cheap novels, a subject of no interest to most readers.

While it would be tempting to write these judgments off as the lingering legacy of late 1950s America, Donna Deitch's screenplay for *Desert Hearts* was treated in much the same way twenty years later. Like Rule, Deitch considered her screenplay, especially the first version of it which was much closer to the novel than the ultimate film, as a story about ethical decision-making. In an application to the National Endowment for the Humanities for funding to support the production of the film, Deitch says "the purpose of raising controversial ethical quandaries is to challenge the audience to discussion and reflection on the larger issues of love and appropriate ethical behavior" (box 1, folder 7). Even though Deitch had the endorsement of a number of highly successful feminist scholars, the proposal was rejected. The rejection letter (written in August 1980) cites (anonymous) panelists who express opinions such as the following: "Of questionable value. Love expressed in lesbian relationships has been done to death already in commercial films. . . . People are bored with the lesbian story now." "The turpid [*sic*] writing of the proposal is matched by the triteness of the dialogue in the script." "Banal and slick on every level: intellectually and emotionally" (box 1, folder 7). Whatever one might think of Deitch's writing, it is surely a gross exaggeration in 1980 to claim that the lesbian story has been "done to death" in commercial films, any more than the heterosexual love story; unless, of course, one assumes that there is only one lesbian story while the variations of heterosexual love are limitless. After significantly revising the screenplay, Donna Deitch raised funding to produce it as a commercial film. Natalie Cooper wrote the screenplay, Donna Deitch produced and directed it, and it was distributed by the Samuel Goldwyn Company, released in late 1985. Now the film has become a cult classic among lesbian audiences in much the way *Desert of the Heart* has been for lesbian readers. Liz Tracey and Sydney Pokorny, in their "how to" book called *So You Want to Be a Lesbian,* included a chapter on things a lesbian needs to know about literature. Under the heading "Jane Rule," they advise the reader that a good question to ask on a first date is, "Which woman is hottest in *Desert Hearts*"; they go on to say that the reader should also read *Desert of the Heart*, adding that Rule wrote other things too: "See Naiad."

Defining Powers

In the opening pages of the novel, when Evelyn checks the clock at the Reno airport, *Desert of the Heart*, the book, is explicitly situated as a reflection on the United States in the late 1950s. The temporal location is also cultural because the novel inscribes power relations that shaped individual consciousness and social structures in conscious and unconscious ways at that moment in North American culture. Reading practices of the late 1990s bring those power relations into sharp focus and suggest why Rule's fictions provided a useful, productive space for lesbian readers to reimagine the meanings of female desire. By now, in the late 1990s, Lacan's ideas about the production of sexual identities and Foucault's analysis of regulatory discourses and the mechanics of power in relation to sexual personhood have so imbued our ways of reading that even those who resist theory have nonetheless incorporated certain of their key ideas. I would like to consider two of those ideas which, like Freud's concept of the unconscious, have permeated our thinking whatever we may think (or not think) of the ways in which Freud, Lacan, and Foucault have been used in theory and in practice.

In Lacan's work, sexual identities are produced by cultural customs and social laws. Even though his own writing often elides the specificities of the historical moment (particularly the social/political construction of race, ethnicity, gender, and sexuality) the self, or as he prefers to call it, the "subject" is not an ahistorical entity and sexuality is not innate, they are, rather, produced. According to Lacan, the subject or sense of self is rooted in a misperception, a pleasurable illusion of wholeness and autonomy when the child recognizes his image in a mirror at the so-called "mirror stage." Autonomy and the pleasure produced at perceiving and claiming one's autonomy are founded on a misperception, the illusion of a whole person created by the mirror image. After the mirror stage, passing through the Oedipal phase, the child enters into the Symbolic or the realm of language and culture. The Symbolic is regulated by the laws of patriarchy and the family. The maturing child is subjected to the "law of the father": a system of prohibitions (the "non" or "no" of the father) and of language (the "nom" or "name" of the father). Sexual identities are thus shaped by specular and linguistic experience (the mirror image, the laws of the father) and are understood as the product of conscious and unconscious customs and images.

Foucault's work on the discourses of sexuality (religious, medical, scientific, political) argues, to borrow Biddy Martin's summary, that "power in the modern world is the relation between pleasures, knowledge, and power as they are produced and disciplined" (*Femininity* 188). Foucault maintains that the medicalization of sexuality shifted sexual practices from the domain of the law to the person. Sexual acts, particularly since the late nineteenth century, are understood as an expression of personhood; sexuality inheres in bodies rather than acts that are codified by the law. We say that one "is" a homosexual rather than that one "did" certain sexual acts. Because sexuality is implanted in bodies, bodies require surveillance, codification, observation in order to discipline and contain unproductive sexualities (Foucault *Introduction* 41–49). Just as Lacan argues that sexual identities are produced by conscious and unconscious customs and images, Foucault argues that power (including the regulation of sexuality) is exercised not only in obvious ways, imposed on the person by the state, but power also permeates the deepest levels of individual consciousness. "But in thinking of the mechanics of power," writes Foucault, "I am thinking of its capillary form of existence, the point where power reaches into the very grain of individuals, touches their bodies and inserts itself into their actions and attitudes, their discourses, learning processes and everyday lives. The eighteenth century invented, so to speak, a synaptic regime of power, a regime of its exercise *within* the social body, rather than *from above* it" ("Prison Talk" 39). The idea of an autonomous self, preexisting or independent from the technologies of power and knowledge that shape it, would be as illusory in Foucault's thinking as the autonomous self in Lacan's formulation, in which the very sense of autonomy is produced by a misperception.

Feminist readings have explored the gender implications of the work of Lacan and Foucault. Feminists contend that the masculinity of the subject in the early work of these theorists goes unnoticed; in Lacan particularly the "feminine" is a product of a masculine, patriarchal system, unthinkable outside of this Symbolic. Further, feminists have been concerned about the political uses and effects of these theories. Is there a place for agency in a system that seems so fully determined by the mutually enforcing powers of the family, the state, culture, and science? Is there a resistance possible that doesn't merely mirror the terms of the master discourses or narratives? One response, available in Foucault particularly, is to consider the multiplicity of discourses. Because they are multiple, discourses overlap and reinforce each other but are not exactly coextensive and are often contradictory in small ways. One can look for breaches, contradictions in the discourses and technologies of power. Sites of resistance can be identified to refigure aspects of subjectivity on a local, discursive level. Biddy Martin and others have argued, however, that to attempt to replace masculinist, heterosexist definitions of "woman," "the feminine," or "lesbian" with feminist definitions that claim to be more authentic merely perpetuates the illusion that one can argue abstracted from one's own material and ideological reality. Instead, Martin defines a different task for feminists:

> The struggle for control over representational and social practices through which and across which sex has been defined and organized has been a heterosexist struggle between and among men in which woman has figured as the object of knowledge and the metaphor for truths. Having achieved a position from which to enter the struggle over definition, we are confronted with the avant-garde's observations that sexual difference, sexual identity, sexuality itself are fictions, and that the perpetuation of those categories can only further enhance the workings of power. . . . A materialist cultural interpretive practice insists that we read not only individual texts but literary histories and critical discourse as well, not as reflections of a truth or lie with respect to a pre-given real, but as instruments for the exercise of power, as paradigmatic enactments of those struggles over meaning. For feminists, the task is to elaborate the ways in which sexual difference, the meaning of woman, figures in these processes by creating alternative points from which to approach traditionally accepted meanings. Feminism does, in fact, provide a context out of which we can pluralize meaning by opening apparently fixed constructs onto their social, economic, and political determinacies. (*Femininity* 199)

Lesbian readers in the early 1960s and lesbian feminist critics today can claim texts like *Desert of the Heart* as an "alternative point from which to

approach traditionally accepted meanings" of femininity and female sexuality. The narrative structure of *Desert of the Heart* enacts a struggle to
pluralize meanings and continually draws attention to the mechanics of
power at both the institutional and individual levels, the "capillary" seepage into the inner recesses of the individual that Foucault identified. Evelyn is presented as a white, middle-class woman belonging to the generation born around 1920, defined by one set of accepted discourses
(moral, religious, and literary texts reinforced by psychology and capitalist commercialism). Ann is presented as a white woman with shifting
class status, belonging to the generation born around 1935, defined by
a slightly different set of discourses. She is more deeply skeptical of the
truth-value of discourses accepted by Evelyn because they have failed
(and literally scarred) her in fundamental ways. Her father committed
suicide and tried to take her with him; her mother abandoned her when
she was a child and remains invisible, unavailable; she has watched
women like her surrogate mother (Mrs. Packer who keeps the boardinghouse where Evelyn stays for six weeks) subscribe to ideals that are blatantly inadequate to the realities of their lives. Ann's cartoons and her
cynical praise of the casino as the most perfected form of capitalism
(there is no product, it is purposeless, based only on the flaws of human
nature) lead her to see all institutions (including Evelyn's university) as
ideologically identical, serving and imposing the same values and meanings. Evelyn is blindly complicit with the discourses and technologies of
power. Ann is lucid, but isolated, unable to resist the flawed but powerful system that surrounds her; she prefers a cynical embrace of its most
useless institution, the casino. The pervasive third-person-narrative presence in the book puts these two embodied narrative perspectives into
play, to dramatize contradictions in the discourses of power and knowledge out of which individuals can imagine sites of resistance. Resistance
in Rule's narrative requires relationship, alliance, beginning with a dialogue to destabilize seemingly fixed ways of knowing and acting in the
world. Desire, for Evelyn and Ann, is both the impulse and the end point
of resistance.

In *This Is Not for You*, Kate understood a heterosexually motivated,
pathological model of lesbian desire as not only dominant but true—true
because she had learned it and true because it reflected her experience.
In *Desert of the Heart*, Rule provides a means for the reader to sort

through the mechanics of power, to distinguish the necessary from the true, the deployment of power by social and cultural institutions from power effects within one's own subjectivity. *Desert of the Heart* opens up a space for multiple, competing meanings for lesbian desire rather than singular, fixed concepts that serve the status quo. I will look at three narrative threads that identify the mechanics of power and provide a site of resistance for the reader. First, I will look at Rule's use of rituals that authorize juridical, social and personal reality through language. An example of a ritual speech act that creates a social and personal reality would be: "I now pronounce you man and wife." Second, two scenes at Pyramid Lake in the desert measure a changing understanding of power over female desire. The characters move from unwitting absorption of masculine, heterosexual norms for female sexuality to a conscious recognition of the means by which institutions exercise power over (and through) intimate relations. Finally, mirrors measure changing relations between individual consciousness and institutionalized power from fully determining to contingent but not definitive.

Ritual Performances

Reno's industries, as Rule's early notes indicate, are gambling, marrying, and divorcing. The rituals that authorize divorce and marriage are exposed in *Desert of the Heart* as powerful fictions overseen by representatives of the law and of God, used to reinforce a particular, masculine and heterosexual hierarchy of power and to stimulate a capitalist economy. In the rituals of divorce and marriage particularly, the state reveals its stake in regulating intimacy, licensing or dissolving unions according to its own requirements and definitions. It is interesting to consider this novel in the context of Judith Butler's discussion of J. L. Austin and performative speech acts. Butler insists we note that even under the most abstract notions is an underlying heterosexual norm. She says: "The centrality of the marriage ceremony in J. L. Austin's examples of performativity suggests that the heterosexualization of the social bond is the paradigmatic form for those speech acts which bring about what they name. 'I pronounce you . . .' puts into effect the relation that it names" (Butler *Bodies* 224–25). Evelyn comes to Reno to dissolve that relation, and by the time she leaves, the "I do" of marriage has become an "I do" of lesbian desire, spoken by Ann as witness in the divorce court. Evelyn's visits to her lawyer and to the court mark the stages of that appropriation of official speech.

When Evelyn visits her lawyer for the first time, she enters into the ritual that will dissolve her marriage. Her lawyer, Arthur Williams, in his extravagant performance of masculine manners (flinging open the door for her, positioning her chair) strikes her as humorous: "He was a caricature of a Southern gentleman. The manners of his background had become in this climate almost hysterical mannerisms" (52). The artifice of masculinity she sees in the lawyer takes on more serious consequences as they discuss the grounds for divorce. She soon realizes that her own understanding of the failure of her marriage (incompatibility) doesn't exist in the legal language of Nevada; she will have to charge "mental cruelty," and even that must be described in terms the law can recognize, terms that are largely determined by standards of femininity and masculinity that neither Evelyn nor her husband George embodied. Perhaps their incompatibility was rooted in their inability to conform to norms for masculine and feminine behavior and at the same time their inability to remain indifferent to those norms.

As she listens to the instructions of her lawyer, Evelyn thinks: "Divorce was not a private symbolic act. Like marriage, it was a social institution. Though she wanted to protest, Evelyn recognized the irrelevance of her morality" (54). The lawyer persists in his questions, trying to establish grounds for mental cruelty in which Evelyn is the victim and trying as well to be certain that her financial interests will be protected in the divorce. Evelyn is perplexed. Has she been unable to sleep or to work? No, but he has. Has he undermined her sense of security? No, but he suffers from a sense of inadequacy. He is unable to support himself; she wants to see to his needs. Williams accumulates enough information to meet the demands of the law and Evelyn realizes that there is no congruence between the reasons for the breakdown of her marriage and the grounds for legal divorce. She must conform to juridical language or the ritual of divorce will not be performed. Alone again in the street she thinks to herself: "George was the real victim of their marriage, so much the victim that he hadn't the courage left to want a divorce. 'Your honor, I charge this man with what I have done to him. I charge this man with being a victim to my circumstance. . . . I charge him with my guilt which

I cannot bear anymore.' . . . If this mock hearing did, in fact, set her free, she would still carry the mark of a strong, intelligent woman like the brand of Cain on her forehead" (58). When she returns to the boardinghouse, Virginia, another woman waiting out the six weeks until divorce, apologizes for having behaved badly the day before. When Evelyn suggests that Virginia read to relieve the boredom and anxiety of her residency, Virginia says she's read every magazine in the house, but they are all about young couples. Evelyn answers: "You're reading the wrong stories," to which Virginia responds, "That's why I've stopped" (60). Virginia can understand on an emotional level what Evelyn will eventually learn: all the stories, whether women's magazines or the great texts of Western literature are the "wrong stories" for a woman who is trying to extricate herself from the defining rituals of feminine success.

Six weeks later, the divorce takes place in the court house with Ann as Evelyn's witness. Swearing to tell "the whole truth," Evelyn answers the same questions she had resisted six weeks earlier, in a more codified version. She answers according to formula in order to meet the ritual requirements of the law. At one point she bursts in with an answer of her own, in an effort to get some truth on the record: "He's bitter and despairing and frightened" (249). But there is only one moment when the legal requirements and her own sense of truth coincide, when she is asked if she no longer loves him: "Suddenly the bewildering and shaming charade was transformed into reality. Before her were the two lawyers, man and woman, like witnesses at a marriage. Beside and above her the judge waited to hear her answer, the one, simple, truthful answer that would speak her failure and set her free. 'No, I don't love him anymore. There is no possibility of reconciliation'" (250). Juridical success requires personal failure; she has performed her role as plaintiff and the divorce is granted.

The mirroring of marriage and divorce, the investment of society in individual lives is further explored in the middle of the book when Sil gets married. The reader is first introduced to Sil as the sometime lover of Ann, former madam, current flamboyant change apron. Her house is presented as a parody of *Good Housekeeping* consumerism. The kitchen is always in a state of (re)construction as her need for the newest appliances or the latest color of appliance changes with the market. The function of the kitchen is less important than its display. The house is a constantly changing stage set for Sil's multiple female subject positions: prostitute, madam, lesbian, bisexual, consumer, bride and—by the time of the wedding—mother-to-be. As such she is the perfect female impersonator, an exaggerated parody of everything that a woman might be. She is also a positive character, protective of Ann, respected by Evelyn, viewed with sympathetic irony by the third person narrator. The burden of her parodic excess is borne by the roles she performs rather than by her own subjectivity.

Sil's wedding is the central event of the chapter preceding Evelyn's divorce. Sil, towering over everyone at the church and her diminutive groom, Joe who "looks like a prize in a shooting gallery" (220), make their way down the aisle surrounded by ex-customers, ex-employees, and representatives of all of Reno's communities. The language of the sacrament alternates in the narrative with Ann's internalized, ironic commentary, for example: "'Wilt thou, Silvia . . . forsaking all others . . . ?' A vow only your enemies would help you keep." The "I do" spoken at the wedding is echoed in the divorce of the following chapter. When Evelyn's lawyer tries to establish that Ann is a suitable witness for Evelyn's residency, he asks: "Do you know this lady?" "Ann looked down at Evelyn, her eyes unguarded. 'I do'" (247).

Desert Visions

The juridical, performative use of language to create and enforce personal realities is a clear imposition of the state on individual lives. But, as Foucault suggests, the deployment of power is much more pervasive and subtle than its purely public displays. From the first trip to Pyramid Lake in chapter 5 to the second one in chapter 7, Evelyn moves from internalized guilt and blame for failing as a woman to a recognition that the ideal of feminine success as wife and mother is regulated by social order; marriage and maternity are expedient but not inevitable expressions of femininity. Evelyn understands that this "idiom of living" is taught through cultural discourses and monitored by the power of the state. When Ann and Evelyn go to Pyramid Lake the first time, they recognize but have not spoken their desire for each other. Evelyn tries to distance herself from her desire by containing it in regulatory discourse. She explains it away in the clichés of psychology: her attraction was a narcissistic projection because Ann resembles her younger self; hers is the repressed need of a childless woman for a daughter, and so forth. Just as she diagnoses her desire through the discourse of psychology, Evelyn can only see the desert through the images of trial and damnation she knows from the *Inferno* and *Pilgrim's Progress.*

The first trip to the lake marks an important turning point in the dialogue for meaning between Evelyn and Ann. This is marked by Evelyn's changing perception of the desert. Ann is helping her see it through her eyes: through local histories of the people who have passed through it and through unexpected views of the landscape. The brilliant, alkaline Pyramid Lake startles Evelyn with its beauty. At first Evelyn resists, somewhat frightened by this alien landscape, but she follows Ann's lead and learns to appreciate it. After a swim Evelyn discusses her feelings about the desert and about womanhood with Ann. For Evelyn the desert looks like the seventh circle of hell and she is afraid of damnation. For Ann, the desert is beautiful and she is afraid of being "saved," enmired in the values of a society she scorns. For Evelyn sterility is the mark of failed womanhood. For Ann, fertility is "a dirty word": "I'm terrified of giving in, of justifying my own existence by means of simple reproduction" (122).

Even as they argue about the meaning of gender, they draw closer in their desire for each other. Ann leans over to kiss Evelyn:

> As Ann bent down toward her, Evelyn took hold of the soft, damp hair at the back of Ann's neck and held her away. But, as Evelyn looked at the face held back from her own, the rain-grey eyes, the fine bones, the mouth, she felt the weight and length of Ann's body measuring her own. Her hand relaxed its hold, all her flesh welcoming the long embrace. Slowly, carefully, almost painfully, she turned Ann's weight in her arms until she could withdraw. (124)

Resisting her desire, trapped by the conventions she has lived by, Evelyn draws back and says: "I live in the desert of the heart . . . I can't love the whole damned world." She tries to dismiss the meanings she might attach to this embrace by clinging to ideas she has learned: "'No relationship is without erotic feeling,' Evelyn said. She had heard it somewhere at a cocktail party." As her feelings persist, she works to contain them, to medicalize her response and therefore dismiss any social or moral significance:

She watched Ann wade out for the bottle of wine, that young, beautiful body she had so carefully admired an hour ago to take her mind off the terrors of the landscape. Its sudden erotic power bewildered and offended her, whose taste and decorum usually governed her private thoughts as firmly as they governed her public living. . . . Physical response was no more significant than a hiccup, a sneeze, a twinge of gas, functional disorders which caused discomfort but not alarm. . . . To exaggerate a single kiss into significant guilt was a real loss of aesthetic distance. (125)

Evelyn may be able, temporarily, to reestablish her aesthetic distance from desire but her unconscious, like the unconscious of the woman in "If There Is No Gate," is less easily contained, explained away, repressed. The night following the first trip to Pyramid Lake she has vivid dreams in which the women of her life walk through a desert landscape charged with literary images intermingled with images of the literal and emotional storms she had witnessed that day. Ann's face and the face of a woman she had once loved merge and dissolve into each other. On waking, she tries to contain and destroy her "perfect knowledge of the dreams' significance," but the images continue to haunt her. Evelyn searches her past for causes and first instances: she recalls her brief affair with another army wife whose husband had been killed, gestures of comfort changing into erotic touch. But, she reasons, these were circumstantial acts, situational, not an expression of latent homosexuality. She is caught in the paradigm of sexual identity Foucault exposes: she assumes a fixed sexuality must be embedded in her body. If she interrogates her past she may discover what was always there. Was her failure at marriage really a failure to mimic heterosexuality, occasioned by her true, lesbian self? She wonders if she is a case of mistaken identity. As a result of her persistent dream images, fragments of poems, and continuing desire, Evelyn realizes that her "moral landscape had altered" (135).

Evelyn seeks to understand how Ann perceives the world and herself. She catches glimpses of the cartoons Ann constructs to make sense of the world. She begins to understand Ann's counterideal of maternity without reproduction: she adopts foster children throughout the world who become known to her through letters and pictures. Eventually Evelyn consents to her own desire, gives up the need to be "saved," and makes love to Ann. Unexpectedly, Ann experiences a crisis of meaning that parallels Evelyn's. Making cartoons and making love had been, for Ann, ways to stay detached, to control her unacknowledged grief for her mother. "She made love, as she made sketches, to keep her free. She made love to break love" (142).

Evelyn, however, can't be reduced to the offending mother figure. Like Evelyn's effort to reduce desire to the status of a functional disorder, a hiccup, Ann turns to regulatory discourse to contain the significance of her desire. Ann thinks to herself: "The sciences of love tell the truth, explaining away in -exes and -ologies and -alities and -isms all myth and private reality" (143). Ann's efforts to dismiss her desire are no more successful than Evelyn's. Again Rule chooses images of language and naming to chart Ann's changing relationship with Evelyn. After their first lovemaking Ann doesn't know "whether she would scrawl 'Evelyn' across the wall like a dirty word or print it with the careful accuracy and pride of a small child for his own name" (143). Later, after a night together, Ann moves beyond control and detachment toward vulnerability by recognizing Evelyn as a distinct other, only partially knowable, rather than as a projection of her own need to punish.

> Ann turned, the longing of her body straining against the last reluctance of her mind, and she felt Evelyn's tentative, almost casual beginning gradually give way to an authority of love. Ann was held urgently, brought into being, then restrained, caught again, held, until she wanted nothing ungiven, until she wanted nothing, until she came to wonder, not asking any longer, but naming, "Evelyn." (165–66)

From that moment, Ann decides to court Evelyn in mind and body, to help Evelyn see the desert through new eyes. Meanwhile, Evelyn turns to Ann's books in an effort to read Ann. Evelyn tries to piece together Ann's identity by studying underlined passages, comments Ann has written on pages in her library. But what she can't read is tone: is Ann reading with reverence or irony?

> These books were like old photograph albums, through which she searched to find the candid or posed moments of Ann's mind. In some of the quotations she could hardly recognize Ann, a blur among dozens of youngsters who identified with the large, euphoric generalizations of western intellectual heroes, but perhaps Ann was being ironic. Where she did not comment, Evelyn could not be sure. (178)

In her effort to know Ann through her books, Evelyn rediscovers her own, lost self. Her awakening body makes her vulnerable, but paradoxically, like Alysoun in "Home Movie," she discovers courage to rethink femininity even as she becomes vulnerable to her body's needs. She thinks to herself:

> It was curious that, at the very time she was giving up all the external images of womanhood, Evelyn should become increasingly aware of her femininity, and it was not a synthetic maternity as she had expected it to be. . . . She had grown almost vain about her body, and she had begun to discover, underneath the strict discipline she had imposed upon her mind, an inventiveness. . . . Evelyn wanted to be charming, provocative, desirable, attributes she had never aspired to before out of pride, perhaps, or fear of failure. Now they seemed nearly instinctive. She was finding, in the miracle of her particular fall, that she was, by nature, a woman. And what a lovely thing it was to be, a woman. (181)

Falling from grace to knowledge, Eve(lyn) acquires a sense of earthly delight. Evelyn no longer sees herself as a failure at femininity but begins to see that the idiom in which she had learned femininity failed to take her into account. Evelyn's refiguring of femininity is motivated by desire but includes a refiguring of maternity and intimacy as well. Her shift in understanding from personal failure and loss to resistance to regulatory discourse makes her want to return to Pyramid Lake with Ann. Before they return, however, Ann makes Evelyn confront fully her feelings about marriage, George, and divorce. Evelyn confesses to Ann the guilt she feels about George. Their conversation becomes the trial she had expected in Reno; she is tried not before a judge, but in front of "this young image of herself, whose arrogance and morality and innocence she curiously believed in" (185). Evelyn later shifts to an interrogation of Ann, forcing her to confront her unacknowledged grief for her mother's betrayal. After this double trial, Evelyn is no longer abject; Ann, no longer melancholic, has acknowledged her grief and loss. They are ready to return to the desert, to a scene of resignification, to experience and examine again the meanings of their kiss.

Back at Pyramid Lake, the duel of examination and cross-examination becomes a duo of lovemaking in the apparent solitude of the desert. First Evelyn choreographs their lovemaking, following Ann into the lake, overcoming her with the aggressive power of her swimming in the sweet weightlessness of water. Returning to the shore, Ann assumes erotic control:

> Her free, inventive wildness, the physical intimacies she demanded, aroused every vague, animal desire in Evelyn that had been left unnamed, her body growing as demanding as Ann's until Ann's ecstatic cry broke the world silence like the cry of some mythical water bird. They lay still then, exhausted and peaceful. (191)

The return to Pyramid Lake shows that Ann and Evelyn have freed themselves from the totalizing grip of social discourse. Inherited images and idioms of living are not erased, however, but displaced. There is no illusion of unmediated access to a "true" self, obscured by the distortions of cultural imperatives. Rule explores instead the often frightening process of negotiating less noxious images and idioms of living. For example, after the first trip to Pyramid Lake, Evelyn was adrift, confused, unable to read herself:

> Even as she scorned the old image of herself, she could not give it up until she could find another to replace it. And, though her mind admitted a number of possibilities, her imagination continually faltered. Sitting across the dinner table from Ann, Evelyn studied her with the intensity and distance she might have given a painting. What she saw was no longer an imperfect reflection of herself but an alien otherness she was drawn to and could not understand.

> Evelyn did not know any longer who she was. Perhaps she had never known. Perhaps her identity had always been made up of bits and pieces of other people, her thumbs, her collarbone, her ears, her left-handedness, even the tones of her voice dictated by the random and absolute coupling of genes. . . . The self was, surely, the will that shaped the arbitrary and meaningless fragments into identity. The will chose. Or was it, too, dictated to by an inherited morality? (134)

Evelyn's first impulse is to replace the inadequate, scorned "old image" with another. But, significantly, she ends with a question generated by multiple possibilities rather than with a willed, chosen clarity. The meaning of who she "is" will remain unclear, open to negotiation, partially but not fully determined by the arbitrary fragments that she has inherited. The meanings of "woman" and "lesbian" remain multiple, unstable, and unclear. Identity for Evelyn no longer requires foreclosure; rather, it requires uncertainty, mobility.

By the second trip to Pyramid Lake, Evelyn and Ann have begun to fashion selves that stand outside the only configurations for femininity they had known; they have done this through insistent but loving interrogation. But Rule is quick to show that no one can stand entirely outside the regulatory forces of the state, the family, patriarchy, and the law. Minutes after they have made love, Evelyn is sitting, barely covered, on the shore while Ann swims out into the water. Suddenly Evelyn hears a motor in the distance. An army helicopter hovers no more than a hundred feet above them with two uniformed men grinning at the exposed, vulnerable women.

> The plane dropped fifty feet and hovered right over [Evelyn's] head. Then it shied off, leaving her in a storm of sand . . . they had seen Ann. Through an open window they were shouting and waving, the plane not twenty-five feet above the water, hanging there like an obscene, giant insect. (192–93)

Language is drowned in the roar of the engine, resistance is futile. At this moment, surveillance has a grinning face, but the ability of masculine power to contain, control, and, potentially, punish female independence is inescapable. With the image of the army helicopter, Rule has effectively moved the site of masculine power from the internal "capillary seepage" that marked Evelyn and Ann in the beginning of the narrative to an external technology of power, temporarily benign but potentially brutal in its deployment. Self-regulation (informed by the dominant masculinist discourses of her culture, secured by fear or loss) is replaced by regulation of the self by external forces of order, secured by force and intimidation. Internalized oppression is now clearly externalized, but Rule refuses to allow her characters (or the reader) a fantasy escape. Even in this remote corner of an unpopulated desert, lesbian pleasure is fleeting, contained by anonymous, grinning masculine forces. At the moment of surveillance (Ann calls it "routine inspection"), Evelyn's gesture of resistance is ineffectual, overwhelmed by the roar of the engine. At the beginning of the novel, however, resistance had been unthinkable. Now the technologies of power have been exposed and a space for resistance has been opened up.

Evelyn's vision of the desert changes along with her vision of herself. In the beginning of the novel, she could only see the desert through the literary and commercial representations that had been available to her just as she could only understand her femininity through the texts that had formed her. The desert was a place of trial and damnation, terrifying in its apparent sterility and indifference to human life. In the last chapter, her vision of the desert has changed. She can smell the sage and see colors where she had only seen bleakness before. The allegories of the desert she had brought with her haven't disappeared, but her relation to them has shifted:

> Evelyn had walked half a mile into her own vision of the desert before she turned and looked back at the . . . town she had left: "When they were got out of the wilderness, they presently saw a town. . . ." And Faithful was tried there and died there, but for defending his convictions, not for giving them up. . . . Evelyn began to walk slowly back the way she had come, neither Faithful nor Christian. There is no allegory any longer, not even the allegory of love. . . . It's a blind faith, human faith, hybrid faith of jackass and mare. That's the only faith I have. I cannot die of that. I can only live with it, damned or not. (230)

The narrative in this passage shifts nearly imperceptibly from third to first person. It begins like other descriptions in Evelyn's chapters, from her point of view but told in the third person. By the end of the passage, the distinction between the third-person perspective, sympathetic but outside of Evelyn's subjectivity, and Evelyn's perspective is dissolved. At the beginning of the novel the distinction was necessary because Evelyn's vision of herself was entirely determined by conventions and clichés that only the third-person narrator could see as contingent. By the end of the novel, Evelyn is no longer prisoner of a language that can't account for her.

Reflections of Power

Rule uses mirrors to measure shifts in her characters' and the readers' perceptions of social power and identity. The first mirror image in the novel captures the role of conventions and of literary language in shaping identity. Before Ann meets Evelyn, Mrs. Packer has told her that they resemble each other. When they are introduced, Evelyn responds to Ann's hello with a line from e.e. cummings: "Hello is what a mirror says . . ." (12). In her own mind, she sees Ann's face as "a memory, not a likeness," a reminder of her younger self. She takes pleasure in the resemblance, but immediately fears that this very pleasure is a mark of her maternal failure.

> Ann was almost young enough to be her own child. But only a parent could be allowed to feel tenderness for his own likeness. In a childless woman such tenderness was at least narcissistic. And Evelyn had learned the even less flattering names applied to the love a childless woman might feel for anything: her dogs, her books, her students . . . yes, even her husband. She was not afraid of the names themselves, but she was afraid of the truth that might be in them. (20)

Already marked by her failure as a wife, Evelyn feels condemned by her inability to reproduce; her twin failure contaminates any tenderness she might feel toward this younger image of herself. Significantly, Evelyn can only see resemblance and self-projection in their first encounter. Resemblance, however, is a false lure; what secures the couple is difference. Only after Ann appears to Evelyn as an "alien otherness" at Pyramid Lake, utterly separate from her, will Evelyn be able to be intimate with her. Lesbian desire is thus staged as desire for the "other" in another woman, rather than a narcissistic bonding with the same. Ann is not a mirror of her younger self, she is another subjectivity who enables Evelyn to love what is different and alien within herself as well as within the other. As is often the case in Rule, difference is marked by age, rather than by role (butch/femme), as is the more frequent case in 1950s lesbian fiction and 1990s queer texts.

The image of Ann as a mirror occurs in the first chapter, told through Evelyn's sensibility. In the second chapter, told through Ann, the most striking use of mirrors is the one-way surveillance mirror in the casino. In the empty casino, Ann looks at the guns, hung decoratively along the walls and then looks up:

> Her eyes shifted away only to catch themselves suddenly in a ceiling mirror. There was her own face separated from her, not magnified as her voice

had been, instead made smaller. What a device of conscience that mirror was, for behind it, at any time, might be the unknown face of a security officer, watchful, judging; yet you could not see it. You could not get past your own minimized reflection. "I do look like Evelyn Hall," Ann thought, "and what does that mean?" (33–34)

In the casino, marked by phallic, antique guns "the shelved violence of another time," Ann's (diminished) image masks the presence of faceless, persistent surveillance. She can't get past her own image to see the hidden authority. Caught in that frame, she can only wonder what it means that she and Evelyn resemble each other. Ann knows that surveillance is part of the environment, built into one's self-image. What she doesn't know yet is what that means, what her resemblance to Evelyn and her recognition of the technologies of power will have to do with a changing image of who she is.

At the very end of the novel, while Ann and Evelyn wait outside the courthouse for the divorce to be made final, Ann reminds Evelyn that "the world's full of mirrors. You can get caught in your own reflection" (250). Recognizing that any attempt they make to create a life together will be precarious, threatened by the faceless power that peers back through the mirrors of social institutions, Ann and Evelyn decide to take the risk. Evelyn acknowledges her assent in the language the court had used to describe her "permanent" residency in Reno, "for an indefinite period of time" (251). The final image of the book follows: "And they turned and walked back up the steps toward their own image, reflected in the great, glass doors" (251).

In the final image, Rule shows her characters resisting the defining, monitoring power of patriarchal, heterosexist institutions while recognizing that they continue to be caught up in them. Whatever the couple may choose, they remain embedded in social institutions. Rule proposes neither individual triumphalism nor romantic escapism. Rather, she illuminates a small space of resistance within the larger social order, a space made possible by personal transformation through relationship, not detachment. Through the multiple narrative frame (Evelyn's perspective, Ann's perspective, and a disembodied lesbian consciousness), Rule imagines a way out of the predetermined meanings of heterosexual plots and beyond a reactive, singular definition of lesbian. She creates through Evelyn and Ann's negotiations lesbian subjectivities that are volatile, but viable.

Rule is careful in *Desert of the Heart* to show that the "indefinite period of time" Ann and Evelyn might have together is contingent on the blindness or benevolence of masculinist order. Men are complicit with institutional power in a way that is fundamentally different from the relation of women to power. At the same time, in the novel, individual men are not finally threatening to women in the way that masculinist institutions are.[2] George is to be pitied rather than feared; Walter, Mrs. Packer's son, is a good-natured, harmless teenager trying to become a man. Arthur Williams presents a near parody of masculine manners and tries to get a narrow legal system to work for Evelyn.

Power may be masculine, but it is anonymous. When Evelyn feels threatened by the army helicopter pilots at Pyramid Lake, they are grinning but faceless, uniformed enforcers of order rather than individuals. Similarly, the casino's one-way mirrors shield the faces of management behind the reflection of employees and gamblers.

At the beginning of the last chapter, even as Evelyn is waiting to finalize her divorce, she becomes aware that social institutions may seem abstract and anonymous, but they serve male interests and can be deployed in their service at any moment. Walter, the meekest male character in the book, informs his mother, who, in turn, alerts Evelyn that power circulates among men. Bill has learned that Ann and Evelyn are lovers. To avenge his hurt feelings, he has threatened to get the names of the helicopter pilots who saw them in the desert, to enlist Walter as a witness, inform George, and finally denounce Evelyn to her lawyer to block her divorce and get her out of town. Evelyn sees immediately that Bill has the power not only to impede her divorce, but to ruin her career and any possible future with Ann in the bargain. She decides to confront him personally. By the time she talks to him he has decided not to make trouble because he's interested in another woman. Throughout the novel, individual women may have equal power with men or even more power in a personal relationship (Evelyn and George, Ann and Bill, Sil

2. I am indebted for this insight to Rachel Keegan, a student who explored this idea in a paper at Smith College in 1995.

and Joe). But men always have access to institutional powers that can discipline female sexuality. Evelyn doesn't fear or dislike individual men, but she fears masculine institutions and her consequent dependence on the generosity of individual men to exercise that power fairly.

What of men whose needs are not met by masculine institutions or, more precisely, the institution of masculinity? This is a question that Rule asks from her very first efforts at fiction and that she returns to as a central, defining question in *Memory Board*, her last novel but one.

Memory Board: Resignifying Gender

Brothers and Sons

In *Desert of the Heart*, the female body and the desert landscape are heavily inscribed with ethical injunctions and epistemological expectations that are partially renegotiated by the novel's end. A historically specific construction of femininity becomes the site for resignifying (female) sexuality. In *Memory Board*, Rule uses a similar narrative structure to refigure gender. As I noted earlier, from the time she started to write, Rule was fascinated by crises of masculinity. In *Memory Board*, a historically specific construction of (hetero)masculinity becomes the site for resignifying gender. In *Desert of the Heart*, the small space opened up for the lesbian couple depends on male indifference or generosity. Male characters in Rule's work are not necessarily served by masculine institutions any more than they are served by the institution of masculinity itself. In *Memory Board* Rule explores this apparent contradiction through David, one of the main characters. By the end of the novel David has made a place for himself in the home of his lesbian sister and her longtime partner, suggesting in the process that domesticity, kinship, and community might be refigured.

Perhaps prompted by the tensions she observed between her brother and father when her father returned from World War II or by her observations of the told and untold stories of men, war, patriotism, and masculinity seen from the "home front," Rule is sympathetic to men who are bewildered by the shifting, conflicting, punishing definitions of what it means to "be a man." "Brother and Sister," a 1967 story included in the 1975 collection *Theme for Diverse Instruments*, is a poignant portrait of a brother and sister in which the brother is alcoholic and depressed and the unmarried sister has achieved professional success. The story is told entirely from the point of view of the drunken brother, visiting his sister. She is preparing a reception in her home at which she needs to impress her guests for an unidentified professional reason. Because everything is seen through the brother's blurred consciousness, the reader never knows for sure what the event is or why it is important to the sister. Through his bleary observations of her and her home and his imperfect memory of (probably) misbehaving at the party, we slowly realize— along with him—that his alcoholism is a symptom of a much deeper, psychological wound. How and why he has come to this point we don't know, though the implication is that he has failed to live up to their father's demands, or has failed in comparison with her; his sister, meanwhile, has either satisfied paternal expectations or is indifferent to them. The story begins playfully and enigmatically as the sister taunts: "My father is bigger than your father." The teasing signals a long history of competition between them, sometimes in jest, sometimes serious. In the course of the narrative, the brother, stumbling through his sister's house, bruises himself on a chest of drawers that had belonged to their grandmother. He recalls that when they were children he had cut his head on the same chest but didn't know he'd been hurt until he heard his sister crying for him. The story ends as the two go out for a walk and the brother looks down at her from a hill shouting, "I am bigger than your father." Then he sees in the mirror of her face, as he had when they were children, that he is wounded: "He saw that she was crying, and then he had to know how badly hurt he was, just for that moment, and to forgive her for it" (62). He forgives her for having come out ahead in their competitive games, but even more, he forgives her for having seen his wound before he knew he'd been hurt.

Twins, especially male/female fraternal twins, make several appearances in Rule's work. In the title story of *Theme for Diverse Instruments*, first published in 1972, several sets of twins mark the progeny of "the Amazonian mother of us all," the narrative center of the story. The assumed narrator of the story, "the rumored Lesbian in the family" (20), playfully named Arachne, granddaughter of the Amazonian mother, is the twin of Orestes. Their father and uncle are themselves twins, military men, decorated and wounded in the war. The story alludes to myths about the special powers and vulnerabilities of twins. Male twins, for example, are said to be blessed with "unusual intelligence, second sight, success in love and war" (25). "But," Orestes warns, "they lose their power if they eat food prepared by a menstruating woman" (25). In *Memory Board*, Rule brings together her preoccupations with brothers and sisters and twins, dividing the narrative between a (heterosexual) brother, David, and (lesbian) sister, Diana, fraternal twins.

Leave Taking

Rule started work on *Memory Board* in 1982, after publishing *Contract with the World*; it was published five years later. During that same period she was gathering stories and essays for *A Hot-Eyed Moderate* and *Inland Passage*, both of which were published in 1985. When she began planning *Memory Board*, she wasn't sure what shape it would take, either in length (a story? a novella? a novel?) or in narrative form (third-person? two first-person narrators? a double autobiography?). According to her notebook, Rule was working on *Memory Board* rather intensively in the fall of 1984. In September 1984, she and Helen took a trip to New England with Rule's parents, in part to visit Lyme, New Hampshire, where Helen's mother, Ruth, had lived for many years with a companion named Florence until Ruth died in 1962. Rule wrote an autobiographical essay called "Leave Taking" (box 12, folder 12) in December 1984, using journal notes she took during the trip. In "Leave Taking" Rule explores questions of aging, mortality, kinship, intimacy, and loss that are emotionally resonant with *Memory Board*.

Rule has a habit of aging her characters prematurely in her fiction; she has a seeming "aging wish" rather than a "death wish," so that characters at thirty undergo midlife crises, at fifty seem elderly, and over sixty are ancients. This can be explained by many circumstances in her life: her arthritis made her feel aging acutely at a relatively young age, her partner is fifteen years older than she, Rule has a special fondness for great age shown in her tenderness toward her grandmothers when she was young. When Rule wrote "Leave Taking" she was fifty-three; Helen had just celebrated her sixty-eighth birthday, and Rule's parents were in their seventies. The trip that Rule writes about in this essay was prompted by a desire to see the autumn leaves and to visit places in which Helen, particularly, had personal investments. They returned to Concord, where Rule and Sonthoff had met thirty years earlier. Helen had grown up in upper New York State and for many years her mother had owned a farm in Lyme where Jane and Helen had spent a number of Christmas holidays. When they returned in 1984, most of the people they had known had left or were, as Rule wrote, "in the graveyard." Florence, Ruth's longtime companion, had planted a maple tree on the site of Ruth's grave. Florence was not buried there: "She must have been taken off by her sister, buried with relatives in Rochester, but her tree is here" (3).

Set against the bittersweet brilliance of the fall foliage, the story Rule tells in "Leave Taking" is imbued with reflections on emotional ties and losses, the past and the present. For Rule, the sights and activities of the present moment often distract her from memories the landscape might hold, or so she says at the beginning of the essay. She characterizes herself as someone who can leave places lightly, having moved often as a child. For Helen, to revisit this place will be to revisit the loss of her mother, the grief of Florence, and the sale and packing up of the farm. In fact, three couples move through the pages of "Leave Taking": Ruth and Florence, Helen and Jane, and Jane's parents.

In the beginning of the essay, the very real pleasures of travel, the eager anticipation of the sights and smells of a New England autumn are slightly tempered by apprehension: what would be the emotional costs of returning to a place that recalls loss as well as fullness of life? Even as she experiences again the autumnal intoxication of childhood, Rule thinks: "How long has it been since I've been old enough to let the weather in, or in again as I must have when I was a child? And how long have I been old enough to return to such a place with no one left alive to call on?" (box 12, folder 12, pages 2–3). To add to a feeling of fragility, Mr. Rule lost a tooth just before they left and required emergency dentistry; Mrs. Rule came down with a heavy cold in New Hampshire and had to stay in bed at the inn for several days.

Two accidents stun the travelers into a more immediate confrontation with mortality. After dinner one evening at the inn, Helen inexplicably falls over from her chair to the floor, unconscious. Nauseous and disoriented, she must be taken by ambulance to the hospital where her mother had died twenty years before. Rule goes with her in the ambulance and Mr. Rule follows close behind in his rented car. At the emergency room there is the usual interrogation about kinship to determine who can legitimately stay with Helen. Rule writes it as follows:

> "I am next of kin," I say firmly.
> "Relationship?"
> "We've lived together for thirty years."
> "The gentleman?"
> "He's my father." (6)

Rule realized that conventional expectations would have led the attendants to assume that Helen was married to Mr. Rule, leaving Jane twice removed as the person who should stay by her side. Recognizing that the hospital has a right to restrict visits to "next of kin," Rule plays on the ambiguity of the term "relationship" to assert the lived reality rather than the legal technicality of her kinship with Helen. After a series of tests for stroke, heart attack, and diabetes, all of which prove negative, Helen is released to return with Jane and Mr. Rule to the inn. The cause of her fainting is never explained.

The other accident involves the twenty-year-old son of the innkeepers whom Rule had seen talking with his mother. The boy was killed in a car accident earlier in the weekend, Rule learns after the fact, which explains the poor service in the inn and enhances the disordering undercurrent in their pastoral retreat when set against Helen's illness. Rule reflects: "By the time he is buried tomorrow afternoon, too young to have learned to let the weather in, too young to have gone back to a place where everyone he's known lies in the graveyard, beneath the flaming trees" (9). Helen's fainting and the death of the innkeepers' son bring past experiences of loss into sharp relief, reminding both Rule and the reader of the fragility of life.

A meditation on intimacy and kinship is bound up with thoughts of mortality and loss in "Leave Taking." Florence's desire to leave a living sign on Ruth's grave by planting a maple tree and Rule's assertion of kinship with Helen at the hospital circumvent conventions that would erase relationships between women that are as central, sustaining and legitimate as Rule's parents' marriage. Rule also considers the complementary roles that longtime partners assume, roles based on temperament and talent rather than gender. Mrs. Rule's role is to entertain; Helen's is to drive. When conditions require it, the partners fill in for each other, or consider the necessity of having to do so. Rule acknowledges the "interdependence and therefore self sufficiency of any long devoted pair" (7), whether or not the couple is recognized by relatives, the law or hospital procedures. Throughout the essay, age and illness blur the lines between generations, between genders and between intimacies that are deemed legitimate or not by public authorities.

Melancholic loss is not the only face of mortality in this essay; a fundamental affirmation of life pervades both the physical and emotional landscape. Ripe apples and the lushness of the short fall season are as much a part of the landscape as the dying leaves. When Rule washes the sour smell of Helen's illness from her hands at the hospital she says that it "isn't offensive to me. It smells of Helen's life, and it is not the first time I've had its primitive reassurance" (6). Reminded of inevitable "leave takings," Rule cherishes the present moment and reaffirms her attachment to life. The essay ends:

> But for me the present sucks up memory, the dead, love, grief, as gusts of wind suck up the leaves. I haven't any longer the heart for light leave taking. I think perhaps Helen never has. (9)

This, then, was the emotional air that Rule was breathing at the time she was beginning to work seriously on *Memory Board*. She was also working on other essays about the vulnerability of age and flesh, and about homophobia in and outside the family. She had been writing essays for several years for *The Body Politic* and had established herself as a political writer as well as a fiction writer. Her notebooks show that she deliberated for quite a while before deciding what the central conflicts in *Memory Board* would be, whether David would be the central character or whether the three "old ones," David, Diana, and Diana's partner, Constance, would be in some sort of subsistence crisis. She had the idea for the title metaphor early, imagining that Constance was losing "her present memory," as Rule called it, and needed a way to track the timing for watering her garden. Rule also knew that the book would include other kinds of memory boards; she imagined David writing about his past, his childhood, and adolescence in an effort to sort through meaning in old age.

In early versions, David is the central character. Rule asks herself in her notebook: "Is this novel in the 1st person, from David's point of view, a 'confession' no one he knows is interested in hearing" (box 37, folder 4)? In early versions, David is struggling with his sexuality. Rule imagines that both twins are gay, but David decides to marry and have a family. She imagines an episode in which, widowed and retired, David is arrested at the baths and scandalizes his daughter in whose home he lives. Rule also imagines writing the book from Diana's point of view, seeing David not as a biological twin but as a "fictional brother, accessible, articulate, moral. . . . David is a woman's name for a man." It is interesting to recall that "David" was the name the young Rule gave to her fantasy lover who had gone to war, as well as to the young homosexual boy in her unpublished college story, "Between the Darkness and the Sun," discussed in chapter 3. Rule imagines Diana saying at the end of the narrative: "David is my fantasy, my real brother was Cain, but he didn't rape or kill me." David, as he is finally conceived in the novel, denies Diana's existence because his wife, Patricia, requires it; he continues to communicate with Diana secretly on their birthday, but he shuts her out as kin. Diana's nieces knew nothing of her, her identity as an aunt foreclosed by her brother's complicity with his wife's homophobia.

Even after Rule had written well into the second chapter, she hadn't decided what the narrative form would be, but she had resolved one of what she called the "foreground problems." Rather than make David's sexuality the crisis that alienates him from his daughter, she would make Diana herself the cause of David's alienation. Lesbian sexuality, then, is the scandal that prompts David to rethink his past, including his marriage and his relationships with his children. In a sense, the fantasy brother and the real brother are brought together as David reworks his past in the present, considering the meanings of his acceptance of his wife's homophobia and its effects on his children and himself, as well as on Diana. By the time Rule had solved that problem, she had decided to alternate point of view from chapter to chapter. It still took several weeks and six chapters for her to see the full plan of the book. Reflecting on her own working methods in her notebook on November 19, 1985, Rule writes:

Because it snowed and we couldn't get to Salt Spring for the dentist, I've finished Chapt VI today and feel the book lifting up and out though I expect it to go on being slow, partly because I can't seem to use a notebook in the ways I have done before, instead scribble notes on yellow pages which get thrown out. It's as if having a detailed plan won't work with this one. But at least I have the major outline in my head finally after 120 pages! It came clear after talking with Helen, again something I've never done before. I suppose one of the things that keeps writing interesting and terrifying is that every time I think I understand my own working methods I have to shift them to get the new job done. (Box 37, folder 4)

Finally, the form that worked for Rule in *Memory Board* is the double-voiced narrative she used in *Desert of the Heart*: a third-person narrative written from two points of view (David's and Diana's) that alternate from chapter to chapter. As in *Desert of the Heart*, there are traces of a third perspective that orchestrates the other two, a lesbian subjectivity that is not contained within any character but that informs the overall structure of the book. *Memory Board* is about personal meanings and intimacies reconsidered after a lifetime of assumed identities. *Desert of the Heart* and *Memory Board* both begin with loss (Evelyn's marriage through divorce, David's through his wife's death) and end with a new sense of personal and social possibilities. The end of his marriage allows David to reconsider who he is, who he has become, and what he can still become. Born in 1920, the same generation as Evelyn in *Desert of the Heart*, David and Diana have just turned sixty-five. Looking back on family fictions, social scripts, and historical accidents, David and Diana renegotiate their relationship and in the process they renegotiate the defining terms of family, gender, sexuality, community, and self.

Composing Selves: Memory and Personal Histories

The story of *Memory Board* is set into motion by a singular act: David comes out as a lesbian's twin. When he reveals to his adult children that he has a hidden history, a shadow self, the family breaks apart along fault-lines that had been covered over by fictions David's wife had required and that he had colluded to maintain. The seismic effect of David's revelation uncovers more than his secret, the novel interrogates memory, identity, and family in a historical moment fractured by uncertainty.

The title metaphor suggests that memory is a way of organizing the present. Constance, who has no short-term memory, needs daily to construct herself in time. At sixty-seven she has clear but fragmented recall of distant memory. Her memory loss, it is suggested, comes from delayed trauma caused by being buried in a bomb shelter in London during the war, lying for hours at the side of her dead mother and sister. Diana, a nurse with the Canadian forces, rescued her from that living death. Now, on a daily basis, Diana rescues her from random disorder as custodian of her memory board. Diana and Constance first appear in the novel in relation to each other, sharing a history as well as a bed:

> Diana, wakened by her absolute interior clock, touched Constance's face, and there were the dark worlds of her eyes, always the first territory of day. Not since they'd shared a war over forty years ago had they been alarmed out of sleep. Waking was silent, intimate, even after all these years faintly arousing. (23)

One of Diana's first tasks, after she has managed to put herself together, is to prepare Constance's memory board:

> Diana took up a small slate, lifted the cellophane to clear it of the crossed off items of yesterday, and began to write the list for today, the first item intended to amuse Constance:
>
> > Put on your clothes
> > Breakfast
> > The morning show
> > Lift bulbs in the bed by the garage. (24)

The disappearing slate, with its rudimentary language, stands in for memory, allowing Constance to live in the present without needlessly repeating tasks that would be redundant or even harmful. Twice in the novel, Constance wanders off, away from her memory board and from the people who watch over her, providing order to her daily life. Familiar landscapes become menacing, the erasure of her history makes her anonymous, a disoriented old woman rather than Constance, with a past and a network of human connections to define her. By the end of the book, David realizes his lifelong ambition to be an actor by assuming a variety of roles to shore up Constance's sense of security. Mistaken by her as a plumber one minute, an investment banker the next, David can pretend to be whatever Constance needs to support her daily life. In Constance's case, history and memory collide, the blitz reaching into her future, now her present, to obliterate the sense of a continuous self. The erasure of short-term memory forces Constance to live totally in the present, constantly reinventing herself, leading the reader to question the concept of a core identity. Her reinventions are not, however, without limits. The eruption of distant memories in her daily life, the presence of intimate witnesses such as Diana and David who remind her of who she has been, the boundaries of her house, and the persistence of talents and tastes inform her daily reenactments of herself.

The novel begins with David creating a different kind of memory board. Alone, retired, living in the basement of what had been his house (now given over to his younger daughter Mary, her husband Ted, and their family) David sits down to write his history, to explore his memory in language:

> "Our father died in childbirth," wrote David Crown, bearer of bad news (retired), as he sat with his hearing aid turned off at his desk in what had been the ironing room in the basement of his own house. (1)

He begins his story with what he calls an "old line" that amused him and annoyed Diana. Their father had died in an automobile accident on the way to the hospital where their mother was giving birth. Having written the line, which links him to Diana and, at the same time, highlights a difference in their attitude toward their family history, David's mind wanders into a series of associations that re-create for the reader his childhood, especially in relation to Diana. In this narrative, David and Diana are presented as a bundled pair, mistaken at times for identical twins in their early childhood until the pressures to conform to gender expectations cause David, especially, to distance himself from his sister. Until they go to school, they consider themselves "two halves of a harmonious nature" (3). When they are twelve their mother remarries, and David feels deposed as the male in the family. In response, he endows his status as a twin with mythical meaning at the expense of Diana: "What he wanted . . . was not identification but proof of absolute difference, to have a negative, a shadow self, a perfect inferior, available to him at all times when comparison was to his advantage, otherwise invisible" (2). As he grows in his awareness of his own masculinity, he shores up his identity by projecting negative difference on his twin. He splits away what had been an undifferentiated part of himself in order to create a sense of autonomy. The female half of the pair is sacrificed to sustain the male.

The othering of Diana had begun when the twins started school and David learned that girls were to be shunned. David's concern is to please other boys, whatever the personal cost. Meanwhile, at least in David's memory, Diana is less impressed with masculinity, sensing that she is less well served by a gender system that clearly values boys at the expense of girls. Rule is careful to show through David's reminiscences that he is bound to Diana in a way that she is not bound to him, precisely because his sense of self-importance depends on his reconstruction of her. Separated into different classes in the third grade, "David missed her with what he later recognized as that mixture of emotions which overcomes people trying not to fall in love" (6). He dreads seeing her at school, and yet if she ignores him "something as sour and heavy as tears lodged in his throat" (6). At home he torments her, unable to leave her alone. As the twins approach adolescence, Diana surpasses David in height and strength, further threatening his fragile masculinity. Finally, the birth of their first half-brother creates a reason for them to bond again, and they are able to become friends at fourteen.

About halfway through the first chapter there is a break in the narrative, where David looks back to see that he has written only one line. The reader, like David, is brought fully into the present. The house in which he lives, nominally his, is in disarray. His daughter's marriage is threatened by an uncertain economy that slowly erodes the sense of security the white middle class considers to be an entitlement. Bound up with that security is the unwritten gender code that gives financial responsibility to the husband/father. It's important to note that the class and gender system that defines family security for David and Patricia's daughters is also racialized. The racialization goes largely unmarked because we are reading through an unself-consciously privileged white point of view. But even that perspective is not undifferentiated. David's position differs from Diana's, and the narrator who orchestrates the action provides still another angle of vision. For example, we learn at one point that Constance goes into business as a gardener after the war in part because "all the Japanese were sent away from the coast and still haven't been allowed back" (42). By coincidence, Laura, David's younger daughter, had hired the "C. Crowley Gardening Service," Constance's business, and makes the following remark to David:

> "She was just wonderful, as good at squatting as a Jap."
> David flinched inwardly as he always did at his wife's vocabulary on his children's lips, but he would have had to correct her to be free to correct them. (50)

David is still trapped into silence by his wife's biases; having failed to participate in the shaping of his family's history, he continues to stand at the sidelines in their present lives.

Discouraged by his inability to write more than his opening line about their father's death in childbirth and sensing the beginnings of a fight above his head, David leaves his basement room to escape into downtown Vancouver for the evening. The city, like his house, is in transition, increasingly unfamiliar to David. As his bus approaches the Granville Bridge to go downtown, David looks at the lights:

> David never got used to this new skyline, its cancerous swiftness obliterating what he wanted to remember, the town of his growing up, modest at the foot of mountains, at the edge of the infiltrating sea, a place for modest lives in the shadow of wilderness and remote snow. But there before him was an inflated city where you had to be at least twenty floors up for a view of the mountains and the water and pay dearly for it by the square inch. (17)

Caught in a history he simultaneously regrets and misses, David is no longer at home in his house or in his city. He broods about the failures and compromises of his life. He gave up his ambition to be an actor, instead reading the news for CBC radio. Too nearsighted to serve in World War II, he stayed behind, always reporting the events of the world, never participating directly. He thinks:

> It was a very odd way to have spent his life—in a soundproof box. Nearly everyone else he knew of in his own generation had taken part, placed the world catastrophe inside their personal experience and learned over the years to contain it. His disqualifying eyesight had spared and deprived him. None of his memories were his own, words rather, falling on him as impersonally as acid rain. (15)

Dressed in his old raincoat and walking aimlessly, David is suddenly misperceived by a stranger who bumps into him on the sidewalk: "Watch where you're going, you old beggar" (19). David takes this as a provocation rather than a humiliation. Removing his upper plate, his glasses and his hearing aid, assuming a slouch, he becomes the beggar the stranger had perceived and panhandles a well-dressed young man walking by. His success as an actor gives him a "comic sense of triumph" (20). He can get out of himself to play a different part. Or is it that he is becoming what others already perceive him to be? His brooding on past compromises and failures of courage continues. When he was twenty-three—the age his father was when he was born—his first child, a son, died inexplicably of crib death. He feels his life is bracketed by these two unrealized male lives, an infant and the young man his father was, both of whom shared his name. He is then led to think about "another pairing of failures" (21), this time two fully realized female lives—his sister and his wife—whom he was unable to reconcile in life. His wife, Patricia, had demanded that Diana be shunned into the very position of an invisible "negative, a shadow self, a perfect inferior" that David himself had wished for in early adolescence. This time, the othering of Diana protects the boundaries of a white, middle-class nuclear family just as David's early dream of othering Diana had protected the boundaries of white, middle-class heteromasculinity. At sixty-five, David realizes that the banning of Diana is a pervasive failure in his life, "a failure which had cleaved his life in two for all these years" (21). For forty years he had furtively visited his sister on their birthday, occasional witness to her success as an obstetrician and gynecologist. At the end of the chapter that begins with his aborted effort to write his past, he resolves to change his present by phoning Diana. In that gesture he forsakes his misplaced loyalty to his fearful and controlling wife and resolves to reconcile with his sister.

David's multiple self-presentations in the first chapter (would-be dominant twin, secret brother, grieving son, passive father, failed actor, retired reader of the news) underscore the effects on one man of a gender system that requires male dominance, a cleaving of the self, repression of the feminine and the erasure of deviant sexuality. Further, to sustain the apparent integrity of the conventional, white, middle-class nuclear family, the heterosexual wife and mother requires the banishment of the lesbian sister. Diana, as the first chapter hints and subsequent

chapters bear out, does not depend on David either positively or negatively to sustain her identity, her sense of who she is. At the most, Diana
envies Constance's memory loss: "Even a year dead, David's wife Patricia was lodged in Diana's memory like a tumor" (25).

There is a self-sufficiency to Diana's life: she has a sustained and sustaining relationship with Constance, a successful career, a life of her own.
But David's family, as defined by Patricia, depends on the exclusion of
Diana. Diana's exclusion provides an invisible support for Patricia's family; Diana may be wistful or melancholy or angry about the absence of
David's family in her life, but she is not defined by it. The situation mirrors the way in which David was bound up in his highly ambivalent rejection of Diana when they were children, while she was relatively indifferent.

The curious episode in which David plays the beggar introduces the
idea of a performative self, produced and policed by public perceptions.
This, in turn, opens up a possibility for moving beyond the bondage of
the gender system that defines David and confines the lives of his two
daughters. The originality of *Memory Board* is the staging of
(hetero)masculinity as a marked category. In David's narrative of masculine initiation, he is troubled even as he is served by male privilege that
depends on female subordination. From his point of view, Diana's distancing from conventional femininity is untroubled; he admires her for
serving in a war that kept him on the home front, he respects her success
in a male-dominated profession, he admires her relationship with Constance. He is especially sensitive to Diana's indifference to convention
when he considers the compromises of his own life. Through a series of
conversations and the sharing of domestic spaces, David redefines his relationship with Diana and, finally, his own identity as a brother, father,
and a man. In his conversational tug of war with Diana, we can see that
his sense of masculine responsibility is profoundly entrenched. Diana
finds him judgmental, moralistic, rigid in his insistence that his son-in-
law Ted repeat the same rituals of masculinity within a conventional family structure as he had. For example, David continues to do all the little
handyman jobs around the house like cleaning the eaves and fixing door
knobs. But he is inwardly censorious of his son-in-law for failing to do
them. His generosity becomes a way of maintaining control in the
household and of infantilizing his son-in-law. More important, David is

incensed when he learns that Ted might consider leaving his marriage when his wife's behavior becomes unbearable. Separation and divorce had been unthinkable for David, and he expects the same of his son-in-law. David feels uncomfortable in his own house (and the middle-class marital domesticity it represents) and yet can't imagine how else to live. Constance's irreverence and Diana's skepticism help him to consider other forms of intimacy. Constance, for instance, insists that her forty-year relationship with Diana is not a marriage, that they are "two very separate fleshes" (84).

A costuming scene that recalls David's performance as a beggar marks his shifting sense of himself, his ability to free himself from past patterns and, ultimately, loosen his hold on the lives of his daughters, a grip he didn't realize he had. In his changed sense of himself, he breaks Patricia's rules (first, by spending too much money for a pair of jogging shoes) and he values both the incongruities and the performative aspect of the role he is taking on. Trying on his expensive shoes, wearing a jogging suit he'd bought earlier, he looks in the store mirror:

> What he saw he could hardly credit. He must be at the fun fair, sticking his head over the cardboard cutout of a jogger, for the body and the feet seemed to belong together, but the head was all he recognized, the head of an old man who had been, one might still be able to see it, a trifle too pretty in youth. (292)

David, widowed, will allow himself adventures, dressed in his new costume, adventures that test social conventions: "He had always honored the ordinary, but he had also always wanted to be peculiar at least some of the time" (294). Eventually, his daughter and son-in-law ask him to move out so that they can rent out his space and subsidize a mortgage that would allow them to make full claim of the house. Having played house with David during a desert holiday, Diana and Constance are ready to take him into their real house, creating a new kind of domestic space. Constance's faulty memory requires David to reinvent himself constantly in contrast to the fixed role he had assumed in his more conventional domestic space. In the newly configured family the three older characters create together, kinship is not assumed, it needs to be negotiated, reaffirmed in the case of Diana and David, invented and reinvented in the case of Diana and Constance and David and Constance. David daily needs to reintroduce himself to Constance, not only as a fellow-lodger but with the words: "I'm David, Diana's brother."

David is not the only character to recompose himself in *Memory Board*. In the course of their negotiations, David pushes back against some of Diana's unexamined certainties. In an effort to learn more about "her world," he reads *The Body Politic*, a newspaper she doesn't even know about. She responds with hostility, saying, "Reading about a homosexual subculture to understand me is insulting" (192). Diana's political sympathies are with women; she would more willingly fight for abortion on demand than for human rights for gays. She rejects alliance with a gay community of which she is ignorant, failing to understand—as both David and other characters try to tell her—that the subculture is the product of the biases of the dominant culture, that she is implicated whether she chooses to recognize it or not. When David's grandson, Mike, introduces her to Richard, a gay friend who has been rejected by his family because he has AIDS, Diana begins, reluctantly, to connect with the gay and lesbian community in an effort to find support for him. In a last effort to resist identification with a subculture, she says to David, but really more for herself: "I wouldn't say, even to that dying boy . . . that, yes, I'm gay or queer or homosexual or lesbian. I am Diana Crown, a proud woman nearly turned to stone, but for Constance" (289).

Diana's assertion about her sexual identity and relation to the gay community is part of a larger conversation in the novel about competing models of sexuality. Diana considers herself to have been born a lesbian: her first attractions were to pretty girls her own age and to demanding women teachers. Narrative details serve to undercut the certainty of Diana's assertion; her exposure to the fragility of the flesh, the presence of death in life came during the war when she ministered to dying male soldiers. Her career as an obstetrician and gynecologist ministers to the bodies of women as givers of life. She admits to herself that her war experience made it impossible for her to be erotically attracted to male bodies. She is not indifferent to social censure, however, even though her privilege and discretion shielded her from the most blatant consequences of homophobia during her career. Because she was relatively sheltered from the material effects of homophobia (with the glaring exception of her sister-in-law's shunning), Diana never needed the support of the gay community and, until she becomes involved in Richard's needs, never had to confront why such a community is necessary.

Constance's understanding of sexuality is more playful. Her erotic needs are multiple and untroubled by social judgment. Her views are summed up in the following paragraph:

> Long before the rhetoric of women's liberation, Constance took the view that linking sexuality with procreation was as misused a piece of information as the splitting of the atom. In the midst of a population explosion, peaceful uses of sexuality should surely finally be considered. (84)

Finally, the causes of sexual orientation are less important in the various strands of discussion about sexuality in *Memory Board* than the effects. Diana's suppression by Patricia and Richard's expulsion by his parents are the most blatant examples of the effects of homophobia. But David's sense of loss and his daughters' infantilized femininity are also the casualties of a gender and sexual system that requires exclusion and repression.

Alongside considerations of gender and sexuality, Rule includes speculation about intimacy. As Constance likes to point out, she and Diana don't have a marriage in which two become one flesh. Rule uses a triangulation of desire to explore the dynamics of intimacy for Constance and Diana, a configuration she uses in a number of other texts, such as the short story "Invention for Shelagh" in *Theme for Diverse Instruments*. Diana, who feels privileged to have been chosen by Constance, doesn't need a variety of sexual partners. Constance, on the other hand, requires variety; erotic adventure and emotional commitment are separate in her libidinal economy. In their early years together, Diana's jealousy and Constance's relative unawareness of her own attractiveness lead to angry quarrels. Finally Diana recognizes the negative patterns of their behavior and determines to break out of her jealousy. Eventually Constance's lovers become part of Diana and Constance's life together, an inclusion that makes them easier for Diana to accept. The new arrangement is not without problems:

> Diana didn't realize for some time that her new sense of security was based on a dangerous smugness, for none of these women had ever been in any

position to offer Constance the blend of security and freedom Diana could once she had established her practice. (41)

A more serious test of their relationship comes when Jill, a woman ten years younger than they are, falls in love with Constance. Diana and Constance accommodate Jill in their lives by including her more fully, choosing a house with enough space to allow them to live together. The triangulation of desire in this more permanent arrangement is not without cost. Constance has a breakdown that hospitalizes her for months during which she undergoes shock treatment. As Diana reminds Constance, "Both Jill and I were so busy with our own heroic stoicism, we hadn't really thought how difficult it must have been for you, even though it was what you thought you wanted—to live with us both, not to have to choose between us" (44). In retrospect, Diana attributes Constance's breakdown more to the delayed effects of the war than the immediate strain of their domestic arrangement, but in her concern for Constance's mental balance, Jill moves out of their house to a more peripheral role in their lives. Through the character of Jill, especially with the ambiguity of Constance's breakdown, Rule presents a possibility rather than an argument about reconfiguring intimacy. She suggests that the instability of forces in contention may be preferable to the stability of static models of the couple based on exclusion. Significantly, David moves into Jill's rooms at the end of the novel, realizing a different sort of kinship rather than the reconfigured intimacy Jill's presence had attempted.

Complacency with familiar, socially sanctioned family forms is repeatedly subjected to criticism in *Memory Board*. When Diana and David reflect on their family of origin, they recognize that the illusion of wholeness was maintained at great cost by their mother. They felt no real kinship with their half-brothers and the pretense to unity dissolved with their mother's death. With the character of Richard the critique is extended. David wants to confront Richard's mother and stepfather, to make them accept their dying son because he needs help. Diana, in spite of her own distancing from the gay community, says that Richard is getting help from people better equipped to support him than his parents: "The last thing in the world he needs is people to reconfirm his own worst judgments of himself, that his is a punishment he must accept in all humility. He's better off angry with them than reconciled to them" (314). A renegotiated self, responsive to the demands of the present, entails a renegotiated sense of family and community.

The dual narrative structure orchestrated by a third-person lesbian subjectivity, which Rule used first in *Desert of the Heart* and returned to in *Memory Board*, allows her to stage identity as a process of negotiation. The terms of negotiation are constrained by social scripts, historical moment, and family narratives, but individual agency is not foreclosed. The present moment is shaped by memory and history, but it is never fully determined by the past. The house that David and Patricia had inhabited with their family and the house that Diana and Constance had chosen with Jill are repositories of history and sites for change. David's move from one to the other signals his changed relationship to his past and his refusal to allow the restrictions of his past choices to determine the present moment. Rule often uses houses, which are both fixed and changeable, public and private spaces, to explore family histories and alternative family possibilities, to explore the connections between private stories and public narratives.

FIVE

Construction Sites

Narratives of Houses and Homes

Going Home (Again)

Since the mid-1980s, feminists have gone home to examine the workings of history, culture, and geography in the making of identity and
community. Minnie Bruce Pratt's autobiographical narrative "Identity: Skin Blood Heart," Biddy Martin and Chandra Talpede Mohanty's collaborative reading of Pratt's essay in "Feminist Politics:
What's Home Got to Do with It?," Martin's return to her own home
and family in the Introduction to *Femininity Played Straight: The Significance of Being Lesbian*, Shane Phelan's revisiting of home and family in "Interlude I: Getting Specific" (1994)—all are part of a rich
constellation of autobiographical essays that theorize the personal particularly by reconsidering the historical, geographic, and social moor-
ings of their families of origin. As Martin and Mohanty argue in their
reading of Pratt and de Lauretis argues in her reading of Cherríe Mor-
aga (1990), these essays (written primarily by lesbians and/or women
of color) break through a number of epistemological and ethical barriers that blocked American feminist theory in the mid-1980s, especially
in the work of white feminists. Among those barriers are the concept
of a "true self," discoverable under layers of patriarchal false consciousness, an idea of community based on sameness rather than coalition, and white guilt stalled in silence that fails to examine its own
racial history. At the same time, these essays reclaim the emotional and
metaphoric power of "home" from the rhetoric of the New Right
without succumbing to the largely unexamined, fixed meanings that
are attached to "home" in popular and some feminist writing.

Biddy Martin and Chandra Mohanty turn to Pratt's essay because it "demonstrates the importance of both narrative and historical specificity in the attempt to reconceptualize the relations between 'home,' 'identity,' and political change" (Martin *Femininity* 164). They look at the ways Pratt uses an apparently conventional narrative to undercut convention, particularly the conventions that sustain the illusion of a coherent, stable "identity," and the safe comforts of "home." They also point out that Pratt does not promote a progressive narrative that denounces past blindnesses in order to arrive at a superior lucidity in the present. Rather than arrive linearly at final answers, she poses questions of identity, home, and community in a different way. Martin and Mohanty describe Pratt's method in this way:

> Geography, demography, and architecture, as well as the configuration of her relationships to particular people (her father, her lover, her workmate), serve to indicate the fundamentally relational nature of identity and the negations on which the assumption of a singular, fixed, and essential self is based. For the narrator, such negativity is represented by a rigid identity such as that of her father, which sustains its appearance of stability by defining itself in terms of what it is not: not black, not female, not Jewish, not Catholic, not poor, etc. The "self" in this narrative is not an essence or truth concealed by patriarchal layers of deceit and lying in wait of discovery, revelation or birth. . . . While Pratt is aware that stable notions of self and identity are based on exclusion and secured by terror, she is also aware of the risk and terror inherent in breaking through the walls of home. (169)

Martin and Mohanty understand that Pratt's reading and rewriting of her personal history, her uncovering of family and social secrets, and her constant shifting of perspective in relation to her multiple social positionings is an interpretive act located in a historical and political field. Martin, in her introduction to *Femininity Played Straight*, incorporates portions of her own personal history to revisit the emotional complexity of going home. With her characteristic resistance to overly neat conceptualization, Martin says:

> I have become frustrated by the excesses of what has been called postmodern or discourse theory, especially with the thin language of subject positions and with critiques of "the subject" that evacuate interiority

altogether, as though the process of subjectification created normalcy without remainders. . . . All this suggests too direct a relationship between "discourse" or "discursive mechanisms" and psychic lives, makes the time of the unconscious coterminus with the time of consciousness and history, and effectively dispenses with the split subject of psychoanalysis. (15)

To enact for the reader what she means by the complex contradictions of interiority and the persistence of remainders, Martin writes about two family crises—the death of one brother and the near death of another—she was living through as she was writing this book. These emotionally charged confrontations with mortality bring to the surface deeply set patterns of family interactions and expectations. Martin tells the story of her own resistance to her family's version of who she is but situates her resistance and studied indifference in the context of her stunned grief after the loss of one brother, killed by the collapse of a dam that her father had spent much of his life trying to shore up, and the nearly fatal disease of another brother. Martin urges her reader to turn to the contradictions, the emotional ambiguities that test theory, to examine frustrations, resistance, and the unexplained in order to understand the limits of theory and, therefore, the directions in which it needs to move.

Coming from a different disciplinary training, Shane Phelan insists that we "get specific": "Getting specific means turning social science and theory on its head; it means working out from the centers of our lives to seeing the connections and contradictions in them" (32). She, too, revisits her childhood homes and family histories as a means to explore privilege and oppression and becoming a lesbian. Because all of the personal narratives I've alluded to are written by feminists, they all work toward a renewed understanding of community and alliances in their interrogations of self, home, and family.

I would like to locate a discussion of "home" in Rule's fiction in this rich field of feminist narratives. Her fictions, like more recent feminist fictions of the self whether they are presented as autobiography or not, examine the specifics of geography, history, family, and home and refuse the illusion of a fixed, prediscursive "self" that awaits discovery. Part of the recent move of theorists toward narrative as a productive mode for developing theory is the need for discourse that is multilayered, metaphoric, and suggestive; narratives don't pretend to be linear, transparent, and conclusive. Personal narratives, sensitively written, engage the reader in the process of discovering connections that the writer herself may not have foreseen. Narratives like Pratt's, Martin's, and Phelan's represent the narrator as a reader of herself within the seemingly familiar, opening up the possibility of multiple, changing interpretations. Like other fictions, personal narratives continue to generate meanings as new readers approach the text or even as a reader returns to the text at different moments and from changed cultural locations.

Homi Bhabha prefaces his reading of Toni Morrison and Nadine Gordimer in *The Location of Culture* by stating that the task of the literary critic is

> to show how historical agency is transformed through the signifying process; how the historical event is represented in a discourse that is *somehow beyond control.* This is in keeping with Hannah Arendt's suggestion that the author of social action may be the initiator of its unique meaning, but as agent he or she cannot control its outcome. It is not simply what the house of fiction contains or "controls" as *content.* What is just as important is the metaphoricity of the houses of racial memory that both Morrison and Gordimer construct. (12–13)

As Bhabha points out, the house as metaphor is particularly suggestive as we reexamine the relation between public and private, masculine and feminine, colonizer and colonized. The home displaces the oppositions it seems at first to maintain. In a move similar to Pratt's homecomings, Bhabha observes:

> The recesses of the domestic space become sites for history's most intricate invasions. In that displacement, the borders between home and world become confused; and, uncannily, the private and public become part of each other, forcing upon us a vision that is as divided as it is disorienting. (9)

The personal narratives I've mentioned and Bhabha's approach to the metaphoricity of home turn on negotiation and situatedness. Identity is a process of negotiations with the living and the dead; home is located in a specific geography traversed by known and unknown or disavowed histories. Home doesn't shut out the world, the walls that mark off private space are permeable. Community, as Martin and Mohanty emphasize, is not a stable entity: "Community . . . is the product of work, of struggle; it is inherently unstable, contextual . . . and it is the product of interpretation—interpretation based on an attention to history, to the concrete, to what Foucault has called subjugated knowledges" (183). These approaches to "home" build also on Foucault's observation about architecture:

> Architecture . . . is only taken as an element of support, to ensure a certain allocation of people in space, a *canalization* of their circulation, as well as the coding of their reciprocal relations. So it is not only considered as an element in space, but is especially thought of as a plunge into a field of social relations in which it brings about some specific effects. ("Space, Knowledge, and Power" 253 in Rabinow)

As I have suggested earlier in discussing "House," "My Country Wrong," and the domestic spaces in *Memory Board*, Rule often situates her narratives in houses, especially houses that are being reconstructed to respond to changing social relations. For interior spaces she favors rooms that are not the conventional center of the home, especially attic and basement rooms like David's in *Memory Board*. Transient spaces are also frequent, such as Evelyn's boarding house room in *Desert of the Heart*, or the anonymous hotel rooms of the narrators in "My Country Wrong" and "Home Movie." Rule's personal history placed her in an unstable and critical relation to "home." Her family moved frequently when she was young. Because her father was in the construction business they sometimes lived in houses that were being built, or lived in other people's houses until they had one of their own. In a recent essay called "Choosing Home" (1996) Rule compares her transient occupation of spaces during her childhood with the more securely anchored houses of grandparents with "attics and basements full of the accumulation of generations" (275). She learned early that values and attitudes that were taken as "the right way to do things," were local; different climates and geographies produced different values. As a transitory resident Rule could see that what was taken to be universal in one town might be absent in another.

Rule doesn't pretend to be unmarked by the places she lived, but to have understood her relation to them differently. In "Choosing Home" she says that her first sense of having a "geographic identity" came when she went to Europe for the first time at nineteen. Others helped her see ways in which she was marked as American that she hadn't seen before: "For the first time in my life I was not simply an outsider. I was an American about whom there were all sorts of negative expectations, a number of which I inadvertently fulfilled" (276). She goes on to say that eventually her adaptive skills earned her the compliment: "You don't seem like an American at all." In Vancouver, Rule first lived in rented rooms. She says: "Like everywhere else I had lived, it was more a stage set than a home." Rule says she was in her thirties before she "learned to make myself at home." This involved rebuilding a house made for a large family into a house adapted to two professional women, including spaces to rent to students or to welcome guests. It also involved learning a neighborhood, participating in the cultural and political life of a young, growing city, becoming Canadian. Carrying a Canadian passport, she is perceived differently at borders than she was as an American. She credits her early rootlessness with providing a certain freedom to "choose what home is, what I have needed it to be" (279). But just as certainly, her early mobility and changing citizenship have made her especially observant of the peculiarities of place, the ways that geography and architecture express and effect social relations without ever completely explaining how identities and communities are formed.

Home Invasion: "A Television Drama"

In 1968, at the same time that Rule was beginning to think about the novel that would become *Against the Season*, she wrote a short story called "A Television Drama" that was eventually included in *Theme for Diverse Instruments*. This brief, taut story dramatizes the reciprocity between social and domestic space and examines different perspectives on and within middle-class domesticity. A housewife named Carolee, running the vacuum cleaner, becomes aware of unusual activity in her quiet, middle-class neighborhood early one afternoon. Police cars are parked in front of her house, she sees "a motorcycle like a slanted stress in the middle of the intersection" (77). Men in uniform carrying rifles and field glasses occupy her neighbor's terrace, police dogs search an empty field. Within the narrative, all of the neighbors are named while the police and reporters are anonymous. Carolee is mystified by the presence of so much fire power in a neighborhood "where every child has a bedroom and most men either studies or basement workshops to retreat into" (78). Then she sees a very young man against her own laurel hedge, clutching at his shoulder; he seems to be sick, injured, or even dead. She has heard fragments of radio reports about a "suspect" and a "house to house search," but when she sees the man, he seems unreal, a product of her imagination rather than the target of the massive police apparatus at her door. She sees him get up suddenly and walk out into the street before falling down, drawing the police and the press toward him like vultures. Carolee watches a television reporter through her window as she listens to the radio. Her visual witness of the scene is out of synch with the report she is hearing, creating a multilayered representation of the event that contains its own internal contradictions. All three versions (what she witnessed, what she is watching of the television reporter, what she is hearing on the radio) are partial; together they create discontinuities that are as meaningful as the efforts to achieve coherence. The wounded young man Carolee has seen has elicited her sympathy and through her, the reader's. The formulas of media reporting (suspect apprehended, robbed a bank, shot a policeman) represent the event solely from the perspective of police, property, and public order, leaving no room for a bleeding young man.

Later, two more perspectives are added to the story. Carolee's husband Pete returns home with the evening paper that has an aerial map of the neighborhood, including their house. A view, as the narrator points out, that Carolee had never seen. Dots and arrows map the afternoon drama, and Carolee notices two details that clash with what she had witnessed. The dots don't go to the hedge where she saw the young man, but arc around to where he ultimately fell; he is represented in the map not as a person but as "a fallen doll." There are no police, no reporters, represented on the map, as if he had fallen all alone, cause of his own injury rather than the object of a massive hunt. The young man seemed "exposed to nothing but a God's eye view" (81). The force of the official version of the story in the paper makes Carolee doubt her own observation and memory. When her husband asks if she got "a good look," she responds: "'I guess not really.' . . . Had he sat there by the laurel hedge at all, his long, stiff legs stretched out in front of him? The map didn't show it" (81).

When her husband mutters that something needs to be done "about all this violence" (82), Carolee realizes that he is perceiving the event from an entirely different perspective. The violence Carolee had witnessed was the invasion of the police and the media on carefully tended private domains. Her husband can only see the violence the suspect represents in the official accounts, all the more frightening because of his anonymity. The suspect becomes all suspects, all those who fail to respect property and state authority. The reader begins to see that the order and privacy the neighborhood represents is secured by the violence that Carolee witnessed rather than threatened by the violence the suspect represents.

The story ends as Carolee and her husband watch the television coverage of the event. A voice-over accompanying a series of fragmented, fast cuts creates a coherent fiction of the event. Again, the image track and the sound track are discontinuous, but here the voice-over is created to suture the gaps between the images. The image of a voice-over and fragments of images becomes a metaphor for the lie of a seamless, comprehensive account of civic life created by the media but covering over contradictions, gaps, the perspectives of the powerless. Sitting in silence, Carolee sees that the official version leaves her out and leaves out the moment she had witnessed when the man lay wounded by the hedge. She wonders if it would be different if she had spoken to the reporter, would her account have altered the official version,

> would the dots in the paper have changed? Would the cameras have climbed into their nearly exposed winter garden? Would she believe now what she couldn't quite believe then, that she stood at that window and saw a man dying in her garden? (82)

Has she colluded in the public lie? The view from within the domestic space is absent from the official version of events and yet it is this perspective that enables the reader to arrive at a changed understanding of the relation between public forces of order and private spaces. The power of the official narrative, told from a "God's eye view" that erases traces of surveillance and terror even as it pretends to an all-encompassing objectivity makes Carolee doubt the reality of her point of view and threatens to erase her memory even as it fabricates public memory. The story ends as Carolee and her husband continue to watch the news, the story of their neighborhood invasion juxtaposed with stories about unfair labor practices in the nation and military invasions in the world: "Carolee wasn't there, but it seemed real to her, terribly real, so that for a moment she forgot Pete's hand in hers, her safe house on a safe street, and was afraid" (83).

By the end of the story, the reader can imagine that more than the illusion of safety has been shattered. Carolee's absence—or, more precisely, her concealed presence—haunts the official narrative. Knowing what we know about the event that Carolee witnessed, what can we imagine about the absences covered over by reports of national and international events? Carolee's perspective provides a different interpretation of the relation between the police and the suspect. The invasion and violence Carolee witnessed were not created by the suspect, but by guns and cameras that were deleted from the newspaper's map. The reader can begin to see that to account fully for the perspective from within the domestic space might lead to a different interpretation of public order.

As Carolee and Pete sit mute in front of the television news at the end of the story, the reader is confronted with multiple interpretive possibilities. The ambiguity of the ending invites the reader to ask if Carolee's fear at the end is more profound, less immediately interested than it at first appears. At several points in the story, Carolee's reflex is to call the police to find out what is happening and to help the wounded man. Then she realizes the absurdity of this well-conditioned reflex: the police have brought this excessive, inexplicable violence into her neighborhood. Home and neighborhood are not havens from violence but are secured by violence. Carolee occupies a gap in the official story, a point of view that, if exposed, would undermine the prevailing myths of home, neighborhood, and country.

Carolee's false sense of security and the threat of force by a faceless police presence recall the hovering helicopter that frightened Evelyn in *Desert of the Heart*. In *Desert of the Heart* outlaw sexuality and unsanctioned intimacy can't escape the surveillance of forces of order; in "A Television Drama" we can see that hearth and home are maintained by those forces, but contain the potential to disrupt a repressive and violent public order. The multilayered dialectic of public and private, legitimate and outlaw, surveillance and repression motivates many of Rule's fictions. The houses and homes in *Against the Season* (1970) and *The*

Young in One Another's Arms (1976), like "A Television Drama," provide metaphoric sites to explore that dialectic even as they begin to displace the binaries that define it.

A House of Language: *Against the Season*

Jane Rule wrote *Against the Season* between 1968 and 1970, during a period of intense productivity and writerly optimism. After three years Rule was finally able to interest a publisher in *This Is Not for You* in 1968; the same publisher, McCall's, expressed an interest in the ideas Rule was working on for a new novel. She had sold several short stories and landed a Canada Council grant to give her time to spend on *Against the Season*. The novel is more ambitious than either *This Is Not for You,* with a single first-person narrator, or *Desert of the Heart,* with two narrative centers; in *Against the Season,* point of view circulates among nearly a dozen characters to create an entire town. *Against the Season,* in fact, is crowded with characters and stories and lacks the intensity of focus of *Desert of the Heart* and the ironic edge of *This Is Not for You.* The point of view is diffuse and sometimes difficult to read. Still, in this apparently conventional narrative, Rule incorporates a number of disruptive elements which, like "A Television Drama," undercut a complacent view of middle-class domestic comfort.

Initially, *Against the Season* seems to be less centrally lesbian than the first two novels. There are several lesbian characters, but they are part of a broader concern in the book to interrogate sexuality and intimacy in many types of relationships. There are no favored models for adult intimacy in the novel; marriage, friendship, sisters, lesbian affairs are among the types of intimacy that are explored: each can be productive, but each can equally well be abused. Rule clearly had a lesbian audience in mind, however, because the second chapter (focused on one of the lesbian characters) was published as a "Chapter from an Untitled Novel in Progress" in *The Ladder* in the October/November 1969 issue. It was later anthologized as "Dina Pyros" in *The Lesbians' Home Journal: Stories from the Ladder* (1976). The more diffuse lesbian presence in the book and the refusal to idealize lesbian desire is consistent with the overall movement in the narrative to resist the temptation to a progressivist view that would correct historic errors and establish a surer model of community. All knowledge in the novel is shown to be partial.

The narrative structure does not promote an entirely relativistic view, however. The orchestrating presence of a lesbian subjectivity makes itself felt in the ways certain characters elicit sympathy and others are hypocritical and controlling. Given the range of characters and issues developed in the novel, the narrative subjectivity might again be characterized as a resisting lesbian subject because the values inscribed in the book resist conventional judgments and interpretations. Further, the resistance often takes a specifically sexual turn. Lesbian desire is incorporated into the narrative through several characters. The narrative frame sets up homophobia, not lesbianism, as a problem in society. The term "homophobia" is, of course, never used; it hadn't been named as a concept in 1968. Narrative values are assumed rather than argued in the novel. Homophobic attitudes are associated with rigid, self-serving or self-loathing characters. Lesbians are not immune from social judgment, but the pleasures and difficulties of lesbian intimacy are shown to be as valid—and as difficult to attain—as the pleasures and difficulties of heterosexual intimacy. Sexuality is not the central defining longing of most of the characters; loneliness and a need for meaning are. Nonetheless, the narrating subjectivity could more appropriately be called lesbian than gay, I think, because although there are allusions to gay male desire, there is more attention paid to women characters and women's sexuality. Men are not excluded, but women are central in a way they aren't in masculine narratives; lesbian desire is assumed to be legitimate in a way that is rarely if ever admitted in heterosexual narratives.

The narrative of *Against the Season* is presented through the perspectives of several characters. Rule succeeds at creating what might be termed a "traveling" narrative perspective in the ninth chapter, which takes place at "Nick's," a Greek restaurant where several important characters are gathered. Point of view moves rapidly from one character to another, illuminating different aspects of their relationships to one another and to the town. That chapter is actually a more intense example of the way point of view is handled in the novel as a whole. Gathering places—especially the Larson house and Nick's—bring characters together in different configurations and facilitate shifts in perspective that are characteristic of the narrative form.

The story told in *Against the Season* takes place in the spring and summer of 1968 in the Pacific Northwest. The specific location is never indicated, and it is interesting that Canadian reviewers said, by and large, that the town is in Canada and American reviewers placed it in the United States. That the town is definitely in the States can be inferred, however, by references to "downstate," and to the dilemma of Cole, one of the young men in the book, who may avoid the draft by going to Canada. The seaside town is a logging port of uncertain definition, neither a town nor quite a city. Even the streets are lettered rather than named. The first center of interest is Amelia Larson, seventy-two, whose older sister Beatrice died six months before the beginning of the narrative at age seventy-seven. Amelia was "born lame" but is not dependent on others for her mobility. Beatrice is repeatedly remembered as a handsome woman, and the prevailing story is that she gave up the possibility of marriage in order to look after her sister. The sisters lived their whole lives in their childhood home, one of the central defining spaces of the novel. Like Rule's grandparents' homes, the house is a family archive, with diaries and artifacts stored in every room that provide clues to histories that are only partially knowable. For many years they had routinely taken in young women from one of the town's institutions—a home for unwed mothers—which is conveniently (for the town's sense of propriety) located at the edge of town at the corner of "F" street and Main. An isolated old hotel, bordering the sea and abutting used car lots and warehouses, the home is run by the Presbyterian church. Following a reciprocal agreement, local girls go elsewhere, and out of town girls come here. The physical and moral confinement of the young women creates a feeling of "house arrest or siege" while protecting the local townspeople from evidence of sexual transgression. The irony of placing this home at the intersection of the forbidden "F" word and the Main street of the town hardly needs comment.

The story begins as one of the girls Amelia has taken in, a self-effacing young woman named Kathy, gives birth, and it ends as Kathy's replacement—a bold young woman named Agate—gives birth while Amelia is dying in the same hospital. The cycle of the seasons (of the year and of life) would appear to inscribe the novel in a normalizing frame, but as the title suggests, there is resistance to what is expected (in nature, in society, in relationships). Originally called *Against the Grain,* the

novel tests expectations, both novelistic and social. While there is a pro-
fusion of stories in the book, there is no predominant plot per se. The
novel is composed of a series of portraits and scenes, each exploring connections (and ruptures) among people and interrogating what constitutes the fabric of a town, how power is used and abused, how histories
are represented or repressed.

Other characters include Cole, the son of Amelia's cousin, who is
spending his college years with her; Harriet Jameson is an unmarried librarian of thirty-six who dates, for their mutual convenience, Peter Fallidon, a bank manager recently arrived in the city. Dina Pyros, in her early
thirties, runs a shop called "George's" where she restores furniture and
provides a gathering place for adolescents, mainly male. Born in Greece,
she subscribes to an elaborate personal mythology according to which
she will marry a Greek and connect again with her motherland, whose
language she doesn't speak. Meanwhile, she has affairs with women. Her
cousin Nick runs a Greek restaurant and bar that welcomes sailors as well
as townspeople. Rosemary Hopwood is a social worker in her forties who
grew up in the town but left because of difficulties with her mother; she
returned after her mother's death to make her life there. She has had a
series of relationships with women and she wants Dina. She counsels the
unwed mothers and provides a link between them and the town. In her
pursuit of Dina, Rosemary tries to expose the incongruity between
Dina's personal belief system (which is a caricature of Greek mythology
and immigrant longing to return, both supporting heterosexual marriage) and her lived reality (as a lover of women, protector of young people, and property owner in the town). Feller Hill is a wealthy businessman whose wife, Grace, is resentful because of her powerlessness in her
family and in the town. She has a secret affair with Dina but compensates
by spreading homophobic rumors about Peter Fallidon. Three other
characters play central roles in the novel: Carl, Ida, and Maud. They are
contemporaries of Amelia's and gather at her house regularly for games
and gossip. Carl is a widower and minister who wants to marry Ida. Ida
has always lived alone, next to the graveyard, and fears that marriage at
her age would appear ridiculous. Maud's primary work is to care for her
ailing husband; she is one of the voices of convention in the novel.

The central character of the novel, in a sense, is the town itself. Like
the other characters, the town is not completely knowable, it isn't even

named, but the reader catches glimpses into the past and follows the ways the town—both as a place and as a field of social relations—has a life cycle of its own. Also, like the other characters, the town is in transition. It will either be revitalized, grow to serve changing needs with a changing population, or it will die, stunted and finally stifled by its history of exclusions and restrictions. The town is a place where lives and choices are under surveillance and subject to judgment. The home for unwed mothers is only the most blatant example. Among the elders, certain unsympathetic characters such as Grace, Maud, and a more amorphous "society," or "they," condemn unconventional behavior, both real and imagined. They make Amelia feel self-conscious about continuing to employ girls from the home. They make sure that Cole and Agate don't inhabit Amelia's house without a chaperoning older presence. Meanwhile, more sympathetic elders like Amelia, Ida, and Carl are flexible and forgiving but not immune to complicity with the conventions they critique. Most of the younger characters are looking for models, teachers, or permission or, like Agate, chafe against arbitrary rules of acceptability. As the title suggests, however, roles are not neatly assigned.

The Larson house, which dominates the novel, is a house of language. As the novel opens, Amelia is going up to the attic to find Beatrice's diaries. The staircase is lined with mottoes "cross-stitched by three generations of Larson women." The walls of the house are inscribed with conventional wisdom, transmitted through women's work. It's interesting to note that the content of the mottoes is never made available to the reader. What might have been amusing or quaint or cliché remains opaque, unreadable; conventional wisdom is ornamental, having lost its force as an interpretive device. Throughout the novel, systems of meaning, like the cross-stitching, remain fragmented, only partially available to interpretation, suggestive rather than conclusive. Amelia and Beatrice are known as "Cousin A" and "Cousin B" to distinguish them, but the abbreviation also signals that they are only partially knowable even to each other, although they lived together for most of Amelia's seventy-two years.

How meanings are made and interpreted is the presenting and most persistent concern of the narrative. When Amelia goes up to the attic six months after her sister asked her (as a dying wish) to burn the diaries, she is caught in a moral and interpretive dilemma. Beatrice explicitly asked that her diaries be burned, but Amelia is convinced from her experience of Beatrice that she would not have wanted the diaries to go unread. Amelia had always understood Beatrice as much by her tone as by her choice of words. Toward the end of her life, however, Beatrice's speech was impaired by a stroke and her tone was unreadable. When Amelia finds the diaries in the attic, amid other artifacts of family history, her dilemma is complicated further. There should be sixty-nine diaries, one for each year since Beatrice learned to write at six. The books for 1913–15 and 1933–35 are missing. The first set corresponds to the only time that Beatrice left home, to go to Seminary; we don't know—and will never know—what happened during the other period, when Beatrice would have been in her early forties. Much later in the novel Agate accidentally finds all the missing books, and through her the reader learns that Beatrice had been unbearably lonely when she was far from Amelia at Seminary; her entry for October 12, 1913, includes: "This morning, walking under the medicinal eucalyptus, I saw a girl with a withered arm and further along, by the bridge, I wept" (128).

We are left to speculate about the stories the other missing books might have contained. Again, gaps and silences (whether accidental or by design) suggest meanings as much or even more than fragments of text. Further, in the overall design of the narrative, gaps serve to illustrate that all readings are interested. Gaps provide a tempting focal point for readers in need of narratives to justify their own lives. For example, Rosemary (the discreet lesbian social worker who works with the "unwed" mothers) is unaware of the missing diaries, but she knows that her knowledge of the lives of the people around her is incomplete. Rosemary wants to imagine that Ida and Beatrice had been lovers, primarily because she wants a bond with Ida, an older, single woman whom she respects. If Ida and Beatrice had been lovers, she imagines, Rosemary might better be able to sort out her own desire for Dina. We might be tempted to think that the missing books would have revealed such a liaison; Beatrice would have been in her early forties in 1933–35, Rosemary's age in 1968, the time represented in the novel. When Rosemary tries to coax a confession from Ida, Ida simply responds: "Leave our graves alone. . . . Ride by" (167). Ida's words seem to echo the verses that Yeats asked to be engraved on his tombstone: "Cast a cold eye/ On life, on death./ Horseman, pass by!" ("Under Ben Bulben," VI, in the *Last Poems*,

1936–39). But the reader knows what Rosemary doesn't know, that Ida (echoing Rosemary's fascinated speculation about her relationship with Beatrice) is very interested in Rosemary and Dina, has observed that they meet and has speculated to herself about what their meetings might mean, not in judgment but in sympathy.

Once she has accumulated most of the diaries, Amelia is faced with another interpretive problem. How should she read them? She begins by reading entries for the month of May year after year:

> She was distracted and heavy with the diaries she had been reading. Her first method, reading through sixty-three Mays, had been arbitrary and frivolous, giving her little of Sister but her hatred of roses and chronic spring envies. So Amelia had started at the beginning. . . . It depressed her, but she felt, by now, committed to the task, as she had been committed to living with Beatrice through all those years the first time. Why? She couldn't explain it to herself except as a moral perversity: love. (51)

Reading produces relationship. Her second method, however, isn't much more satisfying in giving her answers than the first. The effects of reading are more important than the content of the diaries. Agate, who never knew Beatrice, sees that the diaries are disturbing Amelia, upsetting her when she should be resting. Agate reads some of the diaries and has a different interpretation of Beatrice than most of the others. She sees her as spiteful, jealous, and even vaguely incestuous. In Agate's reading, Beatrice shows contempt for Amelia in part because she is dependent on her in ways that Amelia is not. Agate doesn't have the benefit of a shared history in which to locate her reading; her primary motive as a reader is to protect Amelia, and, therefore, she is intent to convince Amelia to burn the diaries unread. Whatever Beatrice's intentions, the language of her text, as Bhabha would say, is beyond control.

The diaries are not the only fragments of texts inviting interpretation in the Larson house. The attic is a repository of signs, some with unbroken links to the past, others less easy to place. At one point Agate puts on old hats and clothing and the house becomes a theater, releasing still other meanings. Some of Agate's costumes recall their original owners to Amelia, some remain mysterious. The clothing takes on new meaning in the changed context, hardly recognizable as the signs of taste and fashion they once were. Agate sings and clowns, leading Amelia to say that she should have been on stage. Agate answers, "I am . . . most of the time" (130). Agate's performance resonates with Amelia whose own life-long performance resurfaces in her half-sleep. Amelia relives a scene from her youth and sees Bill Hopwood, Rosemary's father, crying. She had turned him down as a suitor because Beatrice was coming home from Seminary to stay.

> People had always assumed it was Beatrice who gave up a life of her own for Amelia. Beatrice thought so herself, needing to. It didn't matter. It never had. Then that fragment Agate had been singing repeated itself in Amelia's head: "I've got life! life! life!" Amelia accepted that sentence and was smiling as she fell asleep. (133)

The house is more than a stage for family dramas. Its architecture invites readings that reach out beyond the domestic scene even as they articulate the foundation of that domesticity. From a window high in the attic, generations of women watched ships go to sea and return when the town was a center of merchant activity. In the present, the neighborhood around the house has changed. Other old homes have been transformed into boardinghouses; the Larson gardens are among the last to survive. The town is in decline, stifled by its own history. In the first chapter, Amelia discusses the life cycle of the city with Peter and a few other characters. We can surmise from the house and its placement that the economy of the town was based on shipping and logging. Amelia says that the town's growth had been very fast, its dying very slow: "Giving us time to pay for our sins, my father would have said. His father helped to figure out how to drive out all the cheap Chinese labor, not just from the town, from the whole county. To this day, we have no Orientals, no blacks, no race problems" (15). As with Beatrice's diaries, tone is very hard to catch here. Is Amelia expressing without irony the complacency of the white upper class that could honestly believe that racial exclusion doesn't constitute a "race problem"? Or is she making the connection between racial exclusion and the slow death of the town? The problem of tone isn't made any easier by Peter's rejoinder that the lack of a "race problem" could be "very attractive to industry." When Amelia asks where a labor force would come from, he answers: "It would come. The town doesn't have to die." Survival depends on reversing the exclusions that secured the town's wealth and its demise. Whether or not the characters recognize their own complicity with racism and xenophobia, the house and its history are mute witness to a past that was secured by both.

Muted or repressed sexuality, like racial exclusion, is built into the foundation of the Larson house. Beatrice's hidden diaries and Amelia's refusal to marry are part of that story. Agate, as the most recent in a continuing line of unwed mothers pressed into service at the Larson house, is another example. Like Beatrice's diaries, Agate's body is read in contradictory ways. Agate makes the connection in the following passage:

> "You're the diary of my misspent youth," Agate said to her hard house of a belly.
> "Against the law to get rid of you. Shouldn't have written you in the first place. A couple of bitches, B and me." (191)

In the older generation, Maud (who defines herself through the invalid husband she tends), Grace (frustrated in a marriage in which she exercises little power and who is carrying on a hidden affair with Dina), and "they" are threatened by the presence of "illegitimate" female sexuality. For the heterosexual woman, the body easily becomes a witness against her; to protect legitimacy, she must be banned, sent to another city, confined in the home on the seawall, but certainly not welcomed even as cheap labor into a house like the Larson's. Lesbians represent a different kind of illegitimacy, less legible, but just as threatening. Maud disdains Dina, but Grace, caught in the contradictions of her own unhappiness, desires her. Grace's affair is less an expression of desire than an expression of anger at her husband and at Peter for excluding her from power in her family or in the town. Lesbian desire to her is an active transgression against a social order she covets. Rosemary provides the link in the novel between Agate, the most visible threat to heterosexual legitimacy, and Dina who embodies a more covert threat to the defining legitimacy of heterosexuality. Rosemary is the social worker who works with Agate and the other young women in the home, and, of course, she is courting Dina. Agate, who has keen insight into the desires of other characters like Cole, consistently misreads Rosemary. She recognizes a restless desire in her, but because of her own desire and the social assumption of heterosexuality she assumes that Rosemary wants Peter and is jealous of Harriet (a quiet librarian who dates Peter largely as a matter of convenience to them both).

Male sexuality is explored as a source of scandal, a threat to legitimacy, in the novel as well. Stories have to be invented to account for the fact that Peter has arrived in this town, an attractive man in his early forties, without any apparent history of marriage. Without a woman to legitimate him, his position is never secure. In retaliation at one point, Grace spreads a rumor that a Greek sailor who jumped ship was found at Peter's in a "compromising circumstance" (137). By the end of the novel, Peter is vindicated and he asks Harriet to marry him. Cole, whose desire for Peter is barely repressed, sees Peter's engagement as a failure in courage, a cover to protect his power in the town. Significantly, the Larson house, temporary haven for Agate and source of scandal for the voices of convention, is the locus for celebration of their engagement.

In Biddy Martin and Chandra Mohanty's reading of Minnie Bruce Pratt's autobiographical essay, they show that Pratt uses a seemingly conventional narrative form to undercut conventions and to expose the supports of illusory psychic and cultural stability. As they say in their essay, Pratt doesn't promise lucidity or correctness, but a reevaluation of the present in relation to the past, a new way of interrogating identity, home, and community. Rule's novel urges a similar reevaluation. Conventions, narrative and social, are repeatedly challenged. The central tension of the novel is, precisely, a struggle between convention and the compelling needs of characters like Agate or Cole or Rosemary or of the town itself. Narrative conventions are tested by the priority Rule gives to characters who would traditionally be peripheral: unmarried old women, single mothers, lesbians, retired men (like Carl, a semiretired minister of God). Peter most nearly embodies the masculine ideal that would be central in a masculinist narrative, but his identity is unveiled as a precarious and only partially successful performance. Most important, perhaps, is the undecidability and the core illegibility of key elements in stories that might have provided lucidity, a more complete knowledge. Beatrice's diaries are withheld from the reader and never yield a satisfying reading for any of the characters. Peter's past is hinted at but never made explicit; occasionally, as in "A Television Drama," conversations will be seen but not heard. For example, Agate observes Rosemary and Dina in a decisive conversation at the engagement party, but the words remain out of hearing.

The Larson house serves as an organizing metaphor to demonstrate that prosperity and social order are founded on exclusions and violence, a violence that remains muted precisely because entire groups of people were not allowed to participate in the building of the town. Identity and community are not fixed but produced by negotiation and constantly changing relations. The Larson house is a repository, a theater, a foyer through which the past and present interact and conflict. A symbol of continuity in the town, it is actually a site of changing relationships and conflicting ways of making sense of social relations. The future of the house is uncertain.

Jane Rule finished correcting the proofs for *Against the Season* in November 1970, and soon after she turned to her next novel, *The Young in One Another's Arms*, published in 1976. Here a house again serves as an organizing metaphor, but in an entirely different way. In this novel, house and home become politicized.

Under Siege: *The Young in One Another's Arms*

The years in which Rule wrote *The Young in One Another's Arms* were marked by political and personal change. In the early 1970s Rule and Helen Sonthoff became involved in the women's movement. They helped to organize the first feminist consciousness-raising group at the University of British Columbia where they explored, along with other women (faculty, students, graduate students, staff), what it meant to be a woman in a male-dominated institution. Meanwhile, their social life was becoming so intense that they bought a house on Galiano Island in 1973 for escape on weekends and in the summer. In the academic year 1974–75, Sonthoff took a leave from her position at U.B.C. which allowed them to live full time at their house on Galiano. In 1975, both the short story collection *Theme for Diverse Instruments* and *Lesbian Images* were published. Even at their island retreat, Rule and Sonthoff continued to entertain houseguests such as Del Martin and Phyllis Lyon as well as family, and they traveled to the U.S. desert in the Southwest in the winter to escape the cold damp of British Columbia.

As early as January 11, 1971, Rule wrote in her notebook that she had quickly written 10 pages but hadn't yet shaped the events for the novel. She wrote: "I see that probably this book isn't paced to many 'actions', the process of dailiness more important" (box 37, folder 1). Three days later, having read a negative review of *Against the Season,* she wrote:

> Finished Chapter I yesterday in spite of rage at Kirkus review of *Against the Season.* "Though many of these people relate, nothing much happens." It is like Pauline's [Oliveras, the composer] audience, not hearing, or hearing and not accepting because that order of sound is not for them an event so much as a distraction. Is relationship between two people seen as a distraction from event? I find it hard to believe, even against all the evidence. And I am afraid of the undertow of plot which can drag characters into unbelievable action. Well, that's one question. The other is that what seems to me ordinary truths about relationship seem more bleak to others than they do to me—or more bearable, as if my own tolerance did not relate to the world around me. The anger comes from the indifference to the seriousness and integrity of work, whether successful or not—the gleeful, spiteful put down. But I turn away, climb high into my own head to work, then put myself down in the arms of someone I love. Odd process notes, these.

Difficulties with narrative form and demands on her time for other projects, especially the two books published in 1975, kept her from working full time on *The Young in One Another's Arms.* She was worried, once again, about point of view. She considered using the point of view of Ruth Wheeler (the central character) in every other chapter, alternating with the point of view of other characters. At some point in 1971 she gave up the novel for over a year. Her notes in the summer of 1972 show that she was still thinking about it; in the early fall of 1974 she was brooding about the book and had a breakthrough that allowed her to move ahead.

In a letter she wrote to a friend in Palo Alto in November 1974,[1] Rule talks about the pleasures of getting to know Galiano Island through the fall, saying that it reminds her of her childhood in the redwoods at South Fork on the Eel River in California. She says in the same letter that she has "reluctantly begun . . . a new novel called *The Young in One Another's Arms,* too full of urban sadness, but there to write, and maybe as the winter really sets in, it will be all right to get through the darkness of that ex-

---

1. Letter to Mrs. Robert Anderson, "Gracella," dated November 14, 1974. Given to the author by Marilyn Yalom at the Stanford Institute for Research on Women and Gender.

perience." In 1974 she still considered it a "small book." The break-through that allowed Rule to make progress on the book was the realization that the tragic ending she had envisioned for the book was really the middle, not the end, of the narrative. Rather than end the novel in urban violence and defeat with her main characters fighting against "the system," she would have them regroup and attempt to fight *for* something—a redefined family in the community of Galiano.

The new direction allowed her to incorporate the pleasures of discovering Galiano into the novel. Ruth Wheeler, who is presented as having grown up in the California redwoods near the Eel River, observes the Galiano landscape in the following way:

> Ruth wasn't sure why this tiny island reminded her of the redwood landscape of her childhood. In miniature it seemed done to scale, Douglas firs tall enough to dwarf the hills, here called mountains. The little valley that crossed the island was about the size of the valley she had grown up in, though it had been more dramatically defined by the river as well as the hills. Here there was the sea at the end of every road whether they arrived at the shore or on a hilltop, and on that gentle spring day it did not seem to imprison so much as embrace this island and all the others they could see, a colony of lands in friendly sight of each other, stretching down into American waters. (134)

A brief summary of the characters and events of the novel reveals how plot is related to place, how the house becomes a shaping metaphor in the narrative. In contrast to the nameless city in *Against the Season* hovering between stagnation and potential renewal, *The Young in One Another's Arms* is specifically located in Vancouver, mapped very carefully against the rapid growth of the late 1960s and then, as the above passage shows, on Galiano Island. Rule explores the effects of Canada's dependence and complicity with the United States during the worst years of the Vietnam War. There are ten important characters in the novel and a smaller number of secondary characters who play significant roles in their lives. At the center of the narrative is Ruth Wheeler, a woman of fifty who has survived physical and emotional wounds. She lost an arm, and her daughter, Claire, died at twenty-two, two years before the story begins. By using the insurance from her losses she is able to buy and then improve a boardinghouse. The first paragraph of the novel introduces her to the reader through a series of changing perceptions, *trompe l'œil* illusions that finally dissolve into her portrait:

> In the darkened street, Ruth Wheeler might have been mistaken for a boy of middle growth, spare-bodied, light on her feet. She nearly always wore trousers, and the empty right sleeve of her windbreaker could seem a boy's quirk of style. But if she stepped under a streetlight, looked up and sharply beyond that illuminated space, her face redefined the first impression, the color of false pearl, dark eyes of remarkable size but limited by aging lids, anchored by taut lines to her temples: the face of a seventy-year-old woman. Ruth Wheeler was, in fact, just over fifty.

The shifting perceptions of the opening description reinforce Rule's tendency to counter the reader's expectations in her fiction: you can't always believe your eyes, trained as they are to see gender, age, and bodies according to narrow categories. The first portrait of Ruth Wheeler also recalls an unpublished short story called "The Chosen Two" (signed Jinx Rule) that Rule wrote in 1957 (box 12, folder 3). One of the main characters, Elizabeth Henderson, is described in terms that anticipate the gender ambiguity of Ruth's portrait: "In her pose and rocking, [Elizabeth] might have seemed like a young boy, were it not for the gentle suggestion of desire in the ease of her body, and the repose of her face." In the early portrait, desire reestablishes the character as female.

Like the biblical Ruth, Ruth Wheeler loves her mother-in-law, Clara. The narrator asks: "Did many women marry because they loved their mothers-in-law" (6)? Ruth's husband, Hal, who works on road construction and no longer lives with Ruth, is secondary to the relationship between the women. It's interesting to note that Rule, whose biblical allusions in past narratives had pointed toward alliances that led to betrayal (Cain and Abel or Jesus and Judas), turns here to Ruth and Naomi, a loving alliance. The Ruth and Naomi story is one of the biblical stories that gay and lesbian activists turned to in the 1970s because of the positive valuing of same sex relationships. The other characters in the novel are boarders in Ruth's house: Gladys, object of everyone's desire, a political radical who works with handicapped children; Mavis, a repressed lesbian and PhD candidate writing a thesis on Dickens who defends against her own desire by adopting conservative values; Willard, a middle-aged shoe salesman from Kamloops who appears to be mentally retarded and requires strict routine and obsessive repetition in his daily life in order to hang on to sanity; Joanie, who works as a secretary and wants to marry a wealthy man; Tom, an American who has come to Canada to resist the draft; Stew, who begins as a musician doing drugs but eventually, because of guilt or a bad trip, reverts to his upper middle-class background and becomes a conservative law student; and Arthur, a wounded and brooding young man who has deserted the U.S. Army and has found sanctuary in Ruth's basement. Later in the novel, Rule introduces a character named Boyd Wonder who calls himself "Boy," a gay African American who performs stereotypes of blacks and gays to define and defend himself against racism and homophobia.

The old family house, repository of history and a community monument that dominated *Against the Season,* is transformed in this novel into Ruth Wheeler's boardinghouse, a temporary shelter for social outcasts and political refugees. At the beginning of the novel, Ruth has received notice that a highway is being built through her neighborhood; her house, like all the others in that area, has been "expropriated." The razing of domestic spaces in the name of public progress is the first of many invasions of privacy in the novel and establishes the house as a site of social as well as personal struggle. At the beginning of the novel Ruth is unwilling to launch a full-scale political resistance to the city, as Gladys would have her do; she is trying to figure out how best to survive this loss as she has her other losses, using the compensation offered to her by the city to finance her next step. Once again she will subsidize her future by salvaging what she can from loss.

The novel, however, is much more than the stories of Ruth Wheeler's semipublic house with its odd lot of temporary residents caught in the way of progress. The house and the bodies that inhabit it become sites through which to examine what Foucault calls the mechanics of power. In the previous chapter, I cited Foucault's understanding of capillary forms of power, reaching into all private and public interactions, prompting a reconsideration of the relation between private and public, intimate and social. As Biddy Martin says, "According to Foucault, power comes from below; it is induced in the body and produced in every social interaction. It is not exercised negatively from the outside, though negation and repression may be one of its effects. Power in the modern world is the relation between pleasures, knowledge and power as they are produced and disciplined" (Martin *Femininity* 188). At first *The Young in One Another's Arms* would seem to contest this view of power. Power is most dramatically exercised with brute anonymity from the outside, bearing down on the house and its residents through a collusion of the state, big business, and global alliances. The city, to serve commerce, is destroying a neighborhood to build a road; the national government is colluding with the United States to search out and deport American men resisting the draft or deserting the military. Ruth's house and her boarders are all touched in some way by this invasion and repression by faceless forces of destruction and surveillance. As the narrative develops, however, we can begin to see the operation of capillary forms of power that Foucault has defined as "the point where power reaches into the very grain of individuals, touches their bodies and inserts itself into their actions and attitudes, their . . . everyday lives" (Foucault "Prison Talk" 39). Throughout the novel Rule refuses to resolve the tension between these two understandings of power: anonymous surveillance and imposition of "order" from the state (which serves and is served by capitalist interests) *and* the capillary forms of power which permeate individuals, marking their bodies, their unconscious gestures as well as their interactions with one another.

The defenses that each major character assumes to compensate for wounds and losses sustained before the narrative begins all express the ways in which power has reached into their bodies. Mavis's conservatism and "middle age" posture at the age of twenty-five; Willard's obsessive repetition and routine are among the clearest examples of power permeating the very posture and gestures of individuals. Boy's hyperbolic performance of black and gay stereotypes is an ironic example of resistance to power. Boy acknowledges that white heterosexuality invents blackness and gayness in ways that sustain white heterosexuality as the norm. He resists by playing those roles in such an exaggerated way that they are exposed as masks, as artifice. If that is how he is "recognized" as a black gay man, that is how he will act. But Boy is always performing, he has, in effect, become the character he parodies.

The knot of relations between desire, knowledge, and power is expressed in the relations among the characters as well. Stew, the Canadian musician, who desires Gladys, the feminist radical, feels betrayed when she sleeps with Arthur, the U.S. draft resister, to comfort him in his pain.

To get even, Stew alerts the police to Arthur's presence in the house and he is deported back to the United States. Appalled at the consequences of his own behavior, Stew takes drugs that give him a bad trip. He becomes so frightened by the effect of the drugs and by his role in Arthur's deportation that he abandons his marginal existence, cuts his hair, gives up drugs, and goes to law school.

Another erotic triangle involving Gladys is played out later in the novel when she becomes pregnant after sleeping with Tom, even as Mavis falls in love with her. Much later in the novel, when Gladys gives birth to twins (a boy and a girl), the boy dies in childbirth and Tom becomes enraged with loss because his son has died and with jealousy because of Mavis. He attacks Mavis physically and she fights back. Both are slightly wounded but deeply affected by the events. The effect of violent erotic emotion and the instability of "the couple" on Mavis is contrary to the effect on Stew. She abandons her plan to take the first available academic job (giving up stability and conventional respectability) and chooses instead to remain in a volatile, unpredictable set of relationships. Through difficult and never conclusive negotiation, Mavis stays on Galiano in what has become a very unconventional, reconstituted household.

Ruth Wheeler's house (with Ruth and her mother-in-law, Clara, at the domestic center) in its changing formations and locations defines the transformations of "home" and "family" that underlie the novel. The house moves from a makeshift means to assure Ruth's economic survival (an individual solution to natural and social hardship) to a collectively negotiated space that sustains an alternative kinship network with a vital role in a larger community. In short, in *The Young in One Another's Arms*, the politics of domestic space are exposed and reimagined, first through resistance against power imposed from outside and then through negotiation within to channel the mechanics of power and create less oppressive forms of intimacy and interaction. One of Rule's concerns as she was writing the book was to avoid creating a narrative that is "too politically patterned" (box 5, folder 6). She accomplishes this by refusing to allow neat or final resolutions to conflicts among characters and by using the metaphor of the house to evoke changing power relations without explaining or overdetermining them.

The house in *The Young in One Another's Arms* takes on three forms, each with some variations. At the beginning of the book, Ruth Wheeler's boardinghouse has been condemned in the name of progress. Other houses in the neighborhood have already been abandoned, and all of the residents, Ruth and Clara included, must find another place and way to live. The road builders are not the only threat to the house. The police arrive to check for draft resisters and military deserters. Ruth, who believes more strongly in the decency of individuals than in the sinister effects of power, invites the police in and, to a point, answers their questions. She has adopted a "don't ask, don't tell" policy in her house, never inquiring about the origins or status of her boarders, understanding that for her to know such things might put them at risk. Even though she has an individualistic approach to political struggle at the beginning of the novel, she has the beginnings of a much more systemic analysis of power and how it operates through the dominant stories of a culture as well as through legal authorities. In an interjection that comes from the unspecified narrative presence but that is associated with Ruth's sensibility, Ruth seems to think: "In a world where even God, never mind Abraham, killed his only son as a loving gesture, how could the police understand a young Isaac or Jesus who wouldn't offer himself up to the slaughter" (16)?

Realizing that the house is a target for vandalism in the increasingly abandoned neighborhood, and bowing to the authority of her husband, who returns home unannounced at Christmas, Ruth decides she must think about the next step. In a nostalgic gesture to the temporary connections that have been made among the residents, they decide to celebrate Christmas. Ruth uses the opportunity to give most of the furniture to her boarders who have decided to rent another large house in a different neighborhood and try to live under the same roof. She reluctantly agrees to let her husband take his mother, Clara, to a home. Ruth finds a sterile, anonymous apartment in a new high rise for herself. She decides to take Willard, whose brittle routines are threatened by change, with her. She thinks she might be able to provide a continuity and stability for Willard that will compensate for his fear of change. This dispersion, a sort of diaspora of the socially marginal or resistant residents of her house, is the second form the house takes in the novel. This is the "urban sadness" Rule described in her letter in November 1974. The connections among the residents has been accidental, a result of chance rather than choice. The combined events of the expropriation of the house and Arthur's deportation shake down the residents, leading some to abandon the group and others to try, for material convenience, to share another space together.

Willard, who seems at first to adjust to the new configuration of his domestic life, has planned a more radical resistance than the others. On the day the boardinghouse is to be razed, he barricades himself in the house with a gun and threatens to shoot anyone who approaches. Ruth, notified by the Royal Canadian Mounted Police, goes to try to help. She finds Tom at the scene; as someone who opposes violence and feels protective of Willard he is trying to intervene. Tom is surrounded by a growing crowd of police, journalists, and spectators. In a panic, Willard shoots Tom in the arm, and just as Ruth begins to persuade him to put down his gun, the police shoot him in the face, killing him on the spot. Pried away from Tom, whom she is trying to comfort,

> Ruth wrenched free and stopped over the broken daffodils. Then she raised her shocked face to the man standing tall above her.
>
> "You kill everything," she said, as two flash bulbs exploded. . . .
>
> She needed to bury the flowers there under the lilac with the bones of birds.
>
> "Can she identify them?"
>
> "Don't try to question her now. She's in shock."
>
> "What have you done with Arthur?" Ruth shouted. "What have you done? They're *my* children, *all* of them, *mine*. You kill everything. Bastards! Bastards!"
>
> "Are they both dead?" someone called out.
>
> Ruth crouched on her own front lawn, holding the broken flowers, weeping, in a new burst of flash bulbs aimed over her head at the stretcher being carried down the walk. (116–17)

In this dramatic confrontation with the police Ruth is shocked into a deeper political understanding of power. Arthur's deportation, Tom's wounding, Willard's death are no longer discrete events, but are part of the brute exercise of power over life and death by the police—to protect progress and promote economic development. Private lives are sacrificed for public order. Another dimension of the relation between public and private is also introduced in this passage. The flashbulbs and television cameras capture Ruth's grief, to display her image on the news and in the paper. The event recalls "A Television Drama," in that we have seen one version of the event through Ruth's sensibility and then we see it represented in a partial, but totalizing, way by the media. The transformation of her private grief into a public narrative over which she has no control has two effects on Ruth. First, it frightens her and, eventually, pushes her to act to redefine her life and Clara's, rather than passively accept what seems available to them (the home for the elderly for Clara, an isolating apartment for Ruth). Second, the public representation of her pain overcomes her personal memory of it, at once distancing her from her own experience and making her a captive witness to the events in her head: "Now her throat still ached with her own screaming, and she saw that screaming face, mouth pulled downward in a grotesque stone mask of grief, as it appeared on the front page of the newspaper all over the city" (119–20). She compares the sequence of images that haunt her memory to a film strip that repeats obsessively in her mind. The sanctity of domestic space must give way to public interest; private grief is subsumed into a public narrative even as it is shorn of personal meaning.

In her original conception of the novel, Rule thought she would end with the destruction of the house and the death of Willard. Both would be the victims of change, the house because it was in the way of a bridge access, Willard because he couldn't survive changes in his routine. Urban sadness, as seen in neighborhoods and in fragile people, would be ended by the arbitrary and irrevocable use of force. The ending, however, seemed to her to be too bleak, too pessimistic. She decided instead to explore what might happen if Ruth, Clara, and the remaining boarders tried to create a life together, by choice rather than by chance.

This reworking of the novel leads to the third form the house takes in the book. Ruth, Clara, Tom, Gladys, Boy, and Mavis relocate to Galiano Island and start a café called Jonah's. The naming is more than a nautical reference for a café by a ferry landing. In the biblical story, Jonah resists what is expected of him. When, on shipboard, a storm threatens the travelers, they toss him over as a scapegoat, blaming him for the storm. He survives, in what Christians take as a parable predicting Christ's Passion, when he is swallowed whole by a "great fish" in whose belly he lives for three days before returning to life. In the Bible, Jonah is disgorged at the very place he had tried to leave and he is not chastened by the ordeal. He remains unforgiving and quick to anger even though he has been saved by the generosity of a Lord who is slow to anger. The Lord calls on him to examine the motives of his rage. Just as Jonah tests his fellow travelers, this group traveling to Galiano tests what society will tolerate. But like Jonah, some of them (Tom, Gladys, and Mavis in particular) have yet to look inward to examine the motives of their own anger, their persistent unwillingness to forgive themselves and each other. They reach an internal crisis when Tom and Mavis fight after Gladys gives birth to twins, as I described earlier. This crisis of birth and death forces the self-examination they had avoided when they had been able to locate the primary threat to their survival in outside forces (the city's expropriation, Canadian collusion in American deportation of draft resisters). Jonah's café helps them survive, and the island house they ultimately establish after facing their inner demons might provide a model for survival, though not a model of stability.

The novel doesn't end neatly with a utopian collective in a rural setting, safe from urban life. Boy, under surveillance because of resisting the U.S. military, has to disappear. For a time the group disperses, threatened by their internal dissension as well as outside pressure. By the end of the novel, they are back together again. As Rule wrote in her notebook, they had learned "to fight *for* what they want together" (box 37, folder 1), not just what they need to fight against. Even at the end, the group is not seen as a secure, fixed entity but a loose kinship that must be constantly worked for, renegotiated, reinterpreted. Further, because of Boy's disappearance, police helicopters, recalling the helicopter in *Desert of the Heart*, maintain surveillance over this still threatening odd lot of outcasts and resisters.

The narrative of *The Young in One Another's Arms*, considered through the changing forms and meanings of the house and "home," might seem to provide less space for the lesbian reader searching for ways to reimagine lesbian identity than some of Rule's other narratives. Such a conclusion, however, would oversimplify the politics of the narrative. As I mentioned earlier, Rule struggled for some time before she decided on the narrative structure of this novel. Finally, the novel is told through Ruth Wheeler's point of view, though, like *Desert of the Heart* and *Against the Season*, the novel is not in the first person but orchestrated by an invisible narrative presence. This novel adds a new dimension, however, that further emphasizes that two women (an emotional if not an erotic couple) are at the center of the narrative. From the beginning, a running conversation between Ruth and Clara gives shape to their lives and meaning to their days. When Clara is removed, temporarily, to a home, Ruth begins to have extensive interior monologues, represented in the text by italics, that continue or replace her conversations with Clara. In the entire novel, whether they are together or not, the daily exchange of love and conversation between two women gives shape and meaning to their lives and the lives of their household. Lesbian desire is not divergent in this scheme but consistent with its values.

Through Mavis and in the relation between Gladys and Mavis, the struggle to claim lesbian desire against the pressures of homophobia is seen as part of a larger struggle to understand desire and intimacy. Lesbian desire is neither idealized nor trivialized, it is an integral part of the new kinship network the characters slowly negotiate; it is woven into the newly defined community. To write such a narrative in the late 1970s might be understood as an effort by Rule to resist the utopian sisterhoods, communities defined by the politics of 1970s lesbian feminism that, in her view, were potentially as restrictive as the homophobia they were resisting. In her next novel, *Contract with the World*, Rule explored further the politics of community, and in the process she entered into a more open debate with other lesbian activists about the responsibilities of a lesbian novelist to her community.

| SIX |

Contesting Communities

Parading Differences

As I begin writing this chapter on a sunny day in June, San Francisco is hosting the twenty-seventh annual Lesbian, Gay, Bisexual and Transgender Pride Parade. The theme for the parade is "One Community, Many Faces." On the street, a celebrant was heard to say to an observer: "You don't have to be part of the family to be in the community." The title for the parade, the theme, and the casual comment encapsulate the successes and the tensions of nearly three decades of gay and lesbian politics and public life. On June 27, 1970, twenty to thirty people had marched down Polk Street for the first "Freedom Day" event in San Francisco to commemorate the Stonewall Riot and demonstrate for gay rights (Stryker and Van Buskirk, *Gay by the Bay* 65–67). The following day a much larger group gathered at a 1960s-style "Gay-In" at Golden Gate Park. By 1973 the official name for the parade was the "Gay Freedom Day Parade," though it competed with a rival event, the "Festival of Gay Liberation" at the Civic Center. By 1975 the events were coordinated and the parade became the largest event of its kind in the U.S. The "Gay Freedom Day Parade" subsumes "lesbian" under the generic "gay." In the early 1970s, "bisexual and transgender" weren't yet part of the conversation: bisexuality hadn't been politicized and the term "transgender" hadn't been invented.

The theme for the 1997 parade, "One Community, Many Faces," expresses the increasingly urgent effort of lesbian and gay activists to recognize diversity (racial, ethnic, gender, erotic, age, disability, HIV status, the list goes on) while claiming a community that shares certain political goals. Certainly the floats and contingents that participated in the parade demonstrated a diversity that would have been unthinkable in 1971. From the traditional Dykes on Bikes (now called women on motorcycles) to breast cancer activists, businesses with gay and lesbian caucuses, HIV and AIDS support groups, PFLAG, leather and bondage clubs, and the ubiquitous cross-dressing and undressing, the parade took over Market Street for the entire day.

The comment, "You don't have to be part of the family to be in the community," expresses the effort of many activists to reach out to allies who don't identify as lesbian, gay, bisexual, or transgendered. This outreach contrasts with efforts of other activists to "act up," to challenge rather than reassure the majority culture that continues to be indifferent or hostile to the interests (and even the survival) of lesbians, gays, and other sexual minorities. Perhaps more significantly, the comment also signals a shift from "community" to "family" as an organizing rhetoric for lesbians and gays since the 1980s. "The family" refers to people who identify as lesbian, gay, bisexual, or transgendered; "the community" includes all allies, however they identify themselves. For some the turn to family is a resistance to right-wing, homophobic appropriations of "family values" rhetoric. For others, as Kath Weston argues, family, specifically "chosen families," have supplanted community because community has itself become a vexed term. In the early days of lesbian and gay organizing, community was predicated on a shared sexual identity as a unifying ground; efforts to define community tended to suppress or disregard differences within the gay and lesbian population as unimportant, secondary or, at worst, a threat to political effectiveness. While initially comforting, a validation of difference from the majority culture and a reassuring buffer between the individual at risk and a hostile society, community came to be seen as a "mini-enforcer," to use Weston's term (*Families* 1991), prescribing certain behaviors as correct or authentic and condemning others as inauthentic or the product of "false consciousness." Weston argues: "Defined in opposition to biological family, the concept of families we choose proved attractive in part because it reintroduced agency and a subjective sense of making culture into lesbian and gay social organization" (135).

Recent efforts by scholars such as Susan Krieger, Shane Phelan, Kath Weston, and Arlene Stein, among others, to rethink community (particularly lesbian and gay community) in sociology and political theory tend

| 216 |

to oppose 1970s "lesbian feminist" understandings of community with 1990s reformulations (or rejections) of community as a useful (or harmful) concept. These analyses tend to cast competing definitions of "community" in historical or developmental terms. Lesbian feminist understandings of community in the 1970s, they argue, couple individual identity and community: the community stakes its existence and political effectiveness on a shared sense of identity, and the individual requires the visibility of the community first to discover and then to validate her identity. The models for community that dominated 1970s lesbian feminist thinking, the argument continues, suppressed differences within and, in Iris Young's terms "relie[d] on the same desire for social wholeness and identification that underlies racism and ethnic chauvinism, on the one hand, and political sectarianism on the other" (Weiss and Friedman, *Feminism and Community* 234). In Shane Phelan's argument, the narratives that shaped those communities (the coming-out story, ways to identify or recognize a lesbian) enabled women to claim an otherwise unavailable aspect of themselves but simultaneously required the denial of other aspects of personal history such as heterosexual experience and marriage or erotic fantasies and practices that threatened the community's understanding of lesbian identity (*(Be)coming Out*). Kath Weston describes another consequence of this understanding of the relationship between identity and community: "Whites without a strong ethnic identification often described coming out as a transition from no community *into* community, whereas people of color were more likely to focus on conflicts *between* different identities instead of expressing a sense of relief and arrival" (*Families* 134).

While the opposition of 1990s thinking to 1970s lesbian feminism may serve to expose blind spots of the past and to clarify contemporary issues, it carries with it its own problems. Such an opposition tends to imply a progressivist or developmental model: past formulations are simplistic, flawed, and should be jettisoned, present thinking is more enlightened, more playful and sexier. Further, the documents that social scientists traditionally turn to tend to obscure or discount private, intimate lives and experiences while privileging more visible, less contradictory public narratives. Susan Krieger in her review of social science literature in the early 1980s lamented the fact that social science literature says little about the internal structures of communities and looks more to external boundaries. To understand the "internal intricacy" of lesbian social life, she said in 1982, we must "turn to journalism, novels and personal histories" (Freedman, Gelpi et al., *Lesbian Issue* 238).

The emergence in the 1980s of theory-making through personal narratives (leading to important concepts such as Anzaldúa's "mestiza consciousness" and Teresa de Lauretis's "eccentric subject") has pushed feminist theorists to reconsider the effectiveness of traditional methodology. Shane Phelan, for example, proposes "challenging the lines between philosophy, politics, and literature . . . acknowledging that the public/private split has prevented all of us from seeing the lines of power in our lives and addressing them as matters of common concern" (*Getting Specific* xix). Phelan recognizes that "community is a constitutive category of Western political thought" (*Getting Specific* 76). But she proposes that we "get specific" about community, by resisting unifying, global theories that suppress differences:

> Getting specific does not simply mean pointing to details. It means calling into question the field(s) that organize experience and meaning, problematizing the identities and allegiances that we have come to take for granted. It means coming to see the effects of power and the possibilities for democratic negotiations of that power. To do so requires a social ontology or landscape that can see and address contemporary modes of power. (16)

Fiction, created within a specific historical and cultural moment and consumed or interpreted by a variety of readers at different moments, provides just such a "social ontology or landscape" within which to examine and question "the fields that organize experience and meaning, problematizing the identities and allegiances that we have come to take for granted." *Contract with the World*, written in the late 1970s, and *After the Fire*, Rule's last novel, published in 1989, are particularly useful for examining problems of identity and community within the historical frame of the 1970s and 1980s. Unlike many lesbian feminists who sought to define community in the 1970s, Rule had claimed a lesbian identity both privately *and* publicly nearly a decade before gay and lesbian communities became visible through the political activism of the 1970s. Rule's relationship to lesbian and gay communities is, therefore, different from that of lesbians whose personal and social understanding of sexual identity was formed in the context of visible communities. By the time she wrote *Contract with the World*, Rule was actively involved in feminist, gay, and lesbian politics in Canada, taken by some as a role model and criticized (often by the same people) for taking stands that were seen as threatening to "the community." In her fiction, Rule imagines communities that contest majority culture, but she also contests models of lesbian and gay community that she sees as too restrictive, too inclined to suppress differences and punish nonconformists. The contradictions, dilemmas, and confrontations that Rule explores reveal that 1970s lesbian feminists themselves challenged models of community predicated on sameness. More important, Rule's fictions provide a ground for "getting specific" about community, a site for examining the stakes that individuals and communities have in each other and the way that power operates on and within groupings of people.

As the 1997 "Lesbian, Gay, Bisexual, Transgender Pride" parade inadvertently illustrated, by the time "identities" become publicly available, they are already inadequate to account for the intricacies of individual lives. To put differences on parade, even in celebration, suggests that individuals need to line up with Dykes on Bikes or bisexuals or the leather and bondage group or their business caucus. But what of those who embrace all (or none) of these and yet feel they are not only a part of the family, but in the community? Fiction incorporates contradictions that political demonstrations can't afford. Further, unlike theory, fiction doesn't make an argument; rather, because of its suggestiveness and indirection, fiction continues to produce new meanings in new contexts. And yet, an effective, flexible politics needs to understand the contradictions fiction makes available. Rule's fictions invite the reader to examine the lures and dangers of community, the complexities of the intimate and the social. Her fiction is political because it challenges "what we have come to take for granted," but also because it creates another kind of community. Kath Weston quotes a gay man who said that finding community meant "discovering that your story isn't the only one in the world" (122). Rule's fictions provide that sort of community for her readers, not by providing a single narrative of lesbian identity, but by multiplying narrative possibilities. Two of Rule's essays from the early and late 1970s give a sense of her ambivalent relationship to different kinds of communities during that tumultuous decade.

Mapping Boundaries

In the early 1970s, Rule wrote a spirited essay called "With All Due Respect: In Defense of All Lesbian Lifestyles" that was first published in Karla Jay and Allen Young's anthology, *After You're Out,* in 1975; Rule later included it in her 1981 collection, *Outlander.* The anecdotes Rule uses to frame her argument in the essay concern two women's studies seminars at the University of British Columbia. The first was an informal, noncredit seminar on "Lesbian Life Styles" that she volunteered to set up and host in her home in Vancouver in the early 1970s. The second, a few years later, was on lesbian writers, offered when Rule was working on *Lesbian Images.* She remembers the first seminar as a nearly unmitigated disaster in which a lot of "psychic blood" was spilled. In the second seminar, a somewhat smaller group of women managed to read lesbian writers together carefully and critically, creating in the process a space for companionship and friendship rather than accusation. Her discussion of the first seminar exposes the dangers and consequences of being "a public lesbian," and the second shows the connections that can be made through the bond of reading: between lesbian readers and writers and among lesbian readers as they interrogate lesbian meanings in fiction.

The first seminar produced a number of unpleasant surprises for Rule, who had thought she could facilitate discussion about lesbian lives among a small group of women. Instead, a floating population of around fifty women came in and out of her living room over the weeks of the seminar, vulnerable and increasingly hostile to one another, making of her familiar domestic space a dangerous battlefield. The first surprise for Rule was that so many women showed up, invigorated by the prospect of being in such a large group of women who were willing to call themselves lesbians. The second surprise (another potential asset of the group) was their diversity: in age, class background, marital status, religion, living situation, erotic experience, and politics. Having come to the meetings expecting validation and greater understanding of their own lives as lesbians, the women attacked one another for the differences among them: "One by one every woman who was willing to speak was disqualified by others in the room as inauthentic, not a 'real' lesbian" (174). In the essay, Rule remains bewildered by the experience. Rather than cast or assume blame, she tries to understand the situation in terms of changing expectations between premovement lesbians and women who claimed their lesbian sexuality after the gay and lesbian movement made sexuality more of a public, politicized issue. Premovement "public" lesbians, that is, women who were willing to be known as lesbians in their public and private lives, either by choice or because of exposure, were keenly aware of the hostility of family, workplace, and society to women who were identified as lesbians. They knew that guilt by association with them might put other women at risk, whether they were straight or closeted. She describes her generation of premovement lesbians as having developed a "negative protection" toward one another, not expecting support from sisters who might not be able to afford to offer it, but at the same time protective of one another.

In contrast, she argues, as more and more women became "public lesbians," expectations of what women could expect from one another escalated. Lesbians speaking publicly (even in as protected a space as a living room) were taken to be speaking for all lesbians rather than on behalf of themselves. The women had come looking for support and validation of their own lives; deviation from the way they defined their lives was seen as a threat to the most intimate, vulnerable parts of their identity. Differences in this miniature lesbian community were read as betrayal rather than as confirmation of a healthy diversity. Rule goes on to say: "The conflicts that I saw in my living room are also being played out in the larger public world" (*Outlander* 175). She cites public lesbians such as Robin Morgan, Jill Johnston, and Kate Millett, who were repeatedly discredited for being "politically incorrect" according to an ever-changing set of understandings about how a "real" lesbian should be, look, think, act in the world. Even as the very notion of "lesbian community" was made possible through a political and social movement, the dangers of having the community turn into a "mini-enforcer" were already evident to Rule in the early 1970s.

In the second seminar, Rule experienced an entirely different atmosphere. A smaller group of women were involved, but they, too, had their differences. Their attention, however, was focused on texts rather than on one another. The same sort of judgment might have occurred, however, with readers condemning writers who didn't create lesbian stories that confirmed their own lives in their own terms. Instead, Rule urged them to consider each writer in her particular historical, social, and literary context. The women in the seminar were free to be critical and amused, maddened and delighted by what they were learning from writers such as Gertrude Stein, Radclyffe Hall, Margaret Anderson, and May Sarton. Rule suggests that these women considered the writers they were studying as individual people rather than as advocates or representatives. The writers needn't stand for all lesbian identity but, rather, provide a means for thinking about living and writing as a lesbian in specific times and places. Rule isn't arguing here for uncritical individualism instead of political consciousness. Rather, she is making a case for what Phelan calls "getting specific," trying to understand through the lives and texts of specific women the effects of power, how identities, experiences, and allegiances are organized. The women in the second seminar could establish a bond with the writers they were reading that the women in the first seminar failed to establish with one another: a bond that acknowledged rather than suppressed differences. Fictional texts created not only a mediating buffer, but a complex landscape marked by contradictions, ambiguities, multiple possibilities. Each reader approached these texts in solitude, but together they created meaningful connections not only with the writers but with one another.

Having suggested the dangers inherent in expecting support based on assumed sameness in "With All Due Respect," she explores further the potential tyranny of community in "Stumps." "Stumps" was written for Rule's column, "So's Your Grandmother," in the July 1979 issue of *The Body Politic* (also included in *Outlander*). She contrasts the insular but heterogeneous community of Galiano Island, in which disagreements are expected and cooperation is elicited when shared needs (a volunteer fire department, a community hall) require it, with communities based on sameness (of profession or identity, for example). She says: "All communities are . . . enemy territory for the individual, even those which profess concern for consensus, because none can accommodate comfortably all that anyone is. This community [Galiano] doesn't even try" (187).

She begins the essay by saying that the CBC wanted to portray Galiano as an artists' colony and that rumor had it in San Francisco that Galiano should be renamed Lesbos. Rule's response is: "If I ever did find myself in an artists' colony or lesbian community, I'd move" (187). Rule explains the vehemence of her response by turning to an anecdote from her childhood. Having moved frequently, Rule knew not only that community values change dramatically from place to place, but that to "belong" one needs not only to identify with the local group, but to participate in shunning those who don't meet the local criteria of acceptability. Group identity is forged by exclusion; initiation requires that the new member show solidarity by rejecting an unacceptable candidate. Again, Rule is not arguing for rampant individualism and the privileged protection of island solitude. Rather, she argues for "an environment in political balance" (188). What she means by that is an environment in which people with different and even competing social and political identities can coexist. Coexistence, however, must be informed. She argues that "political balance" can't be founded on denial or ignorance. Rule insists that visibility (in her case, visibility as a lesbian and as a writer on an island where some people despise lesbians and others disdain writers) is necessary to disrupt ignorance. She writes: "Nothing as simple as a parade will change their minds. Only when a community knows that everywhere in all circumstances it is shared by gay people does it learn, as San Francisco has, that it must accept us as part of the political reality" (189).

The various kinds of community described in these two essays and the intense conflicts between communities and individuals that Rule begins to identify here in an expository mode are explored in many of her fictions. Her fiction, in contrast to the essays, doesn't make an argument but creates a landscape in which the reader can examine how identities and communities shape each other, how power is exercised both bluntly by the state and more subtly in the intricate intimacies of everyday life.

Quarrelsome Communities: *Contract with the World*

Rule started to think about the material that would become *Contract with the World* as early as 1975, when she considered writing about "a central woman character who is a portrait painter" (box 37, folder 3), a character, we may recall, who resonates with one of the defining stories of her adolescence. A year later she had come up with the title and the idea that she would write about "six characters in search of a psychiatrist" (box 37, folder 3). It wasn't until the end of 1977, after the publication of *The Young in One Another's Arms,* that she started work on the new novel in earnest; she completed the draft on July 15, 1978, the revisions for her editor by fall 1979, and it was published by Harcourt Brace Jo-vanavich in September 1980.

During these same years she became involved in lesbian and gay politics. She wrote a review essay (the first of many) called "Private Parts" on books about Carson McCullers, Amy Lowell, and George Sand for *The Body Politic* in June 1976, and a provocative essay for the paper called "Teaching Sexuality" in June 1979 that anticipated the regular column, "So's Your Grandmother." By the time *The Body Politic* folded in 1984, Rule had contributed to 52 of the 135 issues published. While she had contributed book reviews and stories to lesbian and gay periodicals such as *The Ladder, Conditions, Branching Out, Lesbian Tide, Christopher Street,* and *Sinister Wisdom* since the late 1960s, her columns for *The Body Politic* established her as an essayist and as a controversial figure in lesbian and gay politics: a lesbian and a feminist who willingly wrote for the predominantly male readership of the paper. Many of the essays she wrote for "So's Your Grandmother" have been collected in *Outlander* (1981) and *A Hot-Eyed Moderate* (1985). Her involvement with *The Body Politic,* including the beginning of a lifelong correspondence and friendship with Rick Bébout, one of the editors, made her more aware of the public and private conflicts that were defining the "gay and lesbian community" even as she entered into them.

Contract with the World is the first novel in which gay and lesbian politics enter into the story as a theme, as well as through references to *The Body Politic* and other periodicals. As Rule anticipated in a "So's Your Grandmother" column called "Reflections," which ran just before the publication of *Contract with the World,* the novel itself stirred up a controversy about the role of lesbian writers in the now very active and vocal lesbian and gay community in North America. The reactions of some activists illustrate very well Rule's tendency to push against limits whether they are dictated by mainstream culture or subcultures that contest the mainstream and with which she is identified. Perhaps more important, the novel itself, in its characterizations and multiple narrative lines, stages the problems that "communities" present to the people who move in and out of them by chance or by choice.

Contract with the World started out as two novels: one about artists and the other about a group of people who are all the same age. Rule wanted to write a book about artists to explore myths and realities about creativity, reception, and commercialism in contemporary North American art. For one thing, she wanted to consider what motivates artists to create, what constitutes an artistic temperament:

> I wanted to say that there is some very fine art that's motivated by pure fury and hatred . . . it goes back to Dante and the notion that inspiration and vision come out of good places—they can do, but often they don't. Often the urge is revenge, the urge is greed. And then also, the sense of how urgent it is to do it. To take a character like Alma, who's not going to do anything, because it's not important to her. There's nothing driving her.[1]

Rule also wanted to dramatize the situation of young artists in a provincial city, far from the centers of power where tastes are shaped and where gallery owners, buyers, agents, and exhibitions or concerts can make a career. She wanted to consider the personal and creative challenges to artists who haven't yet been accepted, who are under pressure by parents, lovers, spouses, and friends to "grow up." A group of artists, rather than a single character, would allow her to explore artists working in different media, the relations among them, and their interactions with others. She wanted to put her characters "in the places of their hardest dilemmas to see how they shape their lives either to be defeated by them or to learn to carry them or to solve them" (Interview I).

The other novel she had in mind was about a group of people in the same age cohort:

> I've always felt this was an awful trap of education that you spend so much of your formative years with your peers, trapped in an age group. . . . And it's always seemed to me that people of the same age are less likely to be sympathetic to each other because they're dealing with a lot of the same anxieties and pressures . . . the support they get from each other is not without its difficulties. (Interview I)

In both cases, the novel about artists and the novel about people the same age, one of the underlying issues is community defined by same-

---

1. Unpublished interview with the author, June 25, 1994, Galiano Island. Subsequent references will be noted as Interview I. Another interview, July 1995 on Galiano Island, will be noted as Interview II.

ness—of profession, of age, of geography. Far from taking a utopian view of community, Rule wanted to explore the dilemmas and difficulties such associations pose for individuals and how they define themselves against the larger social world.

Contract with the World is often linked with *The Young in One Another's Arms* because they are both "Vancouver" novels, and each examines the relations among a group of people who test social conventions and one another. The narrative shapes of the novels, however, are very different; each establishes a different kind of relationship with the reader. The point of view that determines the reader's access to the narrative in *The Young in One Another's Arms* is Ruth Wheeler's, framed and directed, as is the case in all of Rule's novels, by an invisible narrating presence. In *Contract with the World*, Rule perfected a narrative form that she had experimented with in *Against the Season*. She tells the story through six different points of view, in sequence, so that the reader is forced to perceive events and relationships from within the perspective of each of the main characters, some of whom are sympathetic and some of whom are not. Rule has said that some readers love *The Young in One Another's Arms* and hate *Contract with the World*; others, particularly artists, have told her that *Contract with the World* creates a realistic group portrait of the difficulties facing young artists. Rule has described the different reception of the two books in the following way:

> You're never inside the heads of anybody in *The Young in One Another's Arms*. You have a mother figure saying: Love these children. And so you do . . . she is interpreting the whole thing, and you hear them talking. But the loving concern is there as a tone in the book. And in *Contract* there is no mother saying: You have to love these people. You're inside their heads, so you hear all of the mean things, and all of the scary things. You don't get any of that from the characters in *The Young*. (Interview II)

As Rule's correspondence with her editor shows, the final narrative form presented a number of problems. She needed to clarify the passage of time as narrative perspective shifted from one character to another, and she needed to clarify some of the local references (to Canadian artists, to Vancouver neighborhoods) for American readers. More important, the editor, anticipating other readers, was challenged by the shifts in perspective: alternately seduced and repulsed by the central characters, resisting contradictory interpretations of the same event as experienced by different characters. And yet this type of engagement and interaction between the reader and the text was precisely what Rule sought to achieve. Rather than reassure the reader, lull her into a complacent (or triumphal) sense that she had arrived at the right interpretation, that the author is endorsing ways of being in the world that the reader approves, the narrative form requires the reader (particularly a feminist and/or lesbian reader, but also—for different reasons—heterosexual, male, and/or middle-class readers) to inhabit points of view that are antithetical to the ways she or he might want to be in the world. Because of the multiple points of view and the unseen narrator's shifting sympathies among them, no reader will be entirely "at home" in the text any more than she or he would be "at home" in any community.

Contract with the World is divided into six chapters of roughly equivalent length: "Joseph Walking," "Mike Hanging," "Alma Writing," "Roxanne Recording," "Allen Mourning," and "Carlotta Painting." All but Alma's chapter (which is written in the first person) are written in the third person, but within the sensibility of the title character. The first chapter, using flashback to the time when Joseph was twenty-five, covers about four years in the early 1970s, though the precise dates are never specified in the text. Each of the other chapters advances the narrative about one year so that the book ends at a moment roughly contemporary with the date of publication. One of the devices Rule uses to mark the passage of time is birthdays. By the middle of the first chapter, Alma is celebrating her thirtieth birthday, followed by Mike and Joseph at the very end. By the end of the novel, the six main characters are about thirty-five. The passage from youth to early middle age (which, typically, begins early in life for Rule's characters) presents crises in different degrees for each character.

Contract with the World begins with Joseph, who is presented as a craftsman; he teaches shop, works with a printing press, and, in the view of some of the characters, has an artist's temperament but not the ambition or sense of self-importance that would lead him to become an artist. In a move contrary to portrayals of heterosexual men current among lesbian feminists in the 1970s, Joseph is presented as self-effacing, porous in the presence of other personalities. He's a substitute, a stand-in whose words are words learned from his mother—fragments of verse, poems, and songs. He is a fragile vessel: the world, light, life, joy and pain instantly rush to assume the space he occupies, sending him reeling into madness, otherness, and alienation:

> To be an insignificant man in an insignificant place who could carry such ordinary responsibilities as a job and a mortgage was for Joseph a protective coloring that kept him out of the eye of the eagle, for he had no desire to be claimed for a heroic or melodramatic death in service of his country or his own imagination. But insignificance did not keep him from being a man hunted by songbirds and flowers. (26)

To control his manic responses to the world, Joseph takes long walks through the city, mapping Vancouver for the reader and gradually connecting the six main characters to one another.

At the other end of heterosexual masculinity, Mike is presented as a sculptor from a working-class background who has to support his family by working as a bouncer. In his art and sexuality, Mike recalls Oscar in the short story "Dulce." Mike is as aggressive with his wife, Alma, as he is with the materials he shapes into artistic form. He also has definite ideas about what art should be ("form rescued from usefulness") and what a husband and father should be (a provider and protector). Rule wrote in her notebook as she was writing the novel: "His love making is tangled with his sculpting, 'knowing' what's inside the stone/wood/bone; so, when his wife won't come, it is a terrible defeat to his art" (box 37, folder 3). For Mike, making love is very close to rape; in one scene with Carlotta he crosses the line. In response to her editor who had trouble reconciling Mike's and Carlotta's contrasting views of this scene, Rule wrote: "Mike sees himself conquering Carlotta; she sees the rape as the one time he wanted her more than she wanted him. (I think they're both nuts)" (box 6, folder 3). In spite of his loud proclamations, Mike fails as a sculptor and as a father in the terms that he set for himself, terms that are clichés of artistic discourse and of mainstream masculinity. The only sculpture that succeeds in any sense does so when it *becomes* useful as a jungle gym in the backyard of his friend Joseph's children. Mike's wife, Alma, is lavishly supported by her wealthy parents and is indifferent to Mike's sexual energies. In a moment of melodramatic despair over his unhappy marriage and failed art, Mike hangs himself in effigy. At the end of his chapter, Mike leaves Canada for the American Southwest, where he re-makes himself as a successful businessman, selling mobile homes with his brother.

After Mike leaves her, Alma discovers lesbian desire in an affair with Roxanne. Her chapter, as I discussed in chapter 2, dramatizes the dilemma of the lesbian writer searching for a language adequate to her desire. Like Mike, however, she is a failure. As Rule said, her urgency to write is insufficient. Likewise, her need for the continuing approval (and privileges) of her family make it impossible for her to live visibly and un-apologetically as a lesbian. Living for a time in her parents' house after her divorce and then in a house bought for her by her parents, Alma never moves beyond a self-indulgent, infantilized, or narcissistic lesbian sexuality. For example, describing an evening when Roxanne joins her for dinner at her parents' house, Alma writes:

> We could have been back in grade school, Mother asking me to take Rox-anne to my room to leave her coat and even play awhile before dinner, which we did until the boys [her sons] banged on my door like obnoxious little brothers, and Roxanne tumbled into the living room like one of them. I think Dad was on the brink of offering her a Shirley Temple when I told him she likes scotch on the rocks. (142)

Roxanne is one of the few successful artists in the novel. Raised in fos-ter homes, indifferent to the values and restrictions of middle-class morality, she is a composer who creates "sound maps." She does this by attending to the full range of sound, recording sounds with minute pre-cision at different places in the house and in the city; no sound is in-significant:

> Roxanne was making a sound map of the house. What other people might have fixed, a dripping tap or squeaking hinge, she listened to. What other people blanked out—the refrigerator or furnace going on, a plane passing overhead—she heard. She was interested in the difference in tone between eggshells and chicken bones in the garbage disposal. She compared the re-filling times of the two toilets. She recorded the boys' feet up and down the stairs, in and out of the house, and she asked them to spend one rainy afternoon doing nothing but sitting down over and over on different pieces of living room furniture. (181)

She gets the idea to create a sound map of Vancouver, which she represents visually on a wall in Alma's house. Her method is a careful hyperrealism, capturing each detail in its precise reality and then creating a composition that is her own vision of the city. She has trouble trying to explain to people (Allen, a gallery owner, her friends) what it is she is trying to accomplish with her art. Allen, a photographer, has, more than any of the other characters, a reputation and connections outside of Vancouver. Because he recognizes that Roxanne's talent deserves support, Allen helps her present a public concert in order to become eligible for a grant. But the review in the *Vancouver Sun* bears the headline, "Yet to Find Her Audience" (227); the provincial city can't see itself reflected in her sound maps. Eventually Roxanne leaves Vancouver for California, where she finds a language to articulate her vision and a community to understand it. When Roxanne returns to Vancouver in the last chapter, she is energized by the creative world in California, though Carlotta is impatient with the language she has learned to explain her art. She says: "'Everyone there [in California] is doing things, and there's money— not government money, private money, because people really are interested, really believe in the importance of what we're doing. . . .' The greater length of telling, some several hours, was exactly what Carlotta had expected and dreaded. Roxanne had discovered the vocabulary for what she did" (332–33).

The other artist in the book who achieves recognition beyond Vancouver—and therefore recognition *in* Vancouver—is Allen himself. At the beginning of the book his success is commercial and he adopts a glib attitude toward himself and his art: "He called himself vanity's pimp, a political window dresser, a voyeur, a camera for hire" (8). Privileged by looks, background, and class status, Allen circulates among the powerful and reflects them back to themselves as they want to be seen. Allen is carefully closeted, keeping a younger man, Pierre, as a "boy wife" and accompanying women to public events to create the illusion of heterosexual acceptability. In many ways he resembles Alma—his social privilege and sense of entitlement insulate him from the consequences of homosexual visibility, but they also dull his drive to produce anything more ambitious than his photographs for hire. His illusion of safety begins to shatter when the police raid a private party in Toronto. Alma's young son, Tony, shows the newspaper to Roxanne:

Roxanne saw the headline, "Pederasts' Party Over," and took the paper from Tony to read about the vice squad breaking into the apartment of a prominent Toronto businessman to find a number of men in the company of boys as young as twelve. An MP and a college professor were named. So was Allen Dent, one of Canada's best-known photographers, who had attempted with his camera to jump out a twelfth-floor window before he was apprehended and taken into custody. (229)

Once again in Rule's fiction, domestic space is revealed as fragile, the walls of privacy no protection against police surveillance and invasion. At the same time, she shows the "capillary reach" of power in the way that Allen defines himself and, in this instance, attempts to align himself with dominant lines of power. Once caught in the "justice" system, Allen thinks that he can use his professional status to distance himself from the raid even as he has distanced himself from gay visibility and other forms of engagement with the world that would challenge the role he constructed for himself. He colludes with the police in order to save his own skin:

After the initial shock, the sense of somehow mistakenly being caught in the flash of his own camera, Allen had been cool enough, convincing himself as well as his lawyer and then the judge that his presence at the party had been professional, that he had not known ahead of time what kind of party it would be. He did not say his intention would have been to get evidence to turn over to the police, but he didn't stop his lawyer from indicating that might have been his natural course. The photographs were already in police hands. Allen's sharing in the guilt would do nothing to help his host, who had obviously been set up by one enemy or another. Charges against Allen and several others were dropped. (237)

What Allen doesn't know is that the violence of the invasion has already entered his own home; Pierre, having seen the media coverage, has shot himself. After a period of social and emotional paralysis, Allen decides to take his revenge through art. He prepares a retrospective of his work designed to expose by association many of the powerful closeted men he had photographed by exhibiting their portraits side by side with photographs of publicly acknowledged gay men. Pictures of Pierre would be scattered throughout, a final public testimony to his love. The show ultimately transforms Allen from a mere photographer into an artist. In Toronto, the *Globe and Mail* publishes a superb review of the show, which discerns the art without noticing the "outing" of powerful men that Allen had intended; the art is successful but his revenge fails. The novel poses, without resolving them, the politics of collusion, doubly complicated by Allen's efforts first to get himself off and then to expose the hypocrisy of others like him.

The last chapter, Carlotta's, brings the main characters together through another exhibit and poses problems of the politics of art in another way. Carlotta has painted portraits of all of them and of several secondary characters associated with them, such as Joseph's wife and Pierre. Because of public support of the arts, she is able to secure exhibition space in Surrey, a conservative suburb of Vancouver and, as it happens, the town where Allen grew up. When the exhibit opens, the townspeople attack it, prompted by two sexual transgressions. The first is Allen's exposure as a homosexual, not to be forgiven by his conservative hometown. Carlotta's portraits of him and of his lover Pierre are in the show. The second involves Carlotta directly. Needing money and seeking anonymous sex, Carlotta had turned a trick in a downtown luxury hotel with a man who didn't want to be discovered. He is also among the angry crowd, accusing her of being a whore because she is an artist, absolving his own hypocrisy by his accusation. The crowd turns into "one great beast" (336), throws red paint on the portraits, and physically attacks Carlotta, Joseph, Mike, Alma, Roxanne, Allen, and their friends and family. Allen responds with a stunned admiration that art matters so much to these people whom he had disdained. Carlotta recognizes that her portraits represent a vision and a moment that can't be repeated. She could never exactly replicate the portraits in her doomed exhibit because her subjects continue to grow and change in ways that exceed the vision she had captured once on canvas.

Allen's and Carlotta's chapters explore the politics of art and sexuality, particularly the stakes that communities and individuals have in each other. Allen succeeds critically as an artist, because the official arbiters of taste have noticed and praised his work; the political vision he intended, however, was lost in the process. Allen recognizes, ironically, that Carlotta has succeeded to move people deeply with her art because the community (corrupt and self-serving as it is) takes her subjects and her representations seriously. Carlotta's work is destroyed precisely because the crowd would not allow her art to be removed from its meanings for the community. Before Pierre's death, when Allen reflected back images that socially prominent figures wanted to see, he failed as an artist, he was— in his own eyes—a commercial but not an artistic success. When he made more of his work and took revenge on his subjects, he succeeded with the critics, though his intended "message" was lost. At the end of the novel, it is not the crowd that is punished for destroying Carlotta's work, but Carlotta and her "subjects." They are taken away in a police wagon, having been identified as the disrupters of public comfort and order. In the course of the novel, Carlotta moves from a morbid fascination with self-portrait to a more complicated vision of others when she decides to do the portraits of her friends. She is presented as an intensely private artist, creating in the cold solitude of her studio. And yet her art matters (and is destroyed) because it exists in a context, is displayed in a community that can't bear to admit—even on canvas—people who undermine their values.

Seen in this light, there is special irony in the reception of *Contract with the World*. Rule had anticipated problems in "Reflections," published in the September 1980 issue of *The Body Politic* (and reprinted in *Outlander*):

> At the time a new novel is about to come out, I am always more aware of those inevitably disappointed people who want literature to be not only a mirror, but a flattering mirror of themselves and their way of life. . . . I do understand the appetite in the gay community for art which can celebrate, but too often that desire gets translated into a need for narrowly correct propaganda for one lifestyle or another. Any writer who tries to please such an audience is doomed to failure, because within the gay community there are not only different but morally and politically conflicting tastes.

The column goes on to say that "a good writer is not in the business of propaganda." She recognizes in the essay the difficulties of gays and other minorities who have been deprived of positive reflections in literature or, worse, erased completely. But she argues emphatically that an exclusive diet of heroic gay and lesbian characters and happy endings isn't necessarily in the best interests of the community. She concludes by playing on a "mirror mirror on the wall" allusion she used early in the essay:

I will not apologize for us. . . . I will not even give us my exclusive attention. I will bring to us, as I do to each of my characters, all the tenderness,
severity, and humour I can command to show us making our various contracts with the world. My mirror is never a bad joke. In it, if you will look
with compassion, amusement, and hope, you will find that your image is
fair.

In October, a month later, Karla Jay reviewed *Contract with the World*
in Boston's *Gay Community News*. In the beginning of the review, Jay
praises Rule's "fine narrative hand," but when she turns to an analysis of
the politics in the novel, she states that "many (probably most) lesbians
are going to find the characters in this book not only *politically incorrect*,
but distasteful as well" (emphasis added). Jay considers Rule's essay "Reflections" to be a prepublication apologia for the book, but is not per-
suaded by Rule's arguments. In fact, she says that *Contract with the
World* can't be called a lesbian novel because the first two sections focus
on "unrepentantly heterosexual males," and that there is little homo-
erotic content in the book to appeal to lesbians. She concludes by calling
it a "heterosexually dominated novel" and says that Rule's freedom to
create may collide with the freedom of lesbian readers not to buy. Rule
was stung by this review; she and Jay had known each other for years,
Rule had contributed essays to anthologies Jay had edited, and she recognized Jay's power in the U.S. lesbian community, a significant part of
her readership. In an open letter to Karla Jay that was apparently never
published, she called the review "a political prosecution" that distorted
the novel and misled potential readers (box 19, folder 9a).

Today, nearly twenty years after Jay's review of *Contract with the
World*, when the term "politically correct" has become a blunt weapon
in the hands of the cultural *arrière-garde* and lesbian and gay politics and
culture have evolved, it is useful to return to some of the terms of this argument and ask again: is this a lesbian novel and if so, how? Jay, along
with many reviewers and critics at that time, focused on the representation of politics *in* the novel rather than on the politics *of* the novel, that
is, the ways in which the novel engages the reader in an interrogation of
power, about how power works in explicit and implicit ways to shape personalities and social groups. Among other things that Rule objected to
in Jay's reading was that she said "Roxanne, the only one hundred per-

cent lesbian, heads for Los Angeles and disappears from the book." Roxanne may be "the only one hundred percent lesbian in the book," but more significantly for my reading, she is also one of the two characters whose success as an artist is recognized by the critical establishment. Roxanne expresses an artistic vision that both reflects and tests her community. She is very much present in the first five chapters of the book, and, like some of the other characters who slip into secondary roles when other characters are the center of attention, she returns for the final scene. Roxanne distinguishes herself as an artist in the novel by inventing a method of composing, what I've been calling hyperrealism, that captures in minute and accurate detail fragments of the world around her. She then arranges those fragments in a composition that forces the listener to hear differently, to reconsider the quotidian, the mundane, and the familiar. Roxanne's art refuses to idealize the world around her or to sanitize it by omitting details that might offend some people. In fact, she intentionally upsets conventions of taste and politeness; to return to Shane Phelan's definition of "getting specific," Roxanne's methods call "into question the field(s) that organize experience and meaning, problematiz[e] the identities and allegiances that we have come to take for granted" (16).

Roxanne's sound map can be read as a metaphor for Rule's narrative method in *Contract with the World*. Rule, like Roxanne, takes carefully and precisely observed details from the world around her and arranges them in a composition that forces the readers to reconsider themselves and their relation to the world. Like Roxanne, Rule refuses to sanitize her fictional world by excising elements that might be considered offensive to some readers, such as a homosexual who colludes with police repression, a woman who confuses rape with desire, a bluntly heterosexual male character who is abusive in his relations with women. She invents a suggestive social and sexual landscape; she doesn't make an argument. It is the conflicts and differences, the contradictions in ways of seeing the world that interest the novelist even as Roxanne is fascinated by sounds whether they are conventionally beautiful or not. The only clear and final resolution to differences, the ending of *Contract with the World* suggests, is the unthinking imposition of brute force.

Contract with the World, like Roxanne's sound map, is not without values. Just as Roxanne orchestrates her recordings to create a certain

vision of urban life (complex, clashing, fragmented), Rule, through
the narrating presence that orchestrates the six separate points of view,
gives her fictional landscape a distinctly lesbian foundation. Unlike
conventional realist novels, the narrative structure of *Contract with the
World* as expressed through the sequence of events, the ways in which
characters are punished or rewarded, patterns of success and failure,
uses of images and metaphor, assumes that homophobia is a social evil
and that female sexual desire is not determined by male sexuality. As in
Against the Season and *The Young in One Another's Arms*, the orchestrating narrator of *Contract with the World* assumes the legitimacy of
lesbian and gay desire without idealizing it. Alma, who is not sympa-
thetically portrayed, fails at it; Carlotta experiments with it; for Roxanne, it is a way to live. In the plotting of the novel, Allen is punished
for his glib entitlement and his failure to understand his connection to
public gays whom he disdains. His revenge by "outing" gay men and
lesbians is not condoned or condemned in the novel but is presented
as a moral dilemma to be engaged.

The fundamental shift in narrative structure (from an assumption of
male-defined heterosexuality to an assumption of multiple sexual possibilities) allows Rule to develop characters that are not judged by their
sexuality but by other aspects of their character. Because lesbian and gay
sexuality (and heterosexuality) are neutralized as categories of moral
judgment, Rule can explore unsympathetic as well as sympathetic lesbian
characters. More importantly, she can extend the possible meanings of
sexual identities beyond the immediate needs of the lesbian community
as it existed in 1980. Fiction, as I said earlier, provides a means for en-
gaging contradictions and conflicts that expository prose (whether political or theoretical) can't encompass. In "Imitation and Gender Insubordination," Judith Butler argues that the sign "lesbian" should be understood as strategic and provisional rather than as an identity that is fully
knowable:

> If the rendering visible of lesbian/gay identity now presupposes a set of ex-
> clusions, then perhaps part of what is necessarily excluded is *the future uses
> of the sign*. There is a political necessity to use some sign now, and we do,
> but how to use it in such a way that its future significations are not *fore-*

closed? . . . In avowing the sign's strategic provisionality (rather than its strategic essentialism), that identity can become a site of contest and revision, indeed, take on a future set of significations that those of us who use it now may not be able to foresee. (19)

Rule's fictions, her use of precisely observed realistic detail within a frame that assumes the legitimacy of lesbian desire, are located in a specific political moment but leave future significations (and interpretations) of "lesbian" open.

Aside from Karla Jay's review, reviews in gay and lesbian periodicals tended to praise Rule precisely for the complexity of the novel, the way it challenges readers to rethink their own contracts with the world. Larry Goldsmith, in *The Gay Community News,* said: "By omitting a central figure from her story, Rule encourages us to concentrate not so much on characters as on the relationships between them" (February 1984, 2). He also recognized that fiction permits a more subtle examination of political issues than is possible in political essays: "If the writers of political essays sometimes neglect the subtleties, those ordinary details that make the difference between theory and life, a novelist can focus on them, elaborate and transform them, and help us imagine them. . . . Jane Rule does so remarkably well." Jim Marks, in the *Washington Blade* (October 24, 1980, B-9), wrote: "*Contract* is a Gay novel with a message, the manner of its telling enhancing the meaning of the tale. The technique enables Rule, particularly in the opening chapters where two straight characters hold the stage, to escape the ghetto, to see Gay life in relationship to the world and to offer straight readers a means of access to her story."

Many reviews in mainstream periodicals show that straight reviewers were far from thinking that *Contract with the World* is a "heterosexually dominated novel." While many of the reviews in the mainstream press were positive, for some the presence of lesbian and gay characters and, I would argue, the shift from assumed heterosexuality to a lesbian narrating presence was too threatening. *Kirkus*, never kind to Rule, characterized the novel as "the dank ruminations of an erratic writer . . . who often wildly overestimates the interest-level of sexually troubled souls airing their *relationships*" (July 15, 1981). A reviewer in the *Kamloops News* wrote:

[*Contract with the World*] is unquestionably well-written in the technical sense, but a novel dealing with lesbianism needs more than an elegant style to make it into the marketplace in Canada in the year of our Lord 1980.

I read the book from start to finish, even though I found it boring. . . . What I am questioning is whether or not a book devoted entirely to this subject should expect very wide appeal. (Box 33, folder 3, n.d.)

In contrast, Rita Mae Brown wrote a letter to Rule's editor at Harcourt Brace Jovanavitch saying that she enjoyed the novel: "Jane Rule should never lack for contracts with publishers or contacts with readers. She is a precise writer and this is a mature, deeply moral book" (box 33, folder 3).

Nine years after Rule created the fractious urban community in *Contract*, she published *After the Fire*. In this, her last novel, she creates a rural fictional community based on her experience of Galiano Island that recalls the community described in "Stumps."

Alone, Together: *After the Fire*

In the cemetery on Galiano Island, a short walk from the home of Jane Rule and Helen Sonthoff, two worn headstones are inscribed with Japanese characters. On one of them the English word "Japanese" is engraved at the top. The stones bear silent (and to the eyes of most visitors to the island, indecipherable) witness to the historical presence of Japanese fishermen who made the island their home until the Canadian government forcibly moved West Coast Canadians of Japanese ancestry far inland to the Kootenays during World War II. Karen Tasuki, a lesbian nearly thirty years old and one of the three central characters in *After the Fire*, looks to such a headstone to try to find her connection to the past, to family, to ethnic history, and to the island she has chosen as a place to learn to live alone. Daughter of a white mother and a thoroughly assimilated Japanese-Canadian father, Karen can't read the inscription but uses the stone as a screen to project her imagined history and to claim her place on the island. She says that the grave is her great-grandfather's. She realizes that claiming the grave is at once legitimate and a lie. Her great-grandfather was a fisherman who lived on one of the Gulf Islands, but she doesn't know if he lived on this island or if he is buried in this particular grave. Looking for personal definition in the past is both necessary and insufficient, true and false, fact and fiction, a recovery of the past and an invention of the present.

After the Fire is Jane Rule's last novel, published in 1989 by Naiad in the United States and Macmillan in Canada. She started thinking about the novel as early as 1978 when she jotted down some notes for a possible story to be called "Living Alone—A Ferry Story" (box 37, folder 3). Eight years later she considered writing a novel to be called *Alone*, about people living alone who are all touched by death or loss. In the beginning of 1988 she wrote in her notebook: "Having decided to quit on it, I can't. The energy begins to flow toward it again" (box 37, folder 4). What started as a novel about people living alone became a novel about community.

The twin themes of solitude and connection are admirably rendered by a narrative structure invented for this novel. Building on the shifting narrative perspectives of *Contract with the World*, Rule divided each chapter in *After the Fire* into three roughly equal parts: one told through Karen's consciousness, one through Henrietta Hawkins (a white woman in her sixties who becomes a widow during the novel), and one through Milly Forbes (a forty-five-year-old divorced white woman). There are breaks in the text (blanks or occasionally a line of asterisks) when the perspective changes, signaling the gaps that separate the profoundly different ways that the three characters view the world and one another. The sequence of narrative perspectives changes from chapter to chapter, moving among the three characters, not with the formal regularity of a rondeau, but in an interweaving pattern that gives each of the characters an important place in the ongoing story. As in Rule's other novels, an invisible narrative presence orchestrates the text. Here that presence is marked by the gaps that separate the three centers of consciousness, by the sequences set up in each chapter and by the sympathy or alienation the reader experiences in relation to the three main characters. The narrative structure is both discontinuous and sequential, creating for the reader an immediate sense of the psychological separation and social connection experienced by the characters.

The story moves forward chronologically from January or February to August of one year, marked in indirect ways as the late 1980s. The

specific historic moment is less important than in some other novels because island life removes many of the trappings of the late twentieth century. Conditions on the island distill life to basic elements; a phone, a car,
an adequate well, and electricity are not taken for granted by the permanent residents, some of whom have to live without them. To focus the
novel, Rule chose to develop only women characters who live alone. Significantly, however, if men are physically absent, they are virtually present. Each of the major women characters is inhabited by the voices of
men who define to some degree who they are—husbands, fathers, sons,
friends. Henrietta constantly refers in her mind to her absent husband,
Hart, removed physically and mentally after he is taken to a hospital in
Vancouver after a severe stroke; Milly rages internally at her ex-husband
and seeks to prove her continuing appeal to men to counter his rejection
of her. Karen hears her father's voice telling her how to act, what to as-
pire to, how to be a successful Canadian. Part of the women's struggle is
to exorcise or contain those masculine voices, not to be abject to their
power. In addition to the three characters whose perspectives shape the
narrative, there are two other important characters—Red, an eighteen-
year-old white woman without family ties (her mother is in jail and her
father is unknown) who has chosen to be a single mother, and Miss
James, a white woman in her eighties who, for unspecified reasons, chose
to disinherit herself from her wealthy, powerful Virginia father to lead a
life independent of sustained intimate relationships with men or with
women.

Like the house in *Against the Season* or "A Television Drama," the island in *After the Fire* is not cut off from the outside world, but is traversed by people and histories that leave different kinds of traces. There
are permanent residents whose families have lived there for generations,
former residents (like the Japanese fishermen) who were removed, current residents who started out as weekend people or vacationers but who
have (willingly or not) made the island their home, and temporary residents like Karen whose presence is not superficial like the tourists. She
tries to be part of the community by volunteering in the fire department
and by working at the ferry. She will move on having left a part of her
story behind and having taken something from the island with her. Similarly, the three narrative centers are not autonomous, self-contained,
separate in their solitude. The walls of their psyches are porous, often

fragile. Each of the three women inhabits the past as well as the present, has internal dialogues with the absent and the dead, is inhibited or enabled by the imagined or projected presence of others in their psychic and emotional lives.

After the Fire, with its dual narrative focus on subjectivities and communities, provides a potential corrective to recent criticism of postmodern theorizing. It is useful to consider the novel alongside Biddy Martin's critique of discourse theory. She identifies:

> the excesses of what has been called postmodern or discourse theory, especially the thin language of subject positions, and with critiques of "the subject" that evacuate interiority altogether, as though the process of subjectification created normalcy without remainders. Defining psychic life too exclusively in terms of normalization makes apparently "normal" subjects into realizations of norms and putatively "queer" subjects into subversives simply for their failure to take up a proper place in a heteronormative order. All this suggests too direct a relationship between "discourse" or "discursive mechanisms" and psychic lives. (*Femininity* 15)

Psychic lives, Martin is suggesting, are more complex and contradictory than discourse analysis alone can account for. The psyche can simultaneously conform to sexual and gender norms and fail to conform. Further, norms of gender and sexuality are not entirely consistent or without their own internal contradictions. Shane Phelan approaches the same territory from the point of view of a political theorist dissatisfied with postmodern efforts to theorize difference. She points to the need for another thematic to complicate discussions of difference:

> This thematic centers around the replacement of grand narratives not with new narratives of eternal difference or Rorty's pluralist equivalent, but with what Foucault has labeled "subjugated knowledges." The emergence of these subjugated knowledges entails the rejection of grand, total theory in favor of local, specific theories—theories that do not aim at tying all the strands of life and history into one knot but rather try to locate each of us as the concrete embodiment of overlapping networks of power. (*Getting Specific* xvi)

Each of the three narrating subjects in *After the Fire* performs or tests the "heteronormative order" as Martin uses the term. Each represents a different way of enforcing, enacting or contesting normative femininity, whether the norm is defined by the heterosexual majority (as for Milly and Henrietta) or by a lesbian community (as for Karen). The apparently normal subjects, Milly and Henrietta, fail to realize norms of heterosexual femininity and, to a degree, lay bare the stresses and contradictions inherent in those norms for women. They both experience failure as wives and mothers, though in very different ways. The primary lesbian subject in the book, Karen, is an outsider to the heterosexual world *and* to the lesbian community she knew in Vancouver. There is no overarching model for feminine normativity in the novel, but, rather, overlapping and contradictory narratives of gender that shape each narrating subject and that are, in turn, shaped by narratives of sexuality, race, ethnicity, and citizenship. None of the narrating subjects is transparent, easily or adequately explained by "discursive mechanisms." The narrating characters embody, as Phelan would say, "overlapping networks of power," complicating any effort to explain or interpret them with a single theoretical model. They present the reader with complex psychic lives that are marked by networks of power but not reducible to them. The presence of three different narrating subjects unsettles familiar interpretive and identificatory reading strategies. The reader can't easily discount the blatantly racist character (Milly) or identify comfortably with the lesbian who is the target of that racism (Karen). The text challenges the reader to engage the contradictions posed by the multiple narrative perspectives and to consider the ways in which each primary character exceeds understandings of what it means to be a woman. They embody, to return to Martin's terminology, psychic lives with remainders.

After the Fire begins with a community catastrophe: "Fire had bloomed into the winter night before the fire truck could get there, skidding through the slush, spewing out mud from the deep potholes of the dirt road" (1). Through the efforts of the volunteer fire fighters (including Karen), the fire is contained to one house, but they are too late to save the life of Dickie John, the young man who had built the house and lived in it. Community ceremonies occasioned by personal loss mark the beginning, the middle, and the end of the novel. After Dickie's death, Henrietta organizes a funeral at which his friends are invited to commemorate his life. Toward the middle of the book, Henrietta's husband, Hart, dies, and a memorial must be arranged to scatter his ashes in the sea. At the end of the book, Miss James dies and leaves her house to Red, who isn't quite ready to accept the legacy. Red rents the house to Karen to live in for her last month on the island. Karen, just as she prepares to leave the island for a trip to Japan to learn about the language and history of some of her ancestors, organizes a community tea as a wake for Miss James and a housewarming for Red. The interwoven stories of Milly, Henrietta, and Karen play in different ways on the themes of personal loss and community connection signaled by these ceremonies. Each suffers a loss that is apparent but also endures a more private pain, a deep shame occasioned by her sense of failure as a woman, a failure she fears others can read on her body and in her face.

The central question for the three main characters in *After the Fire* is "how to live alone." Each is surviving "after the fire" of a passionate relationship that had defined them. Divorce ended Milly's marriage; her husband's catastrophic illness shattered Henrietta's marriage, and the loss of children through miscarriages and accidental death unsettled Henrietta's social and personal definition as a mother. Karen has been rejected as "boring" after an eight-year relationship with Peggy, a wealthy white woman who lives in Vancouver. Their relationship mimicked some marriages in that Peggy wouldn't let Karen work, insisted that she serve her needs at home, and valued her primarily as an "exotic." The losses each character has sustained reveal and unsettle the models of femininity that had informed their self-definition. During the course of the narrative, each woman experiences another loss that brings her to a crisis of self-definition and realigns her relationship to the community. In (re)discovering how to be alone, each woman must negotiate a relationship to community that is not primarily mediated by a partner, whether the partner is a man or a woman. The three women are alike in that their relationships repeat conventional gender norms and heterosexual habits that each, in turn, finds unbearable.

Milly is the least sympathetic of the three main characters, but she displays the most wit. Her wit, often sarcastic comments at the expense of others, is used to shore up her self-respect after her divorce. Milly experiences her divorce as a wounding, personal failure. She is lucid about the performative nature of her femininity. A woman of forty-five who is able to look ten years younger through the careful use of make-up and costume, she plays for masculine approval. Her husband rejects her for a younger woman and, in her view, exiles her socially and financially to their vacation home on the island—a home not suited for year-round use. Milly experiences her loss in her body, beginning with early menopausal symptoms. She calls her husband her "late" husband because she wishes he were dead, but he continues to define who she is. She tries to prop up her injured sense of self by insisting on her race and class privilege. She disdains Karen as being too foreign and Red for living out working-class stereotypes by choosing single motherhood. Feeling that she has been discarded, Milly assumes the power to judge; she takes on the role of negative social surveillance, dismissing or condemning virtually all the other women on the island. If she has failed as a woman, all the others will be found lacking as well. In a more anonymous, urban setting her judgments wouldn't matter, but island life brings characters together and makes them dependent on one another, subject to one another's gaze.

Milly experiences shame in the imagined judgment of others; she thinks she has been found inadequate, old, no longer the ornament to her husband's virility she had been as a younger woman. Shame is internalized social judgment that undermines her sense of self. She measured her worth by the effect of her body as an object of desire, used to barter for class privilege available only through a man. The crisis that Milly undergoes in the novel is a hysterectomy, irrevocably ending any pretense to reproductive sexuality, making her a postmenopausal woman. Milly's surgery is followed by an infection that fills her with pain and causes hallucinations. Significantly, all of the judging voices she had internalized (her son's, a missing daughter's, her husband's) appear to her as actors around a stage where her body is reduced to an empty sack, filled with pain. Another daughter who has come to help her is less distinct than the absent accusers who pull her toward pain and death. Her accusers are the product of her own suffering, are her emotional projections and are, therefore, clearer to her than the daughter who is there in the room, a participant in her mother's drama, but not solely the creation of it.

When Milly comes through the operation and the infection, she has a new relationship to her aging female body; her body is no longer an antagonist:

Milly had dealt for so long with her body as an aging enemy that it was a largely forgotten experience to be aware of it simply as a servant to her consciousness. She breathed and felt her lungs at work acquiring oxygen for her blood which traveled through her veins carrying nourishing messages. For every conscious effort she made, her body carried out thousands of instructions she was not aware of. She felt amazed by it and grateful. (126–27)

She thinks back to childbirth when the child's body was the miracle and her own body, "a crude and vulnerable vehicle for life," in need of repair before her husband would make use of it again for his pleasure. Recovering from her hysterectomy, she thinks: "Now no one else's need pushed at her. She could lie and rest and let herself heal for herself" (127).

Milly's new relationship to her body helps her to establish a better relationship with her daughter, but her personal transformation doesn't erase her deeply ingrained habits of surveillance and negative judgment informed by racism, class privilege, and a fundamental misogyny. She continues to disapprove of Karen and Red, especially, as a way to maintain her own sense of superiority. Gradually she lets go of her need to disapprove, but only because her own energy is limited, and Henrietta, whose friendship she needs, warns her away from it. The narrative concludes with a recognition that Milly's judgments allowed her to vent her deep displeasure but were ineffectual at best and wounding at worst in relation to others: "The only disapproval that had done Milly any good was her own, and did she really enjoy it?" (184). Milly's character exposes the close affiliation of femininity understood as barter for privileges derived from wealthy white men, with social hatreds such as racism, homophobia, and class bias. To perform femininity in the way Milly always had, using her young body as her chief asset, inevitably leads to alienation from the aging female body and from other women, who are seen as rivals. Henrietta understands the link between Milly's wounded femininity, which is a product of misogyny, and her racism and homophobia:

The unhealed wound in Milly was humiliation, and Henrietta knew no cure for it. She was afraid it was like arthritis, which simply got worse. Physical pain was easier to be resigned to, and one never had the illusion that sharing it around might lessen it. Milly did really hope that by humiliating other people she might get some real relief. She might be abandoned by her husband, neglected by her children, but at least she was white, at least she wasn't a pervert. (69)

Just as Milly's wounding through divorce leads her to take on the role of negative social surveillance in the island community, Henrietta's loss (her husband's catastrophic stroke) confirms her benevolent role of positive surveillance, seeing to it that the community bonds together when its individual members suffer loss and pain. In this she resembles Ruth Wheeler in *The Young in One Another's Arms*. Henrietta organizes Dickie's funeral and enlists Milly to take some responsibility for it. Henrietta's character at first seems relatively easy to read. Her model for femininity is to put others first: her husband, her children, her community. Her fulfillment as a woman is invested in the nurturing of others. But just beneath the surface of her consciousness, the stresses of her investment of self in others threaten the order of her social self. Rule again uses dreams to reveal the demons of the unconscious. Henrietta tries not to doze off during the day:

> She had nothing against sleeping during the day except the dreams she had, embarrassing rather than really nightmarish. In them, she seemed to be drunk, unable to cross a room or navigate stairs without falling down, all the while trying to pretend nothing was wrong, and curiously no one else in those dreams ever did seem to notice either her embarrassment or her distress. They behaved, just as she was trying to behave, as if nothing were wrong. (49)

Inwardly, Henrietta fears being out of control, she fears embarrassment, an emotion that signals the presence of witnesses. But, like Milly, she has internalized her witnesses, she has assumed the gaze of social judgment into her self-definition. She tries also, in her inner, psychic life, to keep her husband and children alive and safe against the passage of time: "Henrietta alone was used to living in a kaleidoscope of time, her husband and children richly inhabiting her only seemingly solitary life" (143). Her memory, revitalized in solitude, provides a defense against the ravages of time, disease, and death. Her husband's stroke has destroyed his capacity for intimacy, he no longer recognizes Henrietta and is incapable of providing companionship. His primary communication with her is irritation. Her twice-weekly visits bring her back to a reality she is unable to accept:

> [H]is physical appearance always came as a shock to her, her memory having sealed over the facts and healed her image of him between visits. Wholly accepting what had happened to him and who he was now might make visiting easier, but it would rob her of his companionship in her mind for all the time she was alone. She didn't lie about his condition even to herself, but she put it out of her mind. (98–99)

When she visits him for what will be the last time, she sees him as an "anonymous old man who did not want her mothering encouragement" (100). She doesn't wake him before she leaves. Awaiting the morning ferry back to the island the next day, she receives a call telling her that her husband has died in the night. The barrier between her conscious life and her unconscious, between her ordered, carefully tended memory and the stark realities of the present is shattered and her reaction is denial. She takes the phone call to be an obscene trick.

Her husband's death, like Milly's hysterectomy, is the crisis that tries Henrietta in the novel and reorders her relationship to herself and to her world. Her reaction seems at first unaccounted for: she feels shame. What shame could there be in losing a husband, in having been a caring wife and mother, a sustainer of community? Henrietta's response is to retreat, to resist the very community ceremonies she had always organized to help people grieve and come back to life. Her shame is caused, in part, by the stark realization that the husband she had loved and the children she tended were largely products of her own need, projections of her imagination. When the old man she had visited twice a week dies, he takes her husband with him. When her son and his wife visit to help her cope with the cremation and scattering of the ashes, she realizes that her only remaining son is a stranger to her, she doesn't really know him as an adult, a husband, father, and banker. He was, nonetheless, "a stranger she trusted" (134). She is incapable for a time of making decisions, seeing friends, speaking her mind. She goes into an emotional and psychological collapse that has immediate social consequences. She circulates in the world in a way that recalls her daytime dreams: seeming to be drunk, out of control, a thick if invisible wall separates her from others. She thinks:

> Why did she have to face this terrible failure of love, this knowledge that she never had really accepted that damaged old man as her husband until he finally managed to die, taking the memory of Hart with him. (134)

Her emotional breakdown takes a physical toll as her body becomes weaker:

> She had no skin. Nearly everything touched some raw place. In that month of crazed apathy, she had not healed but had further damaged herself. Now she knew she had to eat. She had gradually to teach her neglected muscles to do her bidding. But what to do with the running sore of her psyche she didn't know. (179)

Henrietta had tried to act as a mentor to Red in the first part of the novel, by helping her earn her living and find a place in the community. Now Red becomes caretaker of her body and spirit. Red's bluntness counteracts Henrietta's tendency to understate, to compromise. In a moment of clarity prompted by Red's efforts to make her understand her shame she thinks:

> That old man had been her duty, not her love. And what was the reward of all that duty but the shattering of illusion. *I am not a good woman. I didn't wake him because I didn't want to wake him. I didn't know he could kill Hart.* (181)

In a dream that recalls Milly's fever-induced hallucinations, Henrietta imagines that her husband is at peace, that she can see him as beyond the strokes rather than try to hold on to him as he had been before them. Henrietta then gradually regains her strength and the ability to join the community she had sustained for so long. When she emerges from her breakdown, she emerges alone but able now to establish new kinds of relationships with others. Red is not exactly a daughter-substitute; she provides, however, another means for Henrietta to connect with the future through a younger woman whom she can trust, teach, and learn from. They establish a deliberate rather than a biological kinship, tending to each other's needs.

Karen is the least well defined of the three centers of consciousness in the novel. She is the youngest, the character most clearly questing for personal definition and meaning; she hovers self-consciously at the edges of the lives of others, never quite fitting in, never fully present to her own life. When, for example, two women from the Vancouver lesbian community she had known come to visit the island, they invite themselves to Karen's house, and Karen lets them take her bed. Taking her self-effacement for her guests as a metaphor for her life, she thinks: "Even here in her own house, she was alone in the cold and dark while two people she hardly knew usurped the center" (56).

Like Milly and Henrietta, Karen has internalized social surveillance, both real and imagined: she is acutely sensitive to the assessing gaze of her father (a university professor), her ex-lover Peggy, and other people from the lesbian community she knew in Vancouver and the island community where she now lives. Karen's father wants her to achieve a social position that would validate him as a successful professional; she, too, should become a professional with work deemed important by middle-class standards. Peggy had treated Karen as an acquisition, to embellish her life.

Numbed by her failed relationship with Peggy, she has come to the island to learn to live alone, which, like the others, entails learning who she is as a woman without the mediating presence of a dominant partner between her and the world. The models of white femininity that Milly and Henrietta had internalized are recognizable cultural constructions: woman as sexual object, woman living to meet the needs of others. Karen's model of femininity is less recognizable in part because she is racialized differently. She has inherited blue eyes from her absent, white mother and otherwise Japanese features from her father. Karen's father, who spent part of his childhood in the internment camps, had always denied the significance of his Japanese ancestry. Having internalized the racism and xenophobia of the relocation, her father repeats the pattern in his own life, aspiring to become "one hundred and fifty percent Canadian" by suppressing non-white, non-European racial and ethnic origins. Karen learns the meanings of "Japanese" in Canadian society primarily through negative stereotypes, reading the judgments that others make of her.

Karen's mother is known to her primarily through letters from ever-changing locations. The cause of her mother's detachment from her family and from society is never clear; she seems to suffer from a pervasive, increasingly severe anomie. Karen will have to shape her own sense of what it means to be a Canadian woman of biracial descent; she will have to determine the meanings of her sexuality outside of a lesbian community that had allowed her to be silenced as an "exotic." Neither her womanhood nor her ethnicity (inextricably entwined in her sense of self) are givens. Significantly it is a lesbian character who most clearly embodies the dilemma of forging a social and self-definition outside of available models. Like Alysoun in "Home Movie," Karen's sexuality will not be defined primarily by the object of her desire but by her own negotiations as a subjectivity caught in "overlapping networks of power" that are more alienating than enabling.

The other female characters struggle with the contradictions of heterosexual femininity they had passively or unconsciously assumed; Karen struggles from the start to sort through the expectations and judgments of others to shape her life and her relationships. Like Milly and Henrietta, Karen is in part motivated by shame, the internalized judgment of others. Karen's shame is the paralyzing fear of being different in a social context that suppresses difference. In the dynamics of the novel, Karen and Milly are often antagonists, Karen the object of Milly's negative judgment. Even though Karen disdains Milly, she is stymied when she fails to conform to values she doesn't even approve. For example, when Karen brings sushi to Dickie's wake in the beginning of the novel, Milly says it's inappropriate, "foreign" in this community where smoked salmon, fried chicken, homemade bread, and clam chowder were the more common offerings. Challenged by Milly's racism, Karen claims the grave in the local cemetery as her great-grandfather's. But Karen knows that she has invented a history for that particular grave, she is unable to read the inscription. She instantly feels alienated from her own effort to link to an island history that is hers in the general sense (her grandparents lived in the Gulf Islands) even if the specific example of that headstone may be inaccurate. When her two lesbian friends—Sally and Sarah—come to visit from Vancouver, it is Milly's gaze Karen fears, lest she be perceived and dismissed as a lesbian by association with her more overt friends. Karen's challenge is to distinguish her ethnic identity from racist assumptions and her sexual identity from homophobic definition.

Just as Milly pushes Karen negatively to define her subject position as ethnically "other" and lesbian in a racist, homophobic frame, Miss James suggests to Karen the possibility of a different, positive self-definition that exceeds available categories. Like Karen's mother, Miss James had lived alone and moved frequently during her adult life. Unlike her mother, however, Miss James was engaged with the world and made a place for herself in different communities. She had early on rejected the social position and model for femininity that her wealthy, conservative Virginia father expected for her. Miss James's sexuality is never revealed in the book except as outside the heterosexual expectations of marriage and motherhood. Now an old woman, Miss James is surrounded by the artifacts of an active life. Karen discovers when she goes to take care of Miss James, who is ailing, that she has delicate Japanese soup bowls in her cupboard. She asks if Miss James had ever been to Japan. In contrast to Milly who implied that it was shaming to have been interred during World War II, Miss James says: "I bought those in San Francisco before the Second World War it would have been, before the *disgrace* when all their shops were shut down" (138). Karen learns from Miss James that to live alone requires assuming a central place in one's own life:

> Karen sighed as she put the lovely bowls back among the other treasures of the cupboard. She was coming to understand that if she was to have a life, it must be a deliberate one. The exercising of choice at every level still seemed an exhausting and unnatural business, like collecting stage props before a play could begin. But unless she began, she might wait in the wings of her own life forever. (140)

Miss James doesn't provide a role model for Karen or a mirror in which Karen will discover how to be in the world. Rather, she provides a way for Karen to reposition herself vis-à-vis the powers that have traversed her life. The key elements of Karen's insight are signaled by "deliberate," unnatural," and "stage props." There is no "natural," unproblematic, or inevitable way to perform the interweaving scripts of gender, sexual, and ethnic identity. Working within certain conditions, with specific possibilities at hand, agency is required to give shape and meaning to one's life—beyond the repetition of shapes and meanings imposed by the dominant powers of one's historical and social position. Miss James provides an opening, a point from which Karen might resist her father, Peggy, Milly, and other dominant forces in the context of her life.

Miss James gives the impetus and direction that Karen's biological mother couldn't offer her. This substitution is part of a larger dynamic in the novel involving absent parents, lost children, and the need for kinship. Henrietta had lost several babies at birth and a son in his adolescence; Milly has a daughter who has disappeared, haunting her as a reminder of failed motherhood; Red never knew her own father and is pregnant with a child who, in turn, will not know her father; Miss James rejected her father's values and never married or bore children. Yet, by the end of the novel, each of the principal characters has renewed family connections or established new kinship relationships. Milly mends her relationship with the daughter who has stayed in touch; Henrietta takes a protective role toward Red and, to a degree, Karen; Miss James names Red heir to her house and property, and Karen takes up temporary residence in Miss James's house before moving on to Japan. Karen's decision is made emotionally possible by Miss James and financially possible by an inheritance her mother leaves her. Ironically, it is her mother's money that allows her to explore the ethnic inheritance she takes from her father.

The elaborate reworking of kin connections in the novel demonstrates that kinship is not a natural occurrence. Blood ties are not sufficient to make kinship meaningful and are not necessary to establish progeny, continuity, connection with the past or the future. Like kinship, community is produced through a combination of circumstance and choice: the dynamics and meaning of community are never self-evident, and the work of community is never finished. Like *The Young in One Another's Arms*, which also ended on Galiano Island, community building requires both resistance and coalition in order to meet the needs of individuals without repressing the differences among them.

After the Fire ends with a ceremony invented by Karen to celebrate Miss James's life and to confirm her legacy to Red. Karen assumes a role analogous to Henrietta's in the beginning: she organizes a tea to bring people together. She uses her own methods, posting notices throughout the island extending the reach of community as broadly as possible. Just as Karen assumes a position in the community, central to its life rather than a peripheral and usually silent observer, she is preparing to move on.

Again, one might ask, how is this a lesbian novel, dominated as it is by heterosexual characters? While Milly, Henrietta, and Karen all provide centers of consciousness in the narrative, perspectives through which the story is told, the presence of an invisible, shaping narrator is evident in this novel as it was in the earlier novels. Because none of the characters is associated with the first person, the reader is repeatedly reminded of privileged—but controlled—access to the thoughts and judgment of the three central characters. The sequence of the characters' stories in each chapter and the plot elements establish a moral ground that directs values in the narrative without condemning individual characters. The reader can't resolve or reorder social stresses, what Phelan calls overlapping networks of power, simply by demonizing individual characters. Narrative patterns reveal Milly's negative surveillance and constant disapproval to be the distorted defenses of a woman who has been humiliated and misused. The narrative clearly exposes the links among misogyny, homophobia, racism, and class bias in the model for femininity that had shaped Milly's subjectivity and social role. More subtly, the narrative reveals the stresses inherent in the model of femininity lived by Henrietta, the apparently exemplary wife and mother. With Karen's character, as in all of her fiction, Rule refuses to idealize lesbians or to pretend that lesbian community exists apart from the networks of power that define mainstream society and heterosexual relationships.

The most pervasive lesbian presence in the novel articulates the meanings of aging and women's bodies. Throughout *After the Fire*, issues of kinship, community, and self-definition are tied up with changing relationships to women's bodies. Initially presented, through Milly's character, as a source of shame to be denied or disguised, the aging female body becomes a source and object of tenderness in the story. The most evident physical intimacy between women in the book—aside from a brief reference to Sarah and Sally's lovemaking—is the loving care of the younger women for the fragile, sensitive bodies of the older women. The novel recalls an essay Rule wrote in 1977 for *Lavender Culture* called "Grandmothers," which she later included in *Outlander*. Written when she was forty-six, already suffering from arthritis, "Grandmothers" celebrates aging women. Rule talks about caring for her grandmothers, learning to touch their ailing bodies with sensitivity, brush their hair, read their faces defined by time and experience. She connects her tenderness for her grandmothers, her loving familiarity with their bodies, with the fact that "When I was twenty-three, I fell permanently in love with a woman who was not much younger than I am now, whose face had already begun to be defined by time, and who has stayed there fifteen years ahead of me for twenty-three years, half my life" (206).

Reflecting further on the patterns of a lifelong relationship between women separated by age, Rule writes:

> The natural imbalance of our erotic energies, which has plagued, amused, and taught us patience with each other, is not as pronounced as it used to be. As the erotic fuses with the simply physical, we return together to a place which shares with childhood long moments in the present, no future hope of accomplishment as commanding as the sight of eagles in the high air or a sudden colony of mushrooms in the daffodil bed. (206)

Today, more than twenty years after Rule wrote "Grandmothers" and a decade after she returned to the theme of sexuality after the fire of youth in *Memory Board*, important work is being done by lesbian writers (such as Del Martin, Phyllis Lyon, and Peg Cruikshank) on lesbians and aging, on sexuality and advanced age, on patterns of desire and physicality in intimate relationships. In *After the Fire* there is no fully realized lesbian relationship, but the relationships of trust, care, and touch that evolve among the women characters, especially between the younger women (Karen and Red) and the older women (Miss James and Henrietta), establish a framework for thinking about the erotic dimensions of physicality that is not sexual in the conventional sense. In this way the erotic is generous, it is not removed exclusively to the private domain and is not self-centered but infuses a wider network of connections among women. In "Grandmothers" Rule makes this view of the erotic and community life more explicit:

> I have had long apprenticeship as lover; and in the way I can, I will still carry out those patterns of courtship but I am coming into a time when I must be the beloved of children and the young, who will measure their confidence in terms of my growing needs. As my grandmothers taught me the real lessons of erotic love with their beautifully requiring flesh and speaking faces, so I would wish to teach the children I love that they are capable of tenderness and of strength, capable of knowledge because of what they can see in my face, clear in pain and wonder, intent on practicing life as long as it lasts. (206–207)

Conclusion: Redefining the Public Space

Fiction, as feminist and queer theorists inflected by Foucault have argued, is governed by regulatory discourses; it not only reflects but engages and enforces discourses of power. Just as fiction inscribes regulatory discourses, our reading and interpretation are shaped by authoritative discourses: other fictions, theory, the dominant scripts of our social and literary context. For the same reasons, however, fiction is a field in which resistance can be imagined. A resisting writer can invite the reader to consider ways to destabilize the seemingly natural or inevitable configurations of, for example, gender, sexuality, race, ethnicity—and narrative. Understanding the politics *of* the text opens up ways of thinking about politics *outside* the text. Fiction read in this way becomes a ground for enabling social change rather than just reflecting or representing social and psychological lives.

The narrating subjectivity that sets the terms for meaning in Rule's fictions is lesbian in that heterosexual assumptions and expectations are challenged and intimacy between women does not require justification or apology. Her narratives, furthermore, are framed by a *resisting* lesbian subjectivity that challenges both heterosexual norms and the "mini-enforcement" of lesbian communities. Rule's work offers the reader, in Shane Phelan's terms, "a social ontology or landscape that can see and address contemporary modes of power" (*Getting Specific* 16). It is precisely the specifically lesbian subjectivity which underlies Rule's fiction that makes it important for readers who are male and female, straight, gay, lesbian, bisexual, or celibate. Her fictions provide a space for reimagining the modes of power that can hold us hostage because they appear to be natural, necessary, inevitable, or unbreachable. Her earliest fictions gave lesbian readers a crucial site for resisting the desperate, guilty, homophobic patterns of lesbian subjectivity that seemed inevitable in the 1950s. Her later fictions continue to provide that kind of imaginary ground to lesbian readers, but just as important, they provide a site of resistance for all readers to reconsider the networks of power that control the meanings of gender, ethnicity, desire, and so on.

Rule's fictions, like Roxanne's sound map in *Contract with the World*, begin with what is given, the ordinary realities of daily life, and then reorder relations; they open up new psychic and social spaces and, particularly, explore the terrain where the psychic and social merge. Rather than present a blueprint for change or a utopian vision, Rule's work challenges the reader to reconsider the ordinary. In an essay written in 1993 called "Extraordinary Homosexuals and the Fear of Being Ordinary," Biddy Martin discusses the effects of radical antinormativity in some recent queer theory that is linked to a romanticizing of detachment, indifference and death: "To be radical is to locate oneself outside or in a transgressive relationship to kinship or community because those relationships have already been so thoroughly societalized, normalized, and then internalized as self-control and discipline" (*Femininity* 69–70). Martin warns:

> Implicit in these constructions of queerness . . . is the lure of an existence without limit, without bodies or psyches, and certainly without mothers. . . . An enormous fear of ordinariness or normalcy results in superficial accounts of the complex imbrications of sexuality with other aspects of social and psychic life, and in far too little attention to the dilemmas of the average people that we also are. (70)

The constructions of queerness Martin describes here express adolescent revolt that can provide a clarifying perspective on sexuality and social constraint but that risks, as she says, remaining superficial, repressing the "average" that is also a part of who we are. Rule's fictions provide a means for understanding the radical potential of the ordinary as reimagined by a lesbian subjectivity that accounts fully for the female body, for social connectedness, and for life after adolescence. Her tendency to accelerate aging reflects her desire to consider the full lifespan, not just the crises of adolescence and youth that have tended to dominate queer fiction. Rule's fictions in the 1980s, particularly, pay special attention to the perspective of advanced age that brings into focus the poetics of the ordinary. Among Rule's papers there is one page, undated, stuck in with notes made largely in the 1980s. It bears the title "Failing Powers":

> One does not recognize them until they begin to fail: memory, need to succeed, need to be importantly occupied, need to be in passionate connections.

> The Adolescent has a capacity to suffer, love, be great, and is bored by ordinary life.
>
> The failing begin to see birds, flowers, the sun. (Box 37, folder 6)

There is a certain irony in the fact that Rule stopped writing at a time when lesbian, gay, and queer texts—fictional, theoretical, confessional, historical, cinematic, the list goes on—have exploded into public discourse. Her work has been eclipsed in the current wave of queer writing every bit as much as it was marginalized by straight reviewers and critics when she was producing it. Contemporary queer writers and theorists have ignored her for a cluster of reasons having to do with the dynamics of queer culture and the narratives of sexuality that have dominated both academic and popular writing. The unrelenting demand for the latest, newest performances of queerness discounts the fictions of last year, much less the last few decades, especially if transgression is not the primary marker of queer desire. The playfulness of multiple subject positions in recent feminist and queer theorizing privileges some positions over others; exploring whiteness as an effect of racialization, for example, has only recently been legitimated. The constructions of queerness that Martin discusses in the passage quoted above implicitly scorn the embodiment and social locations of sexual subjectivity that are at the center of Rule's narratives. Rule's work is especially important to us precisely in the ways it resists certain tropes of queerness that enjoy currency today. She doesn't celebrate youth over age; she grounds her representations of sexuality in very physical bodies that are gendered, whose mortality is marked by aging as well as by death. And yet, her refusal to reify identity categories, her ability to stage multiple subject positions and competing models of sexuality aligns her in fundamental ways with queer theory.

Rule's writing has always gone against the grain of hegemonic discourses, whether produced by mainstream or oppositional politics. As such it provides a means for identifying what is suppressed or marginalized or oversimplified by discourses even as they claim the authority of the repressed and the marginalized. Literature provides a publicly available discourse for the staging of private fantasy in which sexual identities are structured and restructured. From the beginning, readers have found in Rule's fictions a social landscape in which to reimagine themselves and their relation to the world. Her readers form invisible but passionate communities linked by texts that challenge as much as they confirm. In January 1995, the documentary *Fictions and Other Truths: A Film about Jane Rule* premiered in Toronto. Rule was weak from a bout with pneumonia and was unable to come to the event. The filmmakers sent her a video so that she could see it as it was unveiled to the public. She wrote me a letter on the eve of the première expressing her pleasure with the film and with what the film represented. Her sentiments in the letter summarize the vital connection between creative and political work, private lives, and public space that has always been fundamental in her work:

> As I watched the film, I thought, "And this is about community, too." It will make money for the Gay and Lesbian Archives in Toronto and there is now talk of a Vancouver fund raiser in March for the Little Sisters' defense fund, but it has also made a community of all of us involved in making it, across borders and continents, across years, affirming what we know about the value of the work we all do together, insisting on doing our own defining of the public space.

WORKS CITED

Abelove, Henry. "The Queering of Lesbian/Gay History." *Radical History Review* 62 (Spring 1995): 44–57.

Alwood, Edward. *Straight News: Gays, Lesbians, and the Media.* New York: Columbia University Press, 1996.

Bannon, Ann. *Beebo Brinker.* Tallahassee, FL: Naiad Press, 1986. Originally published 1962.

Barale, Michèle Aina. "Below the Belt: (Un)Covering *The Well of Loneliness.*" In *inside/out: Lesbian Theories, Gay Theories,* ed. Diana Fuss, 237–57. New York: Routledge, 1991.

Benedictus, David. Rev. of *Desert of the Heart,* by Jane Rule. *The Sunday Telegraph* (London), 9 February 1964, n.p.

Bérubé, Allan. *Coming Out under Fire: The History of Gay Men and Women in World War Two.* New York: Macmillan, 1990.

———. "Marching to a Different Drummer: Lesbian and Gay GIs in World War II." In *Hidden from History: Reclaiming the Gay & Lesbian Past,* ed. Martin Duberman, Martha Vicinus, and George Chauncey, Jr., 383–94. New York: Penguin, 1990.

Bérubé, Allan, and John D'Emilio. "The Military and Lesbians during the McCarthy Years." *Signs: Journal of Women in Culture and Society* 9.4 (1984): 759–75. Rpt. in *The Lesbian Issue,* eds. Freedman et al. 279–96.

Bhabha, Homi. *The Location of Culture.* New York: Routledge, 1994.

Bronski, Michael. *Culture Clash: The Making of Gay Sensibility.* Boston: South End Press, 1984.

Brown, Rita Mae. *Rubyfruit Jungle.* Plainfield, VT: Daughters, Inc., 1973.

Butler, Judith. *Bodies That Matter: On the Discursive Limits of "Sex."* New York: Routledge, 1993.

———. "Imitation and Gender Insubordination." In *inside/out: Lesbian Theories, Gay Theories,* ed. Diana Fuss, 13–31. New York: Routledge, 1991.

Castle, Terry. *The Apparitional Lesbian: Female Homosexuality and Modern Culture.* New York: Columbia University Press, 1993.

Colette. "Claudine à l'école." In *Colette: Oeuvres I,* ed. Claude Pichois. Paris: Gallimard, 1984. Originally published in 1900.

Cook, Blanche W. "Women Alone Stir My Imagination: Lesbianism in the Cultural Tradition." *Signs: Journal of Women in Culture and Society* 4.4 (1979): 718–39.

de Lauretis, Teresa. "Eccentric Subjects: Feminist Theory and Historical Consciousness." *Feminist Studies* 16 (1990): 115–50.

———. *The Practice of Love: Lesbian Sexuality and Perverse Desire*. Bloomington, IN: Indiana University Press, 1994.

D'Emilio, John. *Making Trouble: Essays on Gay History, Politics, and the University*. New York: Routledge, 1992.

———. *Sexual Politics, Sexual Communities: The Making of a Homosexual Minority in the United States, 1940–1970*. Chicago: University of Chicago Press, 1983.

Duggan, Lisa. "The Discipline Problem: Queer Theory Meets Lesbian and Gay History." *Gay and Lesbian Quarterly* 2.3 (1995): 179–92. Rpt. in Lisa Duggan and Nan D. Hunter, *Sex Wars: Sexual Dissent and Political Culture*. New York: Routledge. 194–206.

Faderman, Lillian, ed. *Chloë plus Olivia: An Anthology of Lesbian Literature from the Seventeenth Century to the Present*. New York: Penguin, 1994.

———. *Odd Girls and Twilight Lovers: A History of Lesbian Life in Twentieth-Century America*. New York: Penguin, 1991.

Faderman, Lillian, and Ann Williams. "Radclyffe Hall and the Lesbian Image." *Conditions* 1.1 (1977): 31–49.

Farwell, Marilyn R. *Heterosexual Plots and Lesbian Narratives*. New York: New York University Press, 1996.

Felman, Shoshana. *What Does a Woman Want? Reading and Sexual Difference*. Baltimore and London: Johns Hopkins University Press, 1993.

Fetterley, Judith. *The Resisting Reader: A Feminist Approach to American Fiction*. Bloomington: Indiana University Press, 1978.

Foucault, Michel. *The History of Sexuality, vol. 1: An Introduction*. Trans. Robert Hurley. New York: Vintage Books, 1978.

———. "Prison Talk." In *Power/Knowledge: Selected Interviews and Other Writings by Michel Foucault, 1972–1977*, ed. Colin Gordon, 37–54. New York: Pantheon Books, 1980.

———. "Space, Knowledge, and Power." In *The Foucault Reader*, ed. Paul Rabinow, 239–58. New York: Pantheon Books, 1984.

Freedman, Estelle B., Barbara C. Gelpi, Susan L. Johnson, and Kathleen M. Weston, eds. *The Lesbian Issue: Essays from SIGNS*. Chicago: University of Chicago Press, 1985.

Hall, Radclyffe. *The Well of Loneliness*. New York: Covici Friede, 1928.

Hamer, Diana. "'I am a Woman': Ann Bannon and the Writing of Lesbian Identity in the 1950s." In *Lesbian and Gay Writing*, ed. Mark Lilly, 47–75. London: Macmillan, 1990.

Hancock, Geoffrey. "An Interview with Jane Rule" *Canadian Fiction Magazine* 23 (August 1976): 57–120.

Hermes, Joke. "Sexuality in Lesbian Romance Fiction." *Feminist Review* 42 (1992): 49–66.

Jay, Karla, and Allen Young, eds. *After You're Out: Personal Experiences of Gay Men and Lesbian Women*. New York: Links, 1975.

Jeffreys, Sheila. *The Spinster and Her Enemies: Feminism and Sexuality, 1880–1900*. London: Pandora. 1985.

Katz, Jonathan. *Gay American History: Lesbians and Gay Men in the U.S.A.* 1976; Reprint, New York: Harper and Row, 1985.

———. *Gay/Lesbian Almanac: A New Documentary*. 1983; Reprint, New York: Richard Gallen, 1994.

———. *The INVENTION of HeteroSEXUALITY*. New York: Penguin, 1995.

———. "The Invention of Heterosexuality." *Socialist Review* 20 (January/February 1990): 8–34.

Kennedy, Elizabeth Lapovsky. "Telling Tales: Oral History and the Construction of Pre-Stonewall Lesbian History." *Radical History Review* 62 (Spring 1995): 58–70.

Kennedy, Elizabeth Lapovsky, and Madeline D. Davis. *Boots of Leather, Slippers of Gold: The History of a Lesbian Community*. New York: Penguin, 1994.

Krieger, Susan. "Lesbian Identity and Community: Recent Social Science Literature." *Signs: Journal of Women in Culture and Society* 8.1 (1982): 91–108. Rpt. in *The Lesbian Issue*, eds. Freedman et al., 223–40. Chicago: University of Chicago Press, 1985.

———. *The Mirror Dance: Identity in a Women's Community*. Philadelphia: Temple University Press, 1983.

The Ladder. New York: Arno Press, 1975. Reprint of all sixteen volumes of the periodical from October 1956 to August/September 1972.

Martin, Biddy. *Femininity Played Straight: The Significance of Being Lesbian*. New York: Routledge, 1996.

Martin, Biddy, and Chandra Mohanty. "Feminist Politics: What's Home Got to Do with It." In *Feminist Studies/Critical Studies*, ed. Teresa de Lauretis, 191–212. Bloomington: Indiana University Press, 1986. Rpt. in *Femininity Played Straight: The Significance of Being Lesbian*, 163–84.

Miller, Isabel. *Patience and Sarah*. Greenwich, CT: Fawcett Publications, 1972. Originally published as *A Place for Us* by Isabel Miller in 1969.

Miller, Nancy K. *The Heroine's Text: Readings in the French and English Novel, 1722–1782*. New York: Columbia University Press, 1980.

Munt, Sally, ed. *New Lesbian Criticism: Literary and Cultural Readings.* New York: Columbia University Press, 1992.

Newton, Esther. "The Mythic Mannish Lesbian: Radclyffe Hall and the New Woman." *Signs: Journal of Women in Culture and Society* 9.4 (1984): 557–77.

O'Rourke, Rebecca. *Reflecting on the* Well of Loneliness. London: Routledge, 1989.

Parker, Richard G., and John H. Gagnon, eds. *Conceiving Sexuality.* New York: Routledge, 1995.

Penn, Donna. "The Meanings of Lesbianism in Post-War America." *Gender & History* 3.2 (Summer 1991): 190–203.

Phelan, Shane. *Getting Specific: Postmodern Lesbian Politics.* Minneapolis: University of Minnesota Press, 1994.

———. "(Be)coming Out: Lesbian Identity and Politics." *Signs: Journal of Women in Culture and Society* 18 (1993): 765–90.

———. *Identity Politics: Lesbian-Feminism and the Limits of Community.* Philadelphia: Temple University Press, 1989.

Pratt, Minnie Bruce. "Identity: Skin Blood Heart." In *Yours in Struggle: Three Feminist Perspectives on Anti-Semitism and Racism,* eds. Elly Bulkin, Barbara Smith, and Minnie Bruce Pratt, 9–64. New York: Long Haul, 1984.

Radford, Jean. "An Inverted Romance: *The Well of Loneliness* and Sexual Ideology." In *The Progress of Romance: The Politics of Popular Fiction,* ed. Jean Radford. London: Routledge, 1986.

Rich, Adrienne. "Vesuvius at Home: The Power of Emily Dickinson." *Parnassus: Poetry in Review* (1976); also in *On Lies, Secrets, and Silence* by Adrienne Rich, 157–84. New York: W. W. Norton and Co., 1979.

Roof, Judith. *A Lure of Knowledge: Lesbian Sexuality and Theory.* New York: Columbia University Press, 1991.

Ross, Becki L. *The House That Jill Built: A Lesbian Nation in Formation.* Toronto: University of Toronto Press, 1995.

Ruehl, Sonja. "Inverts and Experts: Radclyffe Hall and the Lesbian Identity." In *Feminism, Culture and Politics,* eds. Rosalind Brunt and Caroline Rowan, 15–36. London: Lawrence and Wishart, 1982.

Rule, Jane. *After the Fire.* Tallahassee, FL: Naiad Press, 1989.

———. *Against the Season.* New York: McCall Publishing, 1971; London: Peter Davies, 1972; New York: Manor Books, 1975; Tallahassee, FL: Naiad, 1984.

———. "Choosing Home." In *Writing Home: A PEN Canada Anthology,* ed. Constance Rooke, 274–79. Toronto: McClelland and Stewart, 1997.

———. *Contract with the World.* New York: Harcourt, Brace, Jovanovich, 1980; Tallahassee, FL: Naiad Press, 1982.

———. *Desert of the Heart*. Toronto: Macmillan, New York: World Publishing, London: Secker and Warburg, 1964; Tallahassee, FL: Naiad Press, 1983.

———. *A Hot-Eyed Moderate*. Tallahassee, FL: Naiad Press, 1985.

———. "I Want to Speak Ill of the Dead." *Brick: A Literary Journal* 58 (1998): 52.

———. *Inland Passage*. Tallahassee, FL: Naiad Press, 1985.

———. "Jane Rule." In *Contemporary Authors Autobiography Series*, ed. Joyce Nakamura. Vol. 18, 309–25. Detroit, Washington D.C., London: Gale Research, 1994.

———. *Jane Rule Papers* are located in Vancouver at the University of British Columbia Library, Special Collections and University Archives Division. The collection includes thirty-six boxes (6.1 m) acquired from 1988 to 1993. The collection includes notes, manuscripts, drafts, galleys, and correspondence relating to her published and unpublished novels and short stories; biographical and autobiographical material, nonfiction manuscripts, and personal and professional correspondence; reviews of her work and audio recordings of interviews and readings. Items cited from the collection are identified by box number, folder number, and, where appropriate, page number.

———. *Lesbian Images*. Toronto and Garden City, NY: Doubleday, 1975.

———. *Memory Board*. Tallahassee, FL: Naiad Press, 1987.

———. *Outlander*. Tallahassee, FL: Naiad Press, 1981.

———. *Theme for Diverse Instruments*. Vancouver: Talonbooks, 1975.

———. *This Is Not for You*. New York: McCall Publishing, 1970; Tallahassee, FL: Naiad Press, 1984.

———. "Tolerance: It Isn't Polite Silence." *Mills Quarterly* 75.1 (July 1992): 10–12.

———. *The Young in One Another's Arms*. Garden City, NY, and Toronto: Doubleday, 1977; Tallahassee, FL: Naiad Press, 1984.

Schweickart, Patricinio P. "Reading Ourselves: Toward a Feminist Theory of Reading." In *Gender and Reading: Essays on Readers, Texts, and Contexts*, eds. Elizabeth A. Flynn and Patricinio P. Schweickart, 31–62. Baltimore and London: Johns Hopkins University Press, 1986.

Sedgwick, Eve Kosofsky. *Between Men: English Literature and Male Homosocial Desire*. New York: Columbia University Press, 1985.

———. *Epistemology of the Closet*. Berkeley: University of California Press, 1990.

Smith, Elizabeth A. "Butches, Femmes, and Feminists: The Politics of Lesbian Sexuality." *NWSA Journal* 1.3 (Spring 1989): 398–421.

Stein, Arlene. *Sex and Sensibility: Stories of a Lesbian Generation*. Berkeley: University of California Press, 1997.

Stimpson, Catharine R. "Zero Degree Deviancy: The Lesbian Novel in English." *Critical Inquiry* 8 (1981): 363–79.

Stryker, Susan, and Jim Van Buskirk. *Gay by the Bay: A History of Queer Culture in the San Francisco Bay Area.* San Francisco: Chronicle Books, 1996.

Terry, Jennifer. "The Seductive Power of Science in the Making of Deviant Subjectivity." In *Posthuman Bodies,* eds. Judith M. Halberstam and Ira Livingston, 135–61. Bloomington: Indiana University Press, 1995.

———. "Theorizing Deviant Historiography." *differences: A Journal of Cultural Studies* 3.2 (1991): 55–74.

Tracey, Liz, and Sydney Pokorny. *So You Want to Be a Lesbian? A Guide for Amateurs and Professionals.* New York: St. Martin's Press, 1996.

Vicinus, Martha. "'They Wonder to Which Sex I Belong': The Historical Roots of Modern Lesbian Identity." In *The Lesbian and Gay Studies Reader,* eds. Henry Abelove, Michèle Aina Barale, David M. Halperin, 432–52. New York: Routledge, 1993.

Weeks, Jeffrey, "History, Desire and Identities." In *Conceiving Sexuality,* eds. Richard G. Parker and John H. Gagnon, 33–50. New York: Routledge, 1995.

Weiss, Penny A., and Marilyn Friedman. *Feminism and Community.* Philadelphia: Temple University Press, 1995.

Weston, Kath. *Families We Choose: Lesbians, Gays, Kinship.* New York: Columbia University Press, 1991.

Whitlock, Gillian. "'Everything Is Out of Place': Radclyffe Hall and the Lesbian Literary Tradition." *Feminist Studies* 13.3 (1987): 554–82.

Winterson, Jeanette. *Oranges Are Not the Only Fruit.* London: Pandora Press, 1985.

———. *Written on the Body.* New York: Vintage Books, 1994.

Wittig, Monique. "The Mark of Gender." In *The Straight Mind and Other Essays,* 76–87. Boston: Beacon Press, 1992.

———. *L'Opoponax.* Paris: Editions de Minuit, 1964.

Young, Iris Marion. "The Ideal of Community and the Politics of Difference." In *Feminism and Community,* eds. Penny A.Weiss and Marilyn Friedman, 233–58. Philadelphia: Temple University Press, 1995. Rpt. from *Social Theory and Practice* 12 (Spring 1986): 1–26.

Zimmerman, Bonnie. "Lesbians Like This and That: Some Notes on Lesbian Criticism for the Nineties." In *New Lesbian Criticism: Literary and Cultural Readings,* ed. Sally Munt. New York: Columbia University Press, 1992.

———. *The Safe Sea of Women: Lesbian Fiction, 1969–1989.* Boston: Beacon Press, 1990.

INDEX

ABOUT THE AUTHOR

Marilyn R. Schuster received her B.A. in French from Mills College in 1965 and her Ph.D. in French language and literature from Yale University in 1973. She has been on the faculty at Smith College since 1971, first in the French department and now as Professor of Women's Studies. Her scholarly work has been in the areas of curriculum transformation (bringing feminist and ethnic studies scholarship into the liberal arts curriculum and classroom), women's studies, French, and comparative literature.

Schuster edited her first book, *Women's Place in the Academy: Transforming the Liberal Arts Curriculum,* with Susan Van Dyne in 1985. Her second book, *Marguerite Duras Revisited,* published in 1993 in the Twayne World Authors series, considers sexuality and gender in Duras's fiction and films. Her articles have appeared in the *Harvard Educational Review,* the *French Review, Nineteenth-Century French Studies, Feminist Studies,* and the *Journal of Homosexuality.* She is currently editing letters between Jane Rule and Rick Bébout from 1981–1995 that shed light on feminist, gay, and lesbian politics during that period and that tell the story of a remarkable friendship.